THE GREAT CHINESE TRAVELERS

AN ANTHOLOGY

EDITED AND INTRODUCED

BY JEANNETTE MIRSKY

THE UNIVERSITY OF CHICAGO PRESS
CHICAGO AND LONDON

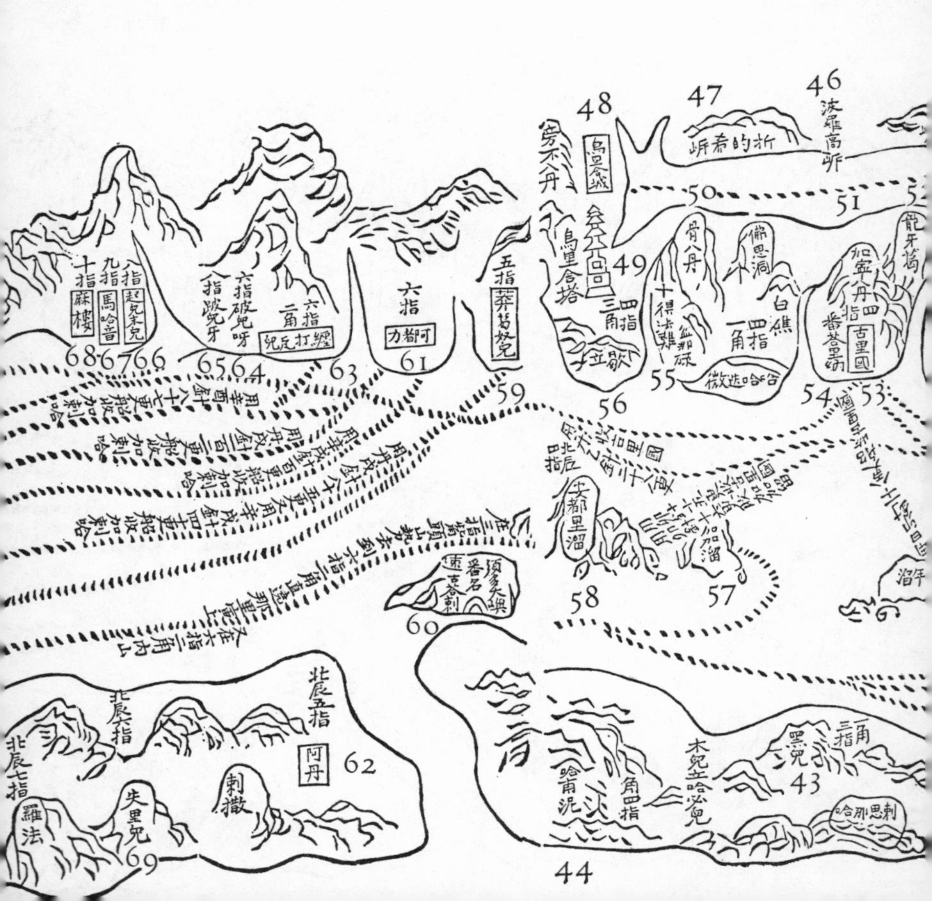

THE GREAT CHINESE TRAVELERS

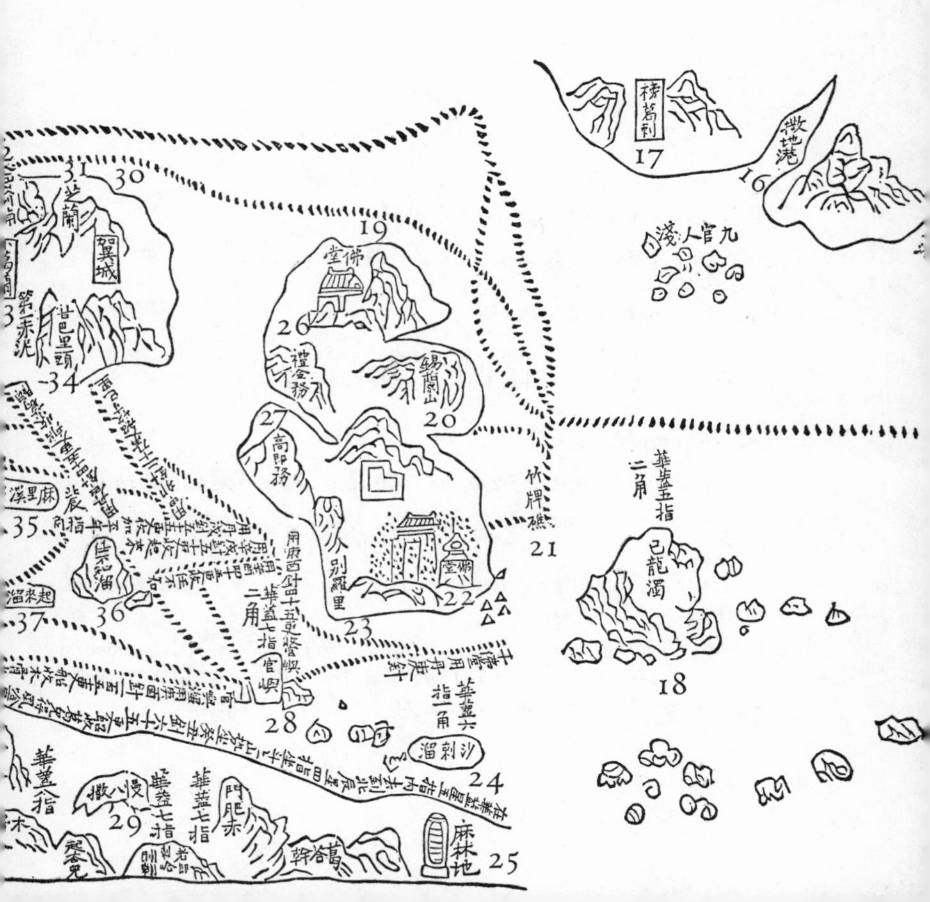

The University of Chicago Press, Chicago 60637
The University of Chicago Press, Ltd., London

Phoenix Edition 1974
Printed in the United States of America

International Standard Book Number: 0-226-53182-1
Library of Congress Catalog Card Number: 64-18345

ACKNOWLEDGMENTS

For permission to reprint from the following, the editor wishes to thank:

George Allen & Unwin Ltd., London, The Real Tripitaka, *by Arthur Waley, 1952*

Routledge & Kegan Paul Ltd., London, The Travels of An Alchemist, *by Arthur Waley, 1931*

Harvard University Press, China's Response to the West: A Documentary Survey, *1839-1923, by Ssu-yü Teng and John K. Fairbank, Copyright, 1954, by the President and Fellows of Harvard College.*

FOREWORD

Our travel literature informs us of the grand design and memorable minutiae of the Age of Discovery. The language of that resounding epic of our civilization created narratives made taut by struggle and search. The language is buoyant with deeds nobly planned and boldly done, sonorous with the sense of mission and destiny, glory and greed, spiced with emotions of wonder and awe, of fortitude and hope, and sustained by a compelling curiosity. From Columbus' *Letter*, announcing his discovery of the New World, down the centuries, we are held by the splendor of the questing. Thus literature and language have persuaded us of the uniqueness of the experience: it was easy to believe that exploration began with Columbus and was peculiar to the West. (In exploration, the term pre-Columbian has the same coloration as the term pre-Christian has in historical dating.) But however familiar and cherished this belief might have been, it is no longer tenable; nor, one can add, fashionable.

Many factors have joined to give us this new attitude. Today we realize that, since European explorers found established human societies wherever it was possible to maintain life, it was obvious that millennia before the Age of Discovery men had crossed the oceans and found the most distant islands and had penetrated mountain systems and forbidding deserts into the innermost recesses of the continents. Then, too, we know from fragmentary records that men of earlier civilizations —Egyptians, Achaemenians, Carthaginians, Greeks, and Polynesians—made purposive, extensive, and daring voyages of discovery. Finally, we are becoming acquainted with the travel literature of other, more recent travelers, Hindus, Arabs, and Chinese. To read the accounts of such non-European travelers is a fascinating experience. Nowhere do they take us into regions different or unknown. Yet even though the landscape across which they move is the same, the language of their records makes it seem utterly different. (One can say lamb is lamb, but a *gigot* prepared by a French chef hardly seems the same animal as appears in a Muslim *kebab.*)

By contrast the language of the Chinese travel literature is lean and laconic. There is a matter-of-factness; it appears to avoid any emotion, and adventures and mishaps are related quite simply. Each of the journeys was undertaken as a mission; but the mission was specific not mystical—to contact a possible distant political ally, to make a pilgrimage, to converse with a world conqueror. Fear and bravery, those prime ingredients of travel literature, are presented obliquely through situation and response. It is the perseverence of the traveler himself that holds the narrative together. Yet despite this muted, prosaic language, the individual quality of the traveler does emerge and prove him brother to our finest hero.

I have omitted the account of the discovery of the country of Fu-sang, named for the gigantic tree found there whose bark furnished the natives with cloth. In A.D. 499, a priest —whether Buddhist or Taoist is not clear—sailed some thirty thousand *li* to the east to reach a land which stretched another ten thousand *li* and bordered on another vast ocean. The natives lived in towns and had writing; they used copper, gold, and silver, but not iron; they possessed horses, milking-reindeer, and seven-foot silkworms. Fu-sang has been identified as America. I have chosen to side-step the arguments and instead give excerpts from Emperor Mu in whose *Travels* a Fu-sang tree with suns hanging like fruit is part of the lands visited.

For quite another reason I have not been able to include one of the most unusual of Chinese travelers. Hsü Hung-tsu (1586–1641, better known as Hsü Hsia-Kó), certainly the equal of any of the Western Arctic explorers, spent more than thirty years traversing the least known and wildest parts of the empire. He explored the mighty mountain regions which radiate from the Tibetan massif and his notes, meticulous and precise, written daily at the end of a long and arduous trek, run to some 750,000 words. Only scattered portions have been translated and I did not feel that summaries and isolated tidbits gave the full quality of this extraordinary scientist.

This anthology of Chinese travelers is offered, therefore, as an introduction and an invitation.

JEANNETTE MIRSKY

Princeton, N. J.
1964

I would like to thank Professor Frederick W. Mote for his encouragement and guidance; however, all mistakes in selection or exposition are mine solely. I am also indebted to Professor T. Cuyler Young who honored me by naming me to a Visiting Fellowship in the Department of Oriental Studies, Princeton University.

J. M.

CONTENTS

ONE *1001-945 B.C.*
TRAVELS OF EMPEROR MU 3

TWO *c. 123 B.C.*
CHANG CH'IEN: THE HAN AMBASSADOR TO BACTRIA 13

THREE *c. A.D. 645*
HSÜAN-TSANG: PRINCE OF PILGRIMS 29

FOUR *c. A.D. 1220*
THE TAOIST CH'ANG-CH'UN
GOES TO VISIT CHINGHIZ KHAN 119

FIVE *c. A.D. 1250*
RABBAN SAUMA VISITS EUROPE 175

SIX *c. A.D. 1297*
RECOLLECTIONS OF THE CUSTOMS OF CAMBODIA 203

SEVEN *early fifteenth century*
CHENG HO'S NAVAL EXPEDITIONS 237

EIGHT *eighteenth century*
THE HAI-LU: AN EIGHTEENTH-CENTURY SEAMAN 263

NINE *nineteenth century*
SCHOLARS, STUDENTS, AND AMBASSADORS 275

CHAPTER ONE

TRAVELS OF EMPEROR MU

TRAVELS OF EMPEROR MU[1]

INTRODUCTION

It seems proper to begin this volume with a sampling from the Travels of Emperor Mu *and disregard the question of whether it is an historical chronicle, or one of the earliest Chinese romances of adventure, or a bewildering mixture of both. Since again and again archeologists and linguistic scholars are finding evidence that events and peoples mentioned in scripture, epic, and saga were indeed part of history and not wholly creations of the imagination, it seems wiser to suspend judgment on Emperor Mu and include him.*

There is another reason. Even a sample of a fragment transports us instantly, magically into a world of travel literature as alien to us as the society that produced it. It trains the eye to grapple with strange names and places and proprieties; it states the deeper differences of a rhetoric that subscribes to its own honorable tradition: the idiom is dry and commonplace, the emphasis is on precise minutiae, the tone is as unemotional as a timetable. Yet in the end, the accounts engage us not with a bravery of language or experience, but simply with the fortitude they imply and with the magnitude of the accomplishment.

Hsün Hsü, whose Preface is quoted below, was ordered by Emperor Wu-ti of the Chin Dynasty to re-edit the "bamboo books" found in the tomb of an ancient king. Among the books was the one entitled The Travels of Emperor Mu.

[1] Excerpts taken from the translation by Cheng te-k'un, *Journal of the North China Branch of the Royal Asiatic Society*, Vol. 64, 1933, pp. 124–142.

The book is made of slips of bamboo, pasted with white silk. The leaves are each two feet, four inches long, containing forty characters written in black ink. According to the Bamboo Annals, *also found in the grave, the tomb belongs to Ling-wang, son of Hui-ch'eng-wang, ruler of the Wei State, c. 245* B.C.

The book records the travels of King Mu of the Chou Dynasty (the fifth emperor of that dynasty, who ruled for fifty-five years, 1001–945 B.C.). "King Mu," *Hsün Hsü quotes a commentary on the* Classic of Spring and Autumn, "wished to satisfy his ambition by touring around the world and by marking the countries under the sky with the wheels of his chariot and the hoofs of his horses.

"The king, having the fine steeds Tao-li and Luh-erh, and the excellent driver Tsao Fu, traveled around the world. He visited the four remote corners of the world, crossing the Flowing Sand Desert on the north, ascending the K'un-lun Mountain on the west and paying a visit to the Royal Mother of the West.

"Unfortunately, the book was not well preserved in Chi-hsien and most of the leaves have been either destroyed or disarranged. . . . Therefore, Your Majesty's servant has carefully translated the old text on yellow sheets of paper two feet in size, and begs that, when at leisure, Your Majesty will order the court secretary to copy it out together with the original text and store it up in the third Hall as one of the Middle Classics."

CHAPTER I

On the day *mou-yin*, Emperor Mu started out for the north by crossing the river Chang. [The Chinese have a special way of counting the years. There are ten characters known as the ten stems of heaven and another twelve characters known as the twelve branches of earth. The combinations of these two sets of characters give names to the sixty years of the Chinese cycle. The days are named and counted the same way. This system has actually been in use since the Yin Dynasty, 1766?–1112? B.C.] Two days later the company reached . . . where the emperor was entertained at a banquet by the people of this country upon a hill . . . the emperor himself did not alight from his chariot. The company then proceeded forward until they arrived at the foot of the Hsing Mountain [in Hopei].

On the day *kuei-wei* it snowed, and the emperor went out hunting on the western ranges of the mountain. Crossing the valley of the mountain he followed a course north to the southern bank of the Ho-t'o River. The emperor proceeded north and . . . arrived at the domain of the Ch'uan-jung (a northern barbarous tribe) and was entertained by the people on the southern bank of the Tang River. He was very pleased. . . . The north wind blew on the day *kêng-yin* and snow fell. The emperor ordered his followers to stop and rest, because the weather was cold.

On *chia-wu*, the emperor proceeded to the west and soon crossed the hills of the Yü Gate or Pass [through the mountains northwest of Tai-chou, Shansi Province], at the frontier. On the day *chi-hai* the company arrived at the plains of Yen-chu and Yu-chih. On the day *hsin-ch'ou*, the emperor marched on to the west and reached the kingdom of Pëng-jen. The people of this country were the descendants of Ho-tsung (the god of the Yellow River). Po Hsü, the duke of P'êng-en, proceeded to Chih-shih to welcome the royal guest, offering as presents ten leopards' skins and twenty-six good horses. Duke Ching accepted the presents by the emperor's command.

On the day *kuei-yu* the company camped in the neighborhood of the Ch'i Lake. The emperor went fishing in the river and paid a visit to the country of Chih-shih. The next day the emperor went hunting and captured a white fox and a black *lo* [a kind of fox] with which he made sacrifice to the God of the River. Two days later a banquet was spread by the river and the emperor reviewed his company, which was composed of six divisions of soldiers. On the day *mou-yin* the emperor made his way to the west, marching on as far as the Yang-yu Mountains, where in ancient days Wu Yi, the God of the River, had established his family, the house of Ho-tsung. [This god has a man's face and rides on two dragons; he lives in the Stream of Ts'ung-chi, which is 300 feet deep.] A member of this house welcomed the emperor . . . offering as presents a piece of silk fabric and a *pi* [an ancient jade badge of office, made round with a hole].

On the auspicious day *mou-wu* the emperor robed himself appropriately in the ceremonial costume, the cap, the gown, the handkerchief, the girdle and the *fou,* with ornamental hangings on both sides [a tablet, about three feet long, made of ivory, precious stones, wood or bamboo that was held before the breast by courtiers at audience, even as late as the Ming Dynasty, 1368–1644]. And, holding a *pi* in his hands, he took his stand . . . facing the south. Tseng Chu was the assistant at the ceremony. When the officials had arranged the sacrifical animals in their proper order, the emperor presented the *pi* to the God of the River. Po Yao received it from him, turned to the west and submerged the present in the river. After performing this he knelt before the Son of Heaven and touched his head to the earth many times. Tseng Chu then submerged the sacrificial animals . . . the ox, the horse, the pig and the sheep. Then the God of the River appeared from the water, and, bearing good tidings from God, he addressed the emperor by name, saying, "Mu Man, be thou forever on the throne and may thy rule be wise and prosperous!" To the south the emperor bowed many times.

"Mu Man," continued the God of the River, "let me show thee the precious articles of the Ch'un Mountain and the beautiful palaces of K'un-lun [this mountain, the center of Chinese mythology, was where all the gods assembled; it is also the name of a range in Chinese Turkestan where there are four plains from which flow seventy springs]. Proceed, then, to the K'un-lun Mountain, and behold the precious articles of the Ch'un Mountain."

The voice dropped low and died away. . . .

CHAPTER 2

On the day *ting-ssŭ* the emperor ascended the . . . mountain on the southwest. It was the domain of Mu Hua, where big trees and large bushes spread wide, and wild animals were abundant. It was a good place for hunting.

On the day *mou-wu,* Chu Yü, of the people of Shou Yü, offered as presents one hundred measures of wine. After the entertainment the emperor advanced and halted at the ridge of the K'un-lun by the southern bank of the Red River. . . . On the auspicious day *hsin-yu* the emperor ascended the K'un-lun Mountain and visited the palaces of the Yellow Emperor [the so-called Father of the Chinese race, who is supposed to have ruled the empire in peace for a hundred years beginning 2697 B.C.]. And, in order to identify the burial place of the God of the Clouds for future generations, he heaped up earth upon his grave. . . . The emperor marched on to the north and halted at Chu-tse, or the Pearl Pond, to fish in the running stream. It is said that the marshes of the Pearl Pond were thirty *li* square, and that in them grew all kinds of reeds and rushes. . . . On the day *ting-mao,* in the last month of the summer, the emperor ascended the Ch'un Mountain on the north, from where he could see the wilderness stretching in all four directions. . . .

It is said that the Ch'un Mountain was the richest mountain in the world, a store of precious stones and valuable jades. It was a place where the most flourishing crops grew and the trees were tall and the bushes beautiful. The emperor gathered some species of these excellent crops so that he might cultivate them in the central kingdom when he returned. It is also said that the emperor rested at the foot of the mountain for five days and amused himself with music. Ch'i then presented to the emperor many beautiful women. Among them, Lady T'ing and Lady Lieh soon became his favorite concubines. It is said that the country of the Red Bird was famous for its beautiful women and valuable jade.

On the day *chi-mao* the emperor marched on to the north, driving forward without taking any rest, until he crossed the Yang River and on the next day arrived at the domain of Ts'ao Nu. . . . On the day *jen-wu* the emperor rode to the north and turned eastward on the way back, arriving at the Black River on the day *chia-shen*. The people of the wild west call the river Hung-lu. It rained for seven days and the emperor stopped to wait for the soldiers of the six divisions. Here he conferred on Ch'ang-kung, a member of the Long-armed People, the right to rule over the western portion of the Black River. . . . On *kuei-ch'ou* the emperor rode westward arriving at Bitter Mountain. The name of the wild west was Garden of Prosperity. The emperor stopped for hunting and here he tasted the bitter herb. On the day *ting-hsü* the emperor marched to the westward and on *chi-wei* the company stayed for the night to the west of Yellow Rat Mountain. . . . They proceeded westward until on *kuei-hai* they arrived at the domain of the Royal Mother of the West [semi-devil, semi-goddess, or, it has even been suggested, the Queen of Sheba].

CHAPTER 3

On the auspicious day *chia-tzu* the emperor, carrying a white *kuei* [a small stone scepter given to nobles as a sign of rank—the size varying with the rank—that is held in both hands during levees] and a black *pi*, paid a visit to the Royal Mother of the West. To her he offered as presents one hundred pieces of embroidered silk and three hundred pieces of *wu* fabric. After bowing many times, the Royal Mother accepted the presents.

On the next day the emperor invited the Royal Mother to a banquet on Emerald Pond. During the occasion she sang extempore:

> "Hills and mountains come in view
> As fleecy clouds ascend the sky.
> Far and wide, divided by waters and mountain ranges
> Our countries separately lie.
> Should long life preserve thee,
> Come again."

To this the emperor responded:

> "When I to east return
> To millions bringing order and peace;
> When they enjoy prosperity and ease
> To thee shall I return;
> From this day count three years
> To this country again I shall come."

The emperor then rode on the Hsi Mountains and on the rocks engraved a record of his visit. He planted a memorial tree of sophora and named the place the Mountain of the Royal Mother of the West.

From here the emperor took his way back to the east. . . . On the day *ting-wei* the emperor took a drink at Hot Mountain and the next day went out fowling. The following day, he drank at the bank of the Ju River and gave orders for the six divisions of soldiers to gather together.

In this region there were forests, marshy swamps and ponds full of water, and there were also smooth plains and high plateaus where birds scattered their feathers. Now the six divisions of soldiers had concentrated in this region where it is said the emperor stayed for three months. The emperor gave a big banquet to the ministers of state, the royal princes, the big feudal lords, the officials and all the companies of the seven regiments in Yu-ch'in, a higher plain in this wide region. . . . The soldiers started out on horseback on their expedition with their hounds before them. The hunting was carried on for fully nine days and they captured all the birds and animals in this region, the number of victims being countless. On the plain Yu-ch'in they presented all they had obtained. The good furs and the beautiful feathers were carefully selected and carried home in their carriages. The emperor had for himself one hundred carriages full. . . .

The emperor hurried on eastward, crossing the desert on the south . . . he was thirsty and water could not be obtained in the desert, so Kao Pên-jung, a member of the seven regiments, stabbed the left horse of his chariot in the neck and presented a drink of pure blood to his royal master. The emperor was very much pleased and gave him a piece of ornamental jade, which the soldier received by kneeling down and touching his head to the ground.

The emperor then proceeded southward and reached the end of the Piled Stone Mountain Range, where he found cypresses growing abundantly.

CHAPTER TWO

CHANG CH'IEN: THE HAN AMBASSADOR TO BACTRIA

CHANG CH'IEN: THE HAN AMBASSADOR TO BACTRIA[1]

INTRODUCTION

However alien the names and novel the setting, The Story of Chang Ch'ien *has a familiar theme: the pioneering of a lengthy, difficult, dangerous and historically important overland trail. In this respect, Chang Ch'ien is like our own explorers who blazed the Santa Fe, the Oregon and the other transcontinental trails. But there are also the differences of time and place, of motive and issue. Where the American trail blazers opened the continent to European settlers, Chang Ch'ien brought the high centers of Old World civilization into direct, purposeful communication, thus accelerating cultural cross-fertilization. For the Indo-Scythians, whom he came in search of, had just conquered the Greeks, who had ruled Bactria from the time of Alexander the Great; they showed themselves to be more interested in maintaining their new kingdom's ties with Syria, Egypt and the Mediterranean than in pursuing the ancient grudge they bore the Huns. By the completion of his mission as ambassador from the Han emperor of China to the king of Bactria, China, the Hellenistic West, India and Persia were brought into fruitful contact.*

He was not only a glorified messenger; the Chinese remember him as the man who brought back the grapevine and alfalfa, welcome additions to their agriculture. Later envoys,

[1] Text and translation of Chap. 123 of Ssŭ-ma Ch'ien's *Shih Chi* by Friedrich Hirth, *Journal of the American Oriental Society*, Vol. 37, 1917, pp. 89–116.

following his example, brought back the chive, the coriander, the cucumber, the fig, the sesame, the safflower and the walnut; and in return China gave the West the pear, peach and orange, and, among our flowers, the rose, peony, azalea, camellia and chrysanthemum.

As great a pioneer as Chang Ch'ien was the historian Ssŭ-ma Ch'ien, the "Herodotus of China," who set the pattern for the writing of history in China. "My narrative," he said in explaining his method, "consists of no more than a systematization of the material that has been handed down to us. There is therefore no creation; only a faithful representation."[2]

The Shih Chi, Memoirs of an Historian, *was completed about 100* B.C. *Like his father, Ssŭ-ma Ch'ien held the post of Court Astrologer; he was a traveler as well as a scholar.*

* * *

Our first knowledge of Ta-yuan [Ferghana] dates from Chang Ch'ien, a native of Han-chung, in the south of Shensi Province. During the Ch'ien-yuan reign [140–134 B.C.] he was a *lang*, a titular officer of the imperial household. At that time the Son of Heaven made inquiries among those of the Hsiung-nu [Huns] who had surrendered and been made prisoners, and they all reported that the Hsiung-nu had overcome the king of the Yeuh-chih and made a drinking vessel out of his skull. The Yueh-chih had decamped and were hiding somewhere, constantly scheming how to revenge themselves on the Hsiung-nu; but they had no ally to join with them in striking a blow.

The Chinese, wishing to declare war on the Huns to wipe them out, when they learned this, desired to establish contact with the Yueh-chih; but the road to them led through the ter-

[2] L. Carrington Goodrich, *A Short History of the Chinese People*, 3rd ed. (New York, Harper and Brothers, 1959), p. 52.

ritory of the Huns. The emperor called for volunteers. Chang Ch'ien, being a *lang*, responded to the call and enlisted in a mission to seek out the Yueh-chih. He took with him Kan Fu, a Tartar who had been a slave of the T'ang-i family, and set out from Kansu to cross the Hun territory. Almost immediately he was caught, taken prisoner, and sent to the Great Khan, who detained him, saying, "The Yueh-chih are to the north of us. How can China send ambassadors to them? If I wanted to send ambassadors to Kiangsi and Chekiang, would China be willing to submit to us?" He held Chang Ch'ien for more than ten years; he gave him a wife by whom he had a son. All this time Chang Ch'ien kept possession of the emperor's token of authority, and when in the course of time he was permitted greater freedom, he watched his opportunity and succeeded in making his escape with his men. He went in the direction of the Yueh-chih. Having marched several tens of days to the west, he arrived at Ta-yuan. The inhabitants, having heard of the wealth and fertility of China, had vainly tried to communicate with it. When, therefore, they saw Chang Ch'ien, they asked joyfully, "Where do you wish to go?" And he replied, "I was sent by the Emperor of China to the Yueh-chih and was made prisoner by the Hsiung-nu. I have now escaped them and would ask your king to have someone guide me to the country of the Yueh-chih. If I succeed in reaching that country, on my return my king will reward you with untold treasures."

The Ta-yuan believed his story and gave him safe-conduct on postal roads to K'ang-chu [Sogdiana] and they sent him on to the Yueh-chih. After the king of the Yueh-chih had been killed by the Huns, the people set up his heir as king (though one authority says it was the queen who named the successor). Since that time they had conquered Ta-hsia [Bactria] and occupied the country. It was a rich and fertile land, seldom harassed by robbers, and the people decided to enjoy this life of peace. Moreover, since they considered themselves too far away from China, they no longer wanted to revenge themselves on the Huns. After having made his way through so many tribes to find Bactria, Chang Ch'ien was unable to persuade the Yueh-chih to move against their former enemy. He remained there for a year and then started for home, skirting the Nan-shan in the hopes of going through the country of the Tanguts. But again he was caught and made a prisoner of the Huns. Thus a whole year passed; the khan died and the "left" highly honored prince attacked the rightful heir and usurped the throne, throwing the country into a state of confusion. This was the time Chang Ch'ien, accompanied by his Tartar wife and Kan Fu, the Tartar and former slave, escaped and made his way back to China.

The Emperor Wu-ti [reigned 140–87 B.C.] appointed Chang Ch'ien Imperial Chamberlain and gave Kan Fu the title of Gentleman Attending the Embassy. Chang Ch'ien was a man of strong physique, magnanimous and trustful, and popular with the foreign tribes in the south and west. The Tartar Kan Fu was an excellent bowman and, when supplies were exhausted, provided food by hunting game. When Chang Ch'ien started on his journey [138 B.C.] he had more than a hundred men in his caravan; thirteen years later, only two had lived to return [126 B.C.]. Of the countries he had visited personally, Chang Ch'ien gave this report to his emperor.

FERGHANA: is to the southwest of the Huns and due west of China at a distance of about 10,000 *li*. The people are settled and engage in agriculture; in their fields they raise rice and wheat. They have wine made of grapes and many good horses. The horses sweat blood and come from the stock of the Heavenly Horse. They have walled cities and houses; the large and small cities belonging to them, fully seventy in number, contain an aggregate population of several hundreds of thousands. Their arms consist of bows and halberds, and they can shoot arrows while on horseback. North of this country is Sogdiana; in the west are the Indo-Scythians; in the southwest is Bactria; in the northeast are the Wu-sun; and in the east Han-mi [?] and Khotan. All the rivers west of Khotan flow in a westerly direction and feed the Western Sea; all the rivers east of it flow east and feed the Salt Lake [Lop-nor]. The Salt Lake flows underground. To the south of Khotan is the source from which the Yellow River [the Ho] arises. The country contains much jade. The river flows through China; the towns of Lou-lan and Ku-shi with their city walls closely border on the Salt Lake, which is possibly 5000 *li* from Chang-an [Wu-ti's capital]. The Western Huns live to the east of the Salt Lake up to the Great Wall in Lung-hsi. They are bounded on the south by the Tanguts, who bar their road to China.

WU-SUN: may be 2000 *li* northeast of Ferghana. Its people are nomads following their herds of cattle; their customs resemble those of the Huns. Of archers they have several tens of thousands, all daring warriors. Formerly they were subject to the Huns, but they grew so strong that though they maintain nominal vassalage they refuse to attend the meetings of the court.

SOGDIANA: is to the northwest of Ferghana, possibly 2000 *li* distant. It also is a country of nomads with manners and customs very similar to those of the Yueh-chih. They have eighty or ninety thousand archers. The country is coterminous with Ferghana. It is small. In the south it is under the political influence of the Yueh-chih; in the east, under that of the Huns.

AORSI: lies to the northeast of Sogdiana perhaps at a distance of 2000 *li*. It is a nomad state and its manners and customs are in the main identical with those of Sogdiana. It has fully a hundred thousand archers. The country lies close to a great sea ["great marsh," the Sea of Azov] which has no limit, for it is the Northern Sea.

INDO-SCYTHIANS: are perhaps two or three thousand *li* to the west of Ferghana. They live to the north of the Oxus. South of them is Bactria; in the west is Parthia; in the north, Sogdiana. They are a nomad nation, following their flocks and changing their abodes. Their customs are the same as the Huns. They may have from one to two hundred thousand archers. In olden times they relied on their strength and thought lightly of the Huns; but when Mao-tun ascended the throne he attacked and defeated the Yueh-chih. Up to the time when Lau-chang, khan of the Huns, killed the king of the Yueh-chih and made a drinking vessel out of his skull, the Yueh-chih had lived between Tun-huang and Ch'i-lien, a hill southwest, but when they were beaten by the Huns, they fled to a distant country and crossed to the west of Ferghana, attacked Bactria, and conquered it. Subsequently, they established their capital north of the Oxus and made it the court of their king. The minority, who were left behind and were unable to follow the main body, took refuge among the Tanguts, who occupied the Nan-shan and were called the Small Yueh-chih.

PARTHIA: [*An-hsi*, the Chinese name, is derived from Antioch in Margiana, Merv.] This country I did not visit personally, but I learned that it may be several thousand *li* west of the Indo-Scythians. The people live in fixed abodes and are given to agriculture; their fields yield rice and wheat; and they make wine of grapes. Several hundred small and large cities belong to it. The territory is several thousand *li* square; it is a very large country and close to the Oxus. Their traders and merchants travel in carts and boats to the neighboring countries, perhaps several thousand *li* distant. They make coins of silver; the coins resemble their king's face. Upon the death of a king the coins are changed for others on which the new king's face is represented. They paint rows of characters running sideways on stiff leather to serve them as records. West of this country is Babylonia; north is Aorsi.

SYRIA AND BABYLONIA: [Syria includes the Media of the Seloucids and possibly Egypt as well as the present Syria] are several thousand *li* west of Parthia and close to the Western Sea [Red Sea]. Babylonia is hot and damp. The inhabitants plow their fields in which they grow rice. There is a big bird with eggs the size of jars. The number of its inhabitants is very large, and they have in many places their own petty chiefs; but Parthia, while having added it to its dependencies, considers it a foreign country. They have clever jugglers. [This is the first mention of the "clever jugglers" from Syria.] Although the old people in Parthia maintain the tradition that the Jo-shui [?] and the Hsi-wang-mu [?] are in Babylonia, they have not been seen there.

BACTRIA: [which Chang Ch'ien did visit] is more than 2000 *li* to the southwest of Ferghana, on the south bank of the Oxus. The people have fixed abodes and live in walled cities and regular houses like the people of Ferghana. They have no great king or chief, but everywhere the cities and towns have their own petty chiefs. While the people are shrewd traders, their soldiers are weak and afraid to fight, so that when the Yueh-chih migrated westward, they made war on the Bactrians, who became subject to them. The population of Bactria may amount to more than a million. Their capital is called Lan-hsï, and it has markets for the sale of all kinds of merchandise. To the southeast of it is the country of India. [And then the chronicler quotes Chang Ch'ien's report verbatim] "When I was in Bactria, I saw there a stick of bamboo from Ch'iung [Ch'iung-chou in Szechuan] and some cloth from Szechuan. When I asked the inhabitants how they obtained possession of these they replied, 'The inhabitants of our country buy them in India.' India may be several thousand *li* to the southeast of Bactria. The people there have fixed abodes, and their customs are very much like those of Bactria, but the country is low, damp and hot. The people ride on elephants to fight in battle. The country is close to a great river. According to my calculation, Bactria must be 12,000 *li* distant from China and to the southwest of the latter. Now the country of India being several thousand *li* to the southeast of Bactria, and the produce of Szechuan being found there, that country cannot be far from Szechuan. Suppose we send ambassadors to Bactria through the country of the Tanguts, there is the danger that the Tanguts will object; and if we send them farther north, they will be captured by the Huns. But by going by way of Szechuan they may proceed directly and will be unmolested by robbers." [Chang Ch'ien had indeed grasped that a route between Szechuan and India via Yunnan and Burma, or Assam, did exist and that trade goods passed along it. What he was suggesting to the emperor was that China could side-step both the Huns and the Tibetans and establish contact with the West.]

The Son of Heaven on hearing all this reasoned thus: Ferghana and the possessions of Bactria and Parthia are large countries, full of rare things, with a population living in fixed abodes [not nomads like the Huns] and given to occupations somewhat identical with those of the Chinese people, but with weak armies and placing great value on the rich produce of China. In the north, the possessions of the Indo-Scythians and the Sogdianans, being of military strength, might be made subservient to the interests of our court by bribes and thus won by the mere force of persuasion. In this way a territory 10,000 *li* in extent would be available for the spread among the Four Seas of our superior Chinese civilization by communicating through many interpreters with the nations holding widely different customs. As a result, the Son of Heaven was pleased to approve Chang Ch'ien's proposal, and, in accordance with his suggestions, gave orders that exploring expeditions be sent out from Szechuan [on the Upper Yangtze]. Four parties were simultaneously to try different routes, one to start by way of the Mang tribe, another by way of the Jan [both barbarous hill peoples occupying the southwestern frontier]; the third by way of Ssu [?], and the fourth by way of Ch'iung-chou and P'o in Szechuan. Each one of these missions had traveled hardly more than a thousand *li* when they were stopped by tribes who had no chiefs and were given to robbery; the Chinese envoys would have been killed or captured. The expeditions could not get beyond that point, but they heard that about a thousand *li* or more to the west there was the "elephant-riding country" called T'ien-yueh [possibly Yunnan], whither the Szechuan traders were accustomed to go, exporting produce surreptitiously [smuggling]. Thus it was that by trying to find the road to Bactria, the Chinese obtained their first knowledge of the T'ien country [Yunnan].

The original idea to penetrate from China through the country of the southwestern barbarians was abandoned because, in spite of the heavy expenses incurred, the passage could not be effected; but as a result attention had been drawn to these barbarians. It had been due to Chang Ch'ien's knowledge of their pasture grounds when, as a subcommander, he served under the general-in-chief sent out against the Huns that the army did not fall short of provisions. For this the emperor invested him with the title "Marquis of Po-wang"; this was in 123 B.C. But the very next year Chang Ch'ien took part in a campaign against the Huns east of Peking; when he failed to come quickly enough to the aid of his commander-in-chief, who was blocked by the enemy and suffered heavy losses, his laxness could have been punished by death. Instead, he was permitted to pay a fine, and be reduced to the rank of private.

That same year China also sent an army against the western *ordo* [encampment, capital] of the Huns. At the head of several tens of thousands of troops, the Chinese general pushed forward and the following year (121 B.C.) the Hun prince [whose encampment had been attacked] with all his people submitted and paid their allegiance to China; to the west and all along the Nan-shan as far as the Salt Lake [Lop-nor], no Huns remained. Occasionally Huns would raid caravans, but such harassment was rare, and two years later the Chinese forced the khan of the Huns to retreat to the north of the desert. After such momentous events, the Son of Heaven consulted several times with Chang Ch'ien about Bactria and other countries. Since Ch'ien had lost his marquisate, he submitted the following report:

"When your servant was living among the Huns, he heard that the king of the Wu-sun was styled *k'un-mo*. At one time the k'un-mo's father was chief of a petty state on the western borders of the Huns. The Huns attacked and killed the father and the k'un-mo, at his birth, was cast away in the wilderness, where meat was brought to him by a blackbird and a she-wolf nursed him with her milk. The khan of the Huns regarded this as a miracle and, having raised the child to manhood, made him a military leader in which capacity he distinguished himself on several occasions. The khan restored his father's people to him and made him governor of the Western Ordo. Once restored to chieftainship of his people, the k'un-mo attacked the neighboring small states with tens of thousands of archers, gained experience in conducting war and, after the death of the khan of the Huns, took his forces to a distant retreat and refused to appear at the Hun court. At this affront, the Huns sent a force of picked troops to attack him; unable to conquer him, they thought of him as a spirit whom they had better keep at a distance and whom they would not seriously attack even though they continued to claim nominal jurisdiction over him. Now since the khan of the Huns has been defeated by China and the Hun prince's former territory has been deserted, and since the barbarians covet the rich produce of China, this is the opportune moment to bribe the Wu-sun with liberal presents and invite them to settle farther east in what had been the Huns' territory. Should they become attached to the Chinese as a brother nation by intermarriage (betroth a Chinese princess to the k'un-mo), the situation would be in favor of their listening to our proposition, and if they do that, it would be tantamount to the cutting off of the western branch of the Hun nation. Once we are connected by marriage with the Wu-sun, the countries to the west of them might be invited to come to us as outer subjects."

The Son of Heaven approved of Chang Ch'ien's proposal and appointed him commander in the Imperial Bodyguard as well as leader of an expedition consisting of three hundred men, each with two horses, and thousands of oxen and sheep. He also furnished him with gifts of gold and silken stuffs worth millions, and with assistant envoys, holding credentials, whom Chang Ch'ien could dispatch to, or leave behind in, other nearby countries.

When Chang Ch'ien arrived at the Wu-sun, he keenly resented the humiliation offered to him, ambassador of China, by a mere k'un-mo of the Wu-sun when he received him in audience with court ceremonial like that adopted with the khan of the Huns. Knowing the greed of these barbarians, he said, "If the k'un-mo does not treat these gifts with due respect, which have come from the Son of Heaven, they will be withdrawn." Whereupon the k'un-mo rose and bowed low before the gifts; but all other ceremonies passed off as before. Then Chang Ch'ien explained the emperor's ideas. "If the Wu-sun are able to move eastward into the Huns' territory, China will send a princess to become the k'un-mo's consort." The Wu-sun were divided. By now the k'un-mo was old and considering China very distant, and being unaware of its greatness, had heretofore submitted for a very long time to the Huns. Furthermore, his country was nearer theirs so that his ministers, who were afraid of the Tartars, did not wish to move away, and, since the Wu-sun k'un-mo was not free to make his own decision, Chang Ch'ien was not successful in persuading him to adopt his suggestion.

The k'un-mo had more than ten sons; the second, Ta-lu, was an energetic leader of the masses. In this capacity he set himself up in a separate part of the kingdom with more than ten thousand horsemen. Ta-lu's older brother, the crown prince, had a son, Ts'on-ts'u. When the crown prince met with an early death, his last words to his father were: "Let Ts'on-ts'u become crown prince and do not allow any other man to take his place." The k'un-mo, in his grief, consented; and so, on the death of his father, Ts'on-ts'u became crown prince. Ta-lu was angry at being prevented from acting as crown prince and, having imprisoned his brothers, led his people against Ts'on-ts'u and the k'un-mo. The latter, being old, was in constant fear that Ta-lu might kill Ts'on-ts'u; he therefore gave the latter more than ten thousand horsemen and told him to settle elsewhere; he retained the same number of horsemen for his own protection.

The population was thus divided into three parts, and, notwithstanding that the majority were under his authority, the k'un-mo did not dare take the full responsibility for concluding a treaty with Chang Ch'ien. Chang Ch'ien, therefore, sent assistant ambassadors in several directions to the countries of Ferghana, Sogdiana, Indo-Scythia, Bactria, Parthia, India, Khotan, Hanmi [?] and the adjacent territories. The Wu-sun furnished guides and interpreters to accompany Chang Ch'ien on his return, and the latter, traveling with several dozen natives and as many horses sent by the Wu-sun in acknowledgement of the emperor's gift, thereby afforded them the opportunity to see China with their own eyes and thus to realize her extent and greatness.

On his return to China, Chang Ch'ien was appointed "Great Traveler," or head of the Office of Foreign Affairs, with rank as one of the nine ministers of state. More than a year after this he died.

The envoys of the Wu-sun, having seen that China was a very populous and wealthy country, reported to this effect on their return home, and this increased the esteem in which she was held there. More than a year later some of the envoys whom Chang Ch'ien had sent to the Bactrian countries returned with natives of those countries, and after this the countries of the northwest began to have intercourse with China. Since Chang Ch'ien had been the pioneer in this, envoys proceeding to the West after him always referred to the Marquis of Po-wang as an introduction in foreign countries, the mention of his name being regarded as a guaranty of good faith.

CHAPTER THREE

HSÜAN-TSANG: PRINCE OF PILGRIMS

HSÜAN-TSANG: PRINCE OF PILGRIMS[1]

INTRODUCTION

How fortunate we are that Johnson had his Boswell; and how fortunate for Boswell that he had in Johnson a subject worthy of his respectful admiration on whom he could spend his considerable talent. His Life *adds a dimension to Johnson's own writings. So, too, the Shaman Hui-li's* Life of Hsüan-tsang, *an act of love and piety, supplements Hsüan-tsang's own account of his sixteen-year quest, the* Hsi-yu-chi Record of Western Countries. *Hui-li wrote his book in 648 or 649, three or four years after Tripitaka had returned from his journey to India. For only in widely spaced intervals of leisure snatched from the great task of translation from Sanskrit into Chinese and after the daily routine of governing a large monastery was concluded, could the master relax and speak of his adventures along the Silk Road route to India. And Hui-li, cherished and devoted, faithfully set down what Tripitaka told of the perils and pleasures of the road, the kingdoms and cities he had seen and the shrines he had visited, the erudite teachers he had studied with, the strange peoples he had met and the stranger*

[1] Both Tripitaka's account and Hui-li's biography were translated by Samuel Beal: *Buddhist Records of the Western World*, 2 vols., London, 1906; and *The Life of Hiuen-tsang* (sic) by the Shaman Hui Li, London, 1911. I have tried to weave these together, being guided and aided in this by constant reference to Arthur Waley's delightful book, *The Real Tripitaka* (London, George Allen & Unwin, Ltd., 1952). This last is primarily concerned with illuminating the religious and doctrinal quest of Tripitaka as it shaped the nature of Chinese Buddhism.

customs—the most interesting items he had experienced as he wandered in the birthplace of his faith.

That Hui-li was a compassionate man is indicated by his being called Shaman, for so the Sanskrit word Shama *is rendered. His reverence for the master is a kind of sunlight warming every scene and situation in which his hero moves. Through Hui-li's eyes we come to know Tripitaka as a brilliant scholar conscious of his worth, a courageous traveler, a dedicated monk whom hermits welcomed and kings were proud to honor. It is pleasant to have his family background sketched in and to learn that the young Tripitaka, who was as "rosy as the evening mists and round as the rising moon; sweet as the odor of cinnamon or the vanilla tree," grew up to be a "tall, handsome man with beautiful eyes and a good complexion, who had a serious but gentle expression and a sedate, rather stately manner."*

The urge to go to the West came to Tripitaka when he was still young. It was part of his precocity to recognize how limited Chinese Buddhism was by the paucity and imperfections of the translations of the Scriptures and learned commentaries: his mind sensed that worlds of holy truth were waiting to be discovered in India and made available to China. And inevitably it is through his biographer that we come under the spell of the fascination Tripitaka exerted—it does not appear on the instant to overwhelm or dazzle us, but rather it is slowly felt as we accompany him on the long, rugged, dogged miles to India, through India, and back. Of the scores of monks who preceded him and followed him, Hsüan-tsang is the true prince of pilgrims. He is also the most human of men—frightened at having to cross a demon-haunted desert alone and unguided; aloof and calm in the face of royal histrionics and the mortal danger of bandit malevolence; and credulous and practical in equal measure, trusting soothsayers and contriving to make miracle-working statues give him the answers he desires.

This personal flavor is almost completely lacking in Tripitaka's classic Record of the Western Countries, *which conforms to the pattern of Chinese travel literature, which was, as Waley characterized it, "in the highest degree impersonal." Detached and emotionally anonymous, the story has none of the European idiom which features moments of suffering or success and exploits the traveler's reaction to frustration, suspense, danger and beauty. Instead he lists the direction and distance traversed, he notes the different terrains and the size, climate, products and noteworthy traits and customs of each of the many regions; he sets down fully and without any editorializing the tradition and legends, both sacred and secular, which he hears. The jungle of mythology he recorded has been useful to modern scholars in their reconstruction of that time when Buddhism, its world and ways, was still dominant in India. Thus, for example, out of this Buddhist hagiography, Sir Aurel Stein, who in his extraordinary Central Asian archeological expeditions claimed Hsüan-tsang as his "Patron Saint," was able to solve the mystery of a rat-headed divinity painted on a panel that Stein recovered from the desert near Khotan: "Hsüan-tsang's account of Khotan preserved for us the story of how sacred rats and their king, by destroying the horses' harness, etc., of an invading Hun host, had caused its defeat and thus saved the land."*[2]

* * *

[1] *History and Life* OF THE MASTER OF THE LAW, TRIPITAKA, HSÜAN-TSANG, OF THE GREAT MONASTERY OF MOTHERLY LOVE, AND OF HIS TRAVELS IN THE WESTERN WORLD. WRITTEN BY THE SHAMAN HUI-LI. C. A.D. 648–649.

The infant name of the Master of the Law was Hsüan-tsang; his ordinary family name was Chin; he was a native of Chin-liu and was born in A.D. 602, the youngest of four sons. The boy

[2] Stein, *On Ancient Central-Asian Tracks* (London, 1933), p. 62.

who was to become known as the Master of the Law came of a family of fairly high officials who could trace their name and positions back to ancestors serving the Han Dynasty (just before the beginning of the Christian era). His father was distinguished for his superior abilities, for the elegance of his manners, and for his moderation. Over six feet in height, he loved to be recognized as a scholar—wearing his dress large and his girdle full. He anticipated the decay and fall of the Sui Dynasty (590–618) and buried himself in the study of his books; and so, refusing all offers of political office, declining all magisterial duties on the plea of ill health, he retired to a remote district.

At eight, Hsüan-tsang started reading the Sacred Books and was charmed with the writings of the ancient sages. His elder brother, Ch'ang-chieh, who had become a Buddhist monk and dwelt in the Pure Land Monastery at Lo-yang, the eastern capital, observed how strongly his young brother was attracted to religious study. He took him to the monastery and taught him the method and practice of the Sacred Books of Buddhism.

The future Tripitaka was but a child when there was an unexpected royal mandate to choose fourteen monks to be supported free of charge. Several hundred candidates applied for this important ordination. Cheng Shan-kuo, the high commissioner supervising the ceremony, had an aptitude for recognizing talent in those he met. He observed the young Hsüan-tsang loitering at the hall gate. "Who are you"? he asked. "Do you wish to be selected?" And the boy told him his name, saying that he longed to be chosen but was excluded because of his youth. The high commissioner asked him why he wanted to become a monk, and Tripitaka said, "My only thought in taking such a step is to spread the Light of Buddhism." This impressed the official. He sensed the eagerness and sincere piety in the boy's reply and, despite his youth, selected him to be one of those ordained. For, as the high commissioner explained to the other officials, "To repeat one's instructions is easy, but true self-possession and nerve are not so common." The high commissioner's wish in the matter prevailed; Tripitaka was one of those selected.

As a recluse he lived with his brother in the Pure Land Monastery. Thus five years passed in concentrated study and the precocious youth won the monks' respect for his ability, his precision and clarity in expounding the most involved principles of the religion. His memory was extraordinary—he had only to hear a book read once to remember it throughout; his understanding was equally exceptional—after a second reading he needed no further instruction. At this time he was but thirteen years old.

Soon after this the Sui Dynasty lost the empire (A.D. 618) and the whole kingdom was in confusion. The capital became the rendezvous for robbers, wild beasts roamed the countryside, magistrates were killed, and congregations of monks either perished or took to flight. The streets of the capital were filled with bleached bones; rebellions and riots, massacre and ruin prevailed everywhere; never had such calamity befallen the empire. Everyone was occupied with the arts of war; the books of Confucius and the sacred writings of Buddhism were forgotten and there were no religious conferences in the capital. Tripitaka, deeply affected by these conditions, said to his brother, "Even if this were our native city, could we during the present state of things avoid death? I have heard that the prince of T'ang has established himself at Ch'ang-an, his new capital. The empire relies on him as on father and mother. Let my brother go there with me." The brother agreed to this and together they went to the northwest.

But in Ch'ang-an, though law and order had been restored, yet the only books being studied dealt with military strategy, and Tripitaka, unwilling to be idle, persuaded his brother to go where they could hope to continue their religious studies. Again his brother consented and they went southwest to Han-chung, where they met two learned monks who had also left the capital. At the sight of them, the brothers wept for joy; they stayed with them for a month and some days receiving instruction, and then pushed on to Ch'eng-tu, situated in a region of abundance and peace, where Buddhist monks from far and near had taken refuge. So great a concentration of learned monks offered the eager students the unique opportunity of studying the different schools of Buddhist knowledge. In two or three years Tripitaka had gleaned all that he could from those masters. It was there that he became twenty, and was fully ordained as a monk. He felt that the time had come for him to return to Ch'ang-an in order to clarify certain points and resolve some difficulties he had met in his studies. But now his brother had reasons for not wanting to leave.

Ch'ang-chieh, too, was well versed in Buddhist writings and other texts, in Chinese literature and history, and in Taoist philosophy. Of noble and commanding presence, an eloquent preacher, he was so loved by the people that the governor of the province sought him out and honored him with admiration and deference. The brother could not be persuaded to leave the city where his talents had won him respect and renown. And because he used his influence with the governor to try to prevent his younger brother from leaving, Tripitaka secretly took passage with some merchants and went by boat down the Chia-ling River to the Yangtze, and so down that mighty river to Chingchow. Known by report to the clergy, the prince of Han-yang and his officers, great numbers of people, both religious and lay, heard him preach and carry on a learned disputation. The prince was ecstatic; he showered Tripitaka with presents, which the monk declined to accept. After this debate

Tripitaka made his way northward, seeking out the most renowned monks: at Hsiang-chou [the modern An-yang] he asked questions of Hui-hsiu, a Master of the Law, and, continuing northward, he went to Chao-chou in order to study a difficult text under another famous monk, Tao-shen. In this way he returned to the capital, Ch'ang-an. There he found two great teachers who had attracted disciples as numerous as the clouds. By this time Tripitaka had visited the most celebrated masters throughout the country, devoured their words, and examined their principles; he realized that each master strictly followed the teaching of his own school. While verifying their doctrines, he finally understood that the holy books themselves had important differences, differences so great that he knew not which to follow. It was then he resolved to travel to the Western world in order to ask about doubtful passages. "Moreover," he said, "Fa-hsien [in India from 399–414] and Chih-yen, the pre-eminent monks of their age, went to India to seek the law for the guidance and profit of the people. Should I not aim to continue their noble example? It should be the duty of a great teacher to follow in their steps."

[By going to India, the home of Buddhism, he would find the teachers who could resolve his perplexities: so his biographer explains. Waley, however, suggests that Tripitaka was well aware that the number of sects in India was even greater than in China, and that since the Indian teachers commanded greater respect and authority, his dilemma would be deepened, not resolved. Rather, one of his main aims in going to India was to secure the Sanskrit text of the *Yoga Sastra*, a monumental compendium of Idealist philosophy, of which only parts had reached China. The Yoga school, as explained by a later pilgrim, taught that "the Outside does not exist, but that the Inside does. All things are mental activities only." And Waley illustrates this by the following example: "Sometimes we think that the odd noises we hear on the telephone were made by the distant person to whom we are talking when in reality they are due to a defect in our own receiving apparatus."][2]

Hearing of the obstructions to be overcome and the dangers of the the Western road, he considered what he should do; he would not, he resolved, give up his intention. Then he entered a sanctuary and there supplicated the holy ones to extend their mysterious influences so that he could make his journey and return safely. In the autumn of 630, he was preparing to start. He yearned for a happy omen. It came to him in a dream as his final plans were made. He dreamt that he beheld Mount Sumeru, the Divine Mountain, rising from the middle of the Great Sea; made out of gold, silver, beryl and crystal, it looked supremely beautiful and majestic. He desired to scale the mountain, but the waves around it rose high and wild and he saw neither ship nor raft. Without a shadow of fear he walked into the waves and at the very instant he did so, a lotus of stone sprang up under his foot, which, as soon as he had placed his foot on it, vanished to reappear in front of him. In a moment, dry-footed, he found himself at the base of the holy mountain. But he could not climb its craggy, steep sides. As he gathered his strength to try to leap forward, a powerful whirlwind lifted him up to the very summit. From there he gazed around and beheld nothing but the boundless horizon. Ravished with joy, he awoke.

On this, forthwith, he started on his journey. He was twenty-eight years of age. He had company as far as Liang-chou, where he was invited to explain some of the Buddhist Scriptures. Now Liang-chou, where he stayed a month and some days, was a city frequented by merchants and traders from Central Asia, from the borders of Tibet and the kingdoms beyond the Pamirs. All these men heard Tripitaka speak

[2] Waley, *The Real Tripitaka*, p. 14.

at the Religious Conference, and, deeply impressed by his learning and manner, returned to their homes to extol him to their rulers. Not only did they laud him, they also announced his intention to travel to India; as a consequence everyone in the most distant kingdoms was prepared with joyful heart to entertain the pilgrim royally as he passed through their lands. But at home, severe restrictions were placed on all persons seeking to go abroad; the governor of Liang-chou, obedient to the royal mandate prohibiting travel, learned from an informer that it was rumored that a monk was planning to go to the West. The governor, full of anxiety, called Tripitaka to his presence and asked him the object of his visit. When the Master of the Law told him that he was on his way to the West, the governor urged him to return to the capital. But Tripitaka, his mind made up, was not to be deterred by either edict or official. It was then he secured the help of Liang-chou's most revered monk, who sent him two disciples to help him on his journey. Tripitaka disappeared from sight; guided by the young monks he hid by day and traveled by night and in due time arrived at Kua-chou [the present An-hsi], the last halting-place with local supplies on the road to Hami. The governor of Kua-chou, greatly pleased at his coming, provided him with all the necessary provisions for his stay.

The Master of the Law, on inquiring about the western routes, was told: "At fifty *li* [three *li* to the mile], marching to the north, one comes to the River Su-lo, of which the lower course is wide and the upper one is very contracted. Its waters are constantly whirling and flow with such impetuosity that they cannot be passed in a boat. Near the widest part the Yü-men Barrier has been established, by which one is obliged to pass and which is the key to the western frontiers. To the northwest, beyond this barrier, there are five signal towers where the guards, entrusted with keeping the lookout, reside. They are a hundred *li* apart one from the other. In the space which separates them there is neither water nor herbage. Beyond these five towers there lie the desert of Mo-ho-yen and the frontiers of I-wu [Hami]." On hearing these particulars he was filled with dread and distress. The horse he had been riding was dead; sad and silent he let a whole month pass while he tried to figure out how he should proceed. While he was in such deep distress, spies from Liang-chou informed the governor of Tripitaka's intentions while bringing him the mandate ordering the monk's detention. The governor, a man of piety, secretly showed Tripitaka the mandate and was so moved by the monk's fervid avowal to risk his life to seek the Law that he destroyed the document before him. Having thus shown him that he would not hinder his going, he said: "And now, sir, you must depart in all haste."[3]

From this moment on all his fears and anxieties increased greatly. Of the two novices who had accompanied him from Liang-chou, one defected and the other was too frail to make so arduous a journey. Though Tripitaka did secure a horse, he was worried at having no guide to accompany him. Going into the temple, he bowed before the image of Buddha and prayed fervently for a guide who would lead him safely past the frontier barrier. Prayers, auspicious dreams and happy omens fortified his heart; suddenly, as he was praying, a foreigner, a man from the West, coming to worship, saluted the Master of the Law by circling him three times. "My personal name is Bandha," he said, and asked Tripitaka to be allowed to take the Five Vows [to become a dedicated layman]. Delighted at having done so, Bandha asked permission to return, which he soon did with a present of cakes and fruit. The Master of the Law, observing that Bandha was intelligent and respectful, devout and strong, told him his need for help

[3] Ibid., p. 17.

in starting for the West. Bandha readily offered to conduct him past the five signal towers. On the morrow at sundown —"when the sun was down among the grass"—Tripitaka rode to a thicket where shortly after Bandha appeared with an old graybeard, also a foreigner, mounted on a lean horse of reddish color. His appearance did not reassure Tripitaka, but Bandha introduced him as a man intimately acquainted with the western routes: "He has gone to and come back from Hami more than thirty times." Then the old man warned him: "The western routes are bad and dangerous. At times streams of drift sand obstruct, at others demons and burning winds. If they are encountered no one can escape. Often big caravans lose themselves and perish. How much worse for you, sir, going alone! I pray you consider this seriously and do not trifle with your life." But Hsüan-tsang remained firm and declared that until he reached the country of the Brahmans he would never turn eastward again for China. "If I were to die on the way I should not regret it." Thereupon the graybeard said, "Master, since you are decided to go, you must mount my horse. More than fifteen times already, going and coming, he has done the way to Hami. He is strong and knows the routes. Your horse, on the contrary, is weak and will never reach there." And because a diviner in Ch'ang-an had told Tripitaka that he would leave for the Western World on just such a horse, red-colored, old and skinny, with a lacquered saddle bound in front with iron, he accepted the exchange as a fulfillment of the omen. The graybeard, rejoicing in the deal he had made, made his respectful obeisance; they separated.

Having packed his baggage, Tripitaka, thus mounted, left Kua-chou and rode through the night with Bandha. In the third watch they came to the river and sighted the Yü-men Barrier from a distance. At ten *li* from the barrier the upper stream is not more than ten feet wide. Here they crossed over a rough footbridge which Bandha made by cutting some wood, spreading the branches and filling it up with sand. Tripitaka was delighted that the river had been crossed, and, being tired, he dismounted. Bandha also, some fifty paces from where Tripitaka was resting, spread his mat on the ground and lay down. And so they both slept. In a little while, Tripitaka awoke to see Bandha approaching him, knife in hand; he watched: the young man stopped when about ten paces away, turned, and went back to his mat. Not knowing the man's intention, Tripitaka had risen from his mat and repeated some Scripture. After that, they both slept again.

Hardly had they started in the morning when Bandha announced that he could go no farther, that he had important family matters to attend to, and that he was not willing to break the laws of his country: Tripitaka knew that he was afraid and let him go. But Bandha was not so easily gotten rid of. He was fearful that Tripitaka would be caught and that, when questioned, would implicate him. He was satisfied only when Tripitaka took an oath: "I swear that though my body be cut up as small as the very dust I will never turn back," and he gave Bandha his hand to seal his words.

Deserted by his guide, utterly alone, he started across the sandy waste, guiding himself by the heaps of bones and horse dung along the way. Suddenly, on the dry plain he saw armed hosts, hundreds of men clad in fur and felt moving in the distance. He saw camels and horses, the glitter of standards and lances; then fresh forms and figures appeared and changed into a thousand shapes: they were the terrifying mirages created by demons for which that desert is famous. Even as his eyes beheld the awful sight, he heard a voice in that vast wilderness crying: "Do not fear, do not fear!" After covering eighty *li*, Tripitaka approached the first signal tower. In order to pass it unobserved he hid himself until nightfall. Then when he was trying to fill his water bottle from the water near the tower, an arrow whistled past his head. Calling out that he was a monk from the capital, the soldiers came and took him before the commandant of the post, a native of Tun-huang, who ordered the fire built up to inspect him closely. Having verified that he was indeed the would-be pilgrim in search of the Law, about whom a report had reached him from Liang-chou, he felt pity and treated Tripitaka kindly. Failing to persuade him to return, the commander bade him get a night's rest, promising to guide him in the morning. At the first light, he gave Tripitaka provisions and water for the journey and instructed him to follow the road straight for the next signal tower, where he commended him to its commander, a relative of his. Arriving there the same night, Tripitaka went through the same experience: he was stopped by an arrow and taken before the commandant. On receiving his relative's message, he welcomed Tripitaka and warned him not to approach the fifth and last signal tower as it was held by men of violent disposition. Instead, he advised him to head for the Spring of the Wild Horses, which was 100 *li* off, there to replenish his water. He provided him with a huge leather water bottle and fodder for his horse.

A short distance from the signal tower he entered the desert called Mo-ho-yen, which has a length of 800 *li* and which in ancient times was called the River of Sand. One sees there neither birds nor quadrupeds, nor water, nor pasture. Again demonic visions assailed him and to protect himself he read from his favorite sacred text. After having covered one hundred *li* he lost his way; he could not find the Spring of the Wild Horses. To add to his panic, in a terrible moment he dropped the water bag and the water that was to have carried him across the desert disappeared into the sand. Besides, as the route made long detours, he no longer knew which direction to follow. He then thought to turn back to the signal tower he had last left. But after he had proceeded about ten *li*, he remembered his oath not to take his way eastward until he had reached India and so, fervently praying for divine help, he headed for the northwest. All around he saw only limitless plains, without a trace of men or horses. At night he was frightened by lights lit by wicked spirits and in the daytime by terrible sandstorms. He suffered cruelly from thirst. Yet in the midst of these severe trials his heart remained a stranger to fear. After traveling without water for four nights and five days, he lay down exhausted. In the middle of the fifth night, after fervent prayers to Kuan-yin, refreshed by a cool breeze, he found rest in a short sleep. A divine vision seen in a dream roused him to fresh effort. After about 10 *li*, his horse, which had also found strength to get on its legs again, suddenly turned in another direction and after a few more *li* carried him to a patch of green pasture. When he had allowed his horse to graze and was about to move on, Tripitaka discovered a pool of water, sweet and bright as a mirror. He drank without stint and so his parched body and vital powers were restored. And there he tarried a day before continuing on his journey. With a supply of water to sustain him and fresh fodder for the horse he emerged two days later from the desert; he had reached Hami.

[In 1907, Aurel Stein, crossing the "Pei-shan Gobi" to Hami, investigated whether the great Chinese pilgrim, whom he calls "our Buddhist Pausanius," could have reached Hami as he said he did. Stein verified the pious traveler's account of the desert route by which he escaped from the closely guarded northwest border of the Chinese Empire. He explained that, while Tripitaka's resolute going to the northwest, continuing on his journey "undaunted by thirst and the perils of the desert," needed all the "religious fervour and courage of the great pilgrim, it was also the wisest course to follow—for one who knows how to keep up that bearing. And that Hsüan-tsang fully possessed that instinct of the compass is abundantly proved by the topographical records he has left us." Stein also confirms the providential dash of the horse, that old skinny veteran of many crossings to Hami and back. "The remarkable way in which horses and camels in the desert can scent water and grazing for considerable distances, or correctly locate such places remembered from previous visits, is too well known to need my personal testimony." He concludes that the "grave perils and quasi-miraculous escape" which marked the beginnings of the pilgrim's travels were neither exaggerated nor fictionalized.][4]

He stopped at a temple inhabited by three Chinese monks; one was an old man whose vestment was without a girdle and whose feet were without covering. The old man embraced the Master of the Law, uttering many cries and piteous exclamations. "How could I have hoped ever to see again a man of my own country?" And the Master of the Law likewise, as he saw him, was moved to tears. The king invited him to his own house and provided him with an abundance of food. Tripitaka's arrival at Hami coincided with the visit of envoys from the ruler of Turfan, a larger, richer oasis to the west.

[Turfan was ruled by a Chinese dynasty that had come there from western Kansu about A.D. 504. Though its government and institutions were based on Chinese models, they were simpler and not encumbered with bureaucratic machinery, thus the king and his sons dealt directly with legal disputes. Confucian classics were taught, and, as in China, Buddhism existed alongside of Confucianism. The Royal Audience Hall had a picture of the "Duke of Lu Asking Confucius about

[4] See Sir Aurel Stein, "The Desert Crossing of Hsüan-tsang, 630 A.D.," *Indian Antiquary*, Vol. 50, pp. 15-25.

Government." Turfanese, a Tocharian language, used Chinese ideograms for native Turfanese words; akin to Sanskrit and Persian, it was also related to Latin and Greek, Irish and German. Waley says: "It sometimes looks like English in Simplified Spelling; for example the word for 'new' was *nu.* Or again, like a kind of Esperanto; *okso* means ox."][5]

When the Turfanese envoys reported to their master that Tripitaka was on his way to India, the king sent an impressive escort to meet him and bring him safely to his city. Though Tripitaka had not planned to visit Turfan, he was obliged to, and, crossing the southern desert, in six days he reached its borders. It was sunset and he wanted to stop there. But the king was waiting and fresh horses were readied to carry him. Leaving his old red horse, which was to follow, he came to the royal city at midnight. The king was notified and the city gate was opened. Despite the late hour the king came out to meet him, and, surrounded by attendants bearing lighted torches, led Tripitaka to a seat under a precious canopy in an elegant pavilion. "I was sure you would arrive tonight," the king said, "and therefore my wife and children with myself have taken no sleep." In a moment the queen with tens of serving-women came to pay her respects. Food was served, and only as the day-dawn came was Tripitaka able to announce that he was utterly fatigued and longed for sleep. Thereupon the king retired to his palace and left several eunuchs to wait on his guest during the night.

All this was done to give proper honor to the man whom the king had decided he wanted to have as the head of the Buddhist Church in Turfan. From the first time the idea was broached Tripitaka declined the king's offer, explaining that he was on his way to the West to seek interpretations of the Scriptures not yet known outside India so that the sweet dew

[5] Op. cit., p. 19.

of the expanded Law might also water the regions of the East. But the king was not accustomed to being denied his wish: "The Ts'ung Ling Mountains may fall down, but not my purpose. Be assured of my sincerity and do not doubt my real affection." And so their wills clashed. First the king tried coddling and cajolery to win his way; to everything Tripitaka gave the same refusal. Finally the frustrated king resorted to threats; in a loud voice he said: "I have another way of deciding this question. If you still think you can go where and when you like, know that I can detain you here by force and send you back to your own country. I commend you to think this over; it will be better for you to obey." To this Tripitaka replied: "I came here for the sake of the great Buddhist Law. Now I have met with someone who opposes me. Your power is only over my body; Your Majesty cannot command my will or my spirit." And then he vowed not to eat or drink in order to affect the king's heart. Three days of his hunger strike passed before the king, seeing him grow fainter and fainter, bowed down before him and said: "The Master of the Law has free permission to go to the West. I pray you take a slight morning meal." Then, after the king had proved his sincerity and had taken an oath by repeating his words with his hand pointed toward the sun, and again in the temple before the Buddha, he made two requests of Tripitaka. "When you return I beg you to stop in this kingdom for three years so that I may be permitted to protect and patronize you. I would also like you to remain here for another month; while you teach us one of the Scriptures I will have garments prepared for your difficult journey ahead." To both requests the Master of the Law agreed. Then he consented to eat.

Once the king had recognized the power of Tripitaka's will, he arranged to equip the monk as he chose. Knowing that he would face regions of extreme cold, he had various articles of suitable clothing made, such as face coverings, gloves, leather boots, and so forth. He also gave him a hundred ounces of gold, thirty thousand silver pieces, and five hundred rolls of silk—enough to endow him for twenty years. Thirty horses and twenty-four servants were put at Tripitaka's disposal and he assigned one of his high officials to escort him to the next kingdom, providing the official with a royal gift of fine silks and luscious fruits—products for which Turfan was justly famed—for the neighboring ruler. And finally, he wrote twenty-four royal letters to be presented at twenty-four different countries, and each letter had a large roll of satin as a credential. Tripitaka was overwhelmed by such munificence—it evoked from him a speech of gratitude. The king's reply was brief. "You have, respected master, allowed me to regard you as a brother, and therefore you have the right to share with me the wealth of my kingdom. Why then offer me so many thanks?" [Even Tripitaka's devoted biographer allows the king the last word.] Certainly Tripitaka, in his long road across the breadth of Central Asia and over the bitter heights of the Pamirs, knew how greatly the king of Turfan had protected him against hardships and dangers. Because of such royal care he traveled as comfortably and safely as was possible at that time and in those regions.

Going westward, they crossed the high Silver Mountain, whence the silver is dug which supplies the Western countries with their silver currency. On the other side the party encountered a band of robbers; after giving the sum the robbers demanded, they departed. That night they camped by the side of a stream, planning to reach Kharashahr the next day. While Tripitaka's party were still asleep, a group of Central Asian traders who had joined their caravan started for the city to make an advantageous sale of their goods; later that morning and but two or three miles from their camp, Tripitaka's party found the bodies of the merchants—robbers had killed them and stripped them of their wealth. Deeply affected by the sight, they were glad when they sighted the royal city.

Hsüan-tsang described the oasis of Kharashahr: "On all sides it is girt with hills. The roads are precipitous and easy of defense. Numerous streams unite, and are led in channels to irrigate the fields. The soil is suitable for red millet, winter wheat, scented dates, grapes, pears and plums, and other fruits. The air is soft and agreeable; the manners of the people are sincere and upright. The written character is, with few differences, like that of India. The clothing of the people is of cotton or wool. They go with shorn locks and without headdress. In commerce they use gold coins, silver coins and little copper coins. The king is a native of the country; he is brave, but little attentive to military plans, yet he loves to speak of his own conquests. This country has no annals. The laws are not settled. The professors of religion read their books and observe the rules and regulations with purity and strictness."

Hsüan-tsang noted at Kucha, the next oasis some fifty miles farther west, that the soil was suitable for rice and grain and also for a kind of rice which is not glutinous. The country produces grapes and pomegranates, and numerous species of plums, pears, and almonds also grow here. The ground is rich in minerals—gold, copper, iron, lead, and tin. The air is soft, and the manners of the people honest. The style of writing is Indian, with some differences. They excel other countries in their skill in playing on the lute and pipe. They clothe themselves with ornamental garments of silk and embroidery. They cut their hair and wear a flowing covering over their heads. In commerce they use gold, silver, and copper coins. The king's wisdom being small, he is ruled by a powerful minister. The children born of common parents have their heads flattened by the pressure of a wooden board. He also reported the wonders pointed out and the marvelous accounts he heard. To the north of a city there is a great dragon lake. The dragons, changing their form, couple with mares. The offspring is a wild species of horse, dragon-horse, difficult to tame and of a fierce nature. The breed of these dragon-horses became docile and this country consequently became famous for its many excellent horses. Former records of this country say: "In late times there was a king called Gold Flower, who exhibited rare intelligence. He was able to yoke the dragons to his chariot. When the king wished to disappear, he touched the ears of the dragons with his whip, and forthwith he became invisible."

From very early time till now there have been no wells in the town, so that the inhabitants have been accustomed to get water from the dragon lake. On these occasions the dragons, changing themselves into the likeness of men, had intercourse with the women. Their children, when born, were powerful and courageous, and swift of foot as the horse. Thus gradually corrupting themselves, the men all became of the dragon breed, and relying on their strength, they became rebellious and disobedient to the royal authority. Then the king, forming an alliance with the Turks, massacred the men, young and old; all were destroyed.

The old records say: "A former king of this country worshiped the 'three precious' ones [Buddha, the Law, the community of monks]. Wishing to pay homage to the sacred relics of the outside world, he entrusted the affairs of the empire to his younger brother on the mother's side. The younger brother, having received such orders, mutilated himself in order to prevent any evil passion. He enclosed the mutilated parts in a golden casket, and laid it before the king. 'What is this?' inquired the king. In reply he said, 'On the day of Your Majesty's return home, I pray you open it and see!' The king gave it to the manager of his affairs, who entrusted the casket to a portion of the king's bodyguard to keep. When the king returned, there were certain mischief-making people who said. 'The king's deputy, in his absence, has been debauching himself in the inner rooms of the women.' The king, hearing this, was very angry, and would have subjected his brother to cruel punishment. The brother said, 'I dare not flee from punishment, but I pray you open the golden casket.' The king accordingly opened it, and saw that it contained a mutilated member. Seeing it, he said, 'What strange thing is this, and what does it signify?' Replying, the brother said. 'When the king proposed to go abroad, he ordered me to undertake the affairs of the government. Fearing the slanderous reports that might arise, I mutilated myself. You have the proof of my foresight. Let the king look kindly on me.' The king was filled with deepest reverence and strangely moved with affection; in consequence, he permitted him free ingress and egress throughout his palace."

While Tripitaka wrote down such events in Kucha's past, his biographer, Hui-li, concentrated on the religious aspects of his hero's debate with Hinayana Buddhists, followers of the Lesser Vehicle, whom Tripitaka considered heretics. [In *The Real Tripitaka*, Waley, in his learned and characteristically delightful account of the debate, presents the religious significance of the exchange between Mokshagupta, the Hinayanist, and Tripitaka and tells why that local pundit was much relieved when the pert young Chinese intellectual left Kucha and took the road for the West.]

Two days out of Kucha the party came face to face with a band of some two thousand strong mounted Turkish bandits. Numerous as they were, the robbers were easily dispersed for they were preoccupied with their own quarrels over the distribution of the booty stolen from the previous caravan. The way to the West took them over stretches of desert—days spent amid a world of sand or stone—punctuated by flourishing oases. Thus they came to the T'ien Shan mountain range; ahead of them lay some forty miles of mountains, steep and dangerous and reaching to the clouds. The glare of the glaciers brought on snow blindness, adding another hardship to be endured in that region of icy peaks. They faced the constant danger of avalanches. Wind and snow, driving in swirling masses, chilled them despite the protection of the heavy fur-trimmed clothes they wore. When hungry or sleepy, there was no dry place where they could halt and rest—they soon learned to hang the pot for cooking and to spread the mats for sleeping on the ice. In the seven days they spent making their way through the [Bedel] Pass, fourteen men—almost half the party—starved and were frozen to death while the number of oxen and horses that perished was still greater. [So high a loss along the main line of communication between the eastern and western Turks is thought to indicate that part of the caravan was blotted out by an avalanche or was lost in an icefall.] Once over the pass, they arrived at the Issyk Kul, a great lake, 1400 to 1500 *li* long, enclosed by mountains; into it many streams empty themselves and are lost. Bluish-black in color, salty and bitter in taste, the waves of the lake break tumultuously on the shores. In its depths, dragons and fishes swim together; scaly monsters rise to the surface, and passing travelers pray to them for good fortune. Although water animals are numerous, no one is foolish enough to try to fish for them.

Following the shore for about five hundred *li* they came to a settlement where Yeh-hu, the khan of the western Turks, was encamped on a hunting expedition. The horses of these barbarous people are very fine. The khan wore a robe of green silk, and his hair, worn loose, was only bound around with a silken band some ten feet in length which was twisted around his head and fell down behind. He was surrounded by about two hundred officers, clothed in robes of brocade, their hair braided. On either side were troops dressed in furs and finespun woolen garments; they carried lances and bows and standards, and were mounted on camels and horses. The eye could not estimate their numbers.

The khan was filled with joy at Tripitaka's coming. "Stay here for a while; after two or three days I will come back." And he assigned a large tent for him and arranged for the monk's comfort. The khan's own tent was a large pavilion decorated with golden floral ornaments so glittering that they blinded the eye. In front of it the officers sat in two rows on long mats spread out for them; they were dressed in garments of shining embroidered silk. Although the khan was but the ruler of a wandering horde, yet there was a dignified arrangement about his entourage.

The Turks, Tripitaka's party learned, worship fire: they do not use wooden seats because wood contains fire and so even in worship they never seat themselves but only spread padded mats on the ground. But for their guest they made a seat out of an iron warming pan covered with thick padding. The khan read the letter they brought and examined the gifts sent by the king of Turfan; he was much pleased. He ordered the visitors to be seated and had wine passed around while music played. The khan and his ministers drank to the visitors, and offered wine to the Master of the Law. After this they drank, toasting one another in succession, filling their cups and emptying them in succession, ever more and more animated, during which time the music resounded in a confused clang. And though the style of the music was of the sort common to the barbarians, yet the Chinese found it was diverting both to the ear and the eye, pleasing the thoughts and the mind. In a little while food was served—boiled quarters of mutton and veal were heaped up before the guests. For the master they had prepared pure foods such as rice cakes, cream, sugar candy, honey sticks, raisins, and so forth. When the feast was over, the wine was again passed around. Then the master was asked to expound the Law. He spoke on the Ten Precepts [Ten Commandments], the love of preserving life, and the righteous life that leads to final deliverance. The khan raised his hands to his head, signifying a delighted acceptance of such teaching. "Sir," he said, "you shouldn't go to India. That country is very hot. I am afraid you will succumb to the heat. The people are like savages, without any decorum. It's not worth going all that way to see them."

When Tripitaka respectfully rejected this advice and restated his intention to gaze on the sacred places and search for the Law, the khan attached to his party a young soldier who had spent some years in China and spoke Chinese and would serve as an interpreter as far as Afghanistan. He also presented him with a complete set of clothes of crimson satin and fifty pieces of silk. Then, with all his officers, he accompanied him a little to start him on his way.

Next, Tripitaka came to a little town. Now deserted, it once had about three hundred households. Made up of Chinese who had been carried off forcibly by the Turks, a few, after a time, had come together to start this small community. Tripitaka noticed that though they had adopted the Turkish dress they had preserved their own language and customs. Farther on they passed the Thousand Springs, named for its numerous ponds and springs, and admired the trees, so wonderful for their luxuriant foliage and height. The cool refreshing climate of this spot was enjoyed by the khan when he wanted to avoid the heat of the summer. Abruptly, this delightful region ended at a great sandy desert in which there was neither water nor grass. The road was swallowed up in the waste, which appeared boundless; only by aiming for a particular mountain and following the bones which lie scattered about can the route be followed. The next important city where they were received was Samarkand.

Hsüan-tsang described this kingdom whose Chinese name meant "the peaceful, or happy." "It is," he noted, "completely enclosed by rugged land and very populous. The precious merchandise of many foreign countries is stored up here. The soil is rich and productive, and yields abundant harvests. The forest trees afford a thick vegetation, and flowers and fruits are plentiful. The *shen* horses are bred here. The inhabitants are skillful in the arts and trades beyond those of other countries. The climate is agreeable and temperate. The people are brave and energetic. This country is in the middle of the Tartar people. They are copied by all surrounding peoples in point of politeness and propriety. The king is full of courage, and the neighboring countries obey his commands. The cavalry is strong and sizable, composed principally of men of Chih-chia, who are naturally brave and fierce, and meet death as a way to salvation. When they attack, no enemy can stand before them.

Hui-li related what occurred in Samarkand, where the king and the people were fire worshipers. In the city there were two Buddhist temples, but neither had monks, and if an occasional wandering monk sought shelter in either of them, the barbarians followed him with burning firebrands and drove him off. Tripitaka's party at first was treated with little respect; but after a day or two the king invited him to preach to him about the Buddha. So great an impression did his talk make that the king asked to take the Vows of Abstinence, and from that time on showed the Chinese monk the highest respect. Soon after, two novices in the party went to a temple to worship. The people drove them away by setting it on fire.

Tripitaka mentioned the incident to the king, who immediately ordered the arsonists arrested. Then before all the people, he sentenced them to have their hands cut off. Hearing what their punishment was to be, Tripitaka interceded, asking that they not be mutilated and that their sentence be changed to flogging and expulsion from the city. After this display of mercy, many people, both high and low, asked to be instructed in Buddhism. "Accordingly," his devoted biographer said, "he ordained many of them as monks and set them up in monasteries. The Master of the Law transformed their heretical hearts and corrected their evil customs. And so it was whereever he went."

Fifteen hundred *li* farther to the west, and having crossed five kingdoms, the party reached Kesh. "From this place," Tripitaka wrote, "we enter the mountains; the road is steep and precipitous, and the passage along the defiles dangerous and difficult. There are no people or villages, and little water or vegetation. Going along the mountains 300 *li* or so southeast, we enter the Iron Gates. The pass so called is bordered on the right and left by mountains. These mountains are of prodigious height. The trail is narrow, which adds to the difficulty and danger. On both sides there is a rocky wall of an iron color. Here there are set up double wooden doors, strengthened with iron and furnished with many bells hung up. Because of the protection afforded to the pass by these doors, the name of *Iron Gates* is given. This is the barrier against the advance of the Turks.

"Passing through the Iron Gates we arrive within Bactria. On the east it is bounded by the T'ien Shan Mountains, on the west it touches on Persia, on the south are the great Snowy Mountains [the Hindukush], on the north the Iron Gates. The great river Oxus flows through the midst of this country in a westerly direction. For many centuries past the royal race has been extinct. The several chieftains have by force contended for their possessions, and each held their own independently, relying only upon the natural divisions of the country. Thus they have constituted twenty-seven states, divided by natural boundaries, yet as a whole dependent on the Turks. The climate of this country is warm and damp, and consequently epidemics prevail.

"At the end of winter and the beginning of spring, rain falls without intermission. With regard to the character of the people, it is mean and cowardly; their appearance is low and rustic. Their knowledge of good faith and rectitude extends so far as relates to their dealings one with another. Their language differs somewhat from that of other countries. The number of radical letters in their language is twenty-five; by combining these they express all objects around them. Their writing is across the page, and they read from left to right. Their literary records have increased gradually. Most of the people use fine cotton for their dress; some use wool. In commercial transactions they use gold and silver alike. The coins are different in pattern from those of other countries."

They had arrived at Kunduz, that part of Bactria [now northern Afghanistan] whose ruler, Tardu, was the eldest son of Yeh-hu, the khan of the western Turks, who had entertained them at his rich hunting encampment. Tardu was also the brother-in-law of the king of Turfan, from whom Tripitaka brought glowing letters of introduction. Tardu was mourning his wife, the Turfanese princess who had recently died, and, unhappy and ill, begged Tripitaka to stay with him until he had regained his health, when he would himself conduct him to India. While Tripitaka was his guest, Tardu married his late wife's younger sister and was, almost immediately, poisoned by her. With Tardu dead, the queen and her lover took over the kingdom. [Waley remarks that it must have been "discouraging for Tripitaka, after successfully winning the patronage of Tardu, to have to begin all over with Tardu's murderers; but he seems to have adapted himself to the situation."][6] During the weeks when the funeral ceremony and the installation of the new ruler were taking place, Tripitaka met Dharmasimha, a monk who had traveled to India for instruction in Buddhism and who, on the western side of the Pamirs, was called "the Lawmaker"; he overawed the monks of Sogdiana and Khotan, who dared not meet him in discussion. Hui-li, to demonstrate Tripitaka's superiority, related how his hero, seeking to know the depth of Dharmasimha's knowledge, sent messengers to inquire of him the number of Scriptures and religious treatises the lawmaker knew. His disciples were annoyed at such presumption, but Dharmasimha quietly answered, "I can explain any of them you like." Tripitaka, confining his questions to the school to which the Lawmaker belonged, asked questions that were not easy to solve. When Dharmasimha admitted that he could not answer the questions easily or satisfactorily, his disciples were filled with shame; but his honesty cleared the way for him to enjoy Tripitaka's company. "He ceased not to praise the master," Hui-li wrote, "acknowledging that he was by no means his equal."

When at last the new khan had established his rule, Tripitaka thought he could properly continue on his way to India. The khan urged him to take the time to make a detour and visit his city of Balkh, saying it was famous for its many sacred Buddhist sites. [Balkh was indeed a city long famous. Long ago it had been a capital of Khorasan, a Persian satrapy, and then of Bactria, as the kingdom was called under its Greek rulers. At Balkh was celebrated the splendid wedding of Alexander the Great to Roxana, daughter of a Bactrian noble. "The most famous wedding in ancient history," Waley calls

[6] Op. cit., p. 23.

it. Since the beginning of the second century A.D. Balkh yielded only to the Magadha capital as a great Buddhist center.] Among its sacred relics Tripitaka found the washbasin which Buddha had used; about the size of a peck measure, it was of colors that dazzled the eyes. There was also a tooth of Buddha, about an inch long and about eight- or nine-tenths of an inch in breadth, yellowish white, pure and shining; and Buddha's sweeping brush, made of the Ka-she plant, two feet long, its handle set with many gems. It was there that Tripitaka met Prajnakara, a monk of the Lesser Vehicle, and a native of Takka [that part of the Punjab that borders on Kashmir]. He was truly a man of singular wisdom and learning. Unlike the previous local celebrities, he was able to explain with extreme clarity Tripitaka's questions on the doubtful and difficult passages he had encountered in some of the Lesser Vehicle scriptures. He remained in the New Monastery with Prajnakara for a month, and then, with his new friend, headed southward for India. Together they made the difficult crossing of the Hindukush. The hardships they endured in traversing those high mountain passes can be glimpsed through Tripitaka's quiet phrases. "The Snowy Mountains are high and the valleys deep; the precipices and crevasses are very dangerous. A blizzard keeps on without intermission; the ice remains through the full summer and the snowdrifts fall into the valleys and block the road. The demon spirits send, in their rage, every kind of calamity; robbers waylay and kill travelers. Going with difficulty the six hundred *li* or so, we gradually arrived at Bamiỹan, a kingdom located deep in a valley of the Hindukush. The capital leans on a steep hill bordering on a valley. On the north it is backed by high precipices. The country produces spring wheat and few flowers or fruits. It is suitable for cattle, and affords pasture for many sheep and horses. The climate is wintry, and the manners of the people hard and uncultivated.

The clothes are chiefly made of skin and wool, which are the most suitable for the country. These people are remarkable, among all their neighbors, for a love of religion; there are ten monasteries and about a thousand monks, belonging to the Lokotarra sect." [A little-known Transcendental School of Hinayana Buddhism. And Waley remarks that "Tripitaka must have felt the sort of thrill on coming on these sectarians . . . as an entomologist feels when he lights upon a rare butterfly."]

He described the colossal statues carved into the cliff. Impressive, though mutilated, they still make Bamiy̆an famous. "To the northeast of the royal city there is a mountain on which is placed a stone figure of Buddha, erect, in height 140 or 150 feet. Its golden hues sparkle on every side, and its precious ornaments dazzle the eyes by their brightness.

"To the east of this spot there is a standing figure of Sakya Buddha, made of metallic stone [brass or bronze] in height 100 feet. It has been cast in different parts and joined together, and thus placed in a completed form as it stands.

"To the east of the city there is a figure of Buddha lying in a sleeping position, as when he attained nirvana. The figure is in length about 100 feet or so. The king of this country every five years assembles the great congregation. He sacrifices all his possessions, from his wife and children down to his country's treasures; he gives, in addition, his own body. Then his ministers and the lower order of officers prevail on the monks to barter back those possessions; and in these matters most of their time is taken up."

From Bamiy̆an, they entered the defiles of the Snowy Mountains, crossed the black ridge of the cloud-swept mountain pass, and, fifteen days later, after having become lost in a driving snowstorm, reached the borders of the kingdom of Kapisi. [About forty miles north of Kabul. In the second century A.D. it had been part of the Indo-Scythian kingdom whose great king, Kanishka, had been the patron of Mahayana Buddhism, the Greater Vehicle, to which Tripitaka adhered.] This region, Tripitaka said, "produces cereals of all sorts, and many kinds of fruit trees. The *shen* horses are bred here, and there is also the scented root of the turmeric. Here also are found objects of merchandise from all parts. The climate is cold and windy. The people are cruel and fierce; their language is coarse and rude; their marriage rites a mere intermingling of the sexes. Their literature is like that of the Tocharian country, but the customs, common language, and rules of behavior are somewhat different. For clothing they use wool garments trimmed with fur. In commerce they use gold and silver coins, and also little copper coins, which in appearance and stamp differ from those of other countries. The king is of a shrewd nature, and being brave and determined, he has brought into subjection the neighboring countries, some ten of which he rules. He cherishes his people with affection, and reverences much the three precious objects of worship. Periodically, he makes a silver figure of Buddha eighteen feet high, and at the same time he convokes an assembly, called the Moksha Mahaparishad, when he gives alms to the poor and wretched, and relieves widows and the bereaved.

"There are about a hundred monasteries in this country and some six thousand priests who mostly study the rules of the Great Vehicle. There are also some ten temples and a thousand or so heretics [Jains and Hindus]; there are naked ascetics, and others who cover themselves with ashes, and some who make chaplets of bones, which they wear as crowns on their heads."

According to tradition, Kanishka, having subdued all the neighboring provinces and brought into obedience people of distant countries, governed a territory that extended east of the Pamirs; he received hostages from tribes who occupied the territory between those mountains and China. Even a son of a Han emperor, Hui-li says, was a hostage. Kanishka treated him with singular attention, providing him with different establishments for the different seasons—during the cold months he resided in India, in the summer in Kapisi. This dwelling, a monastery, was still known as Serika, their word for China. Built for the Chinese hostage, his portrait had been painted several times on the wall—the features, clothing, and ornaments were those of a Chinese. After the Chinese prince was allowed to return to his own country, his sojourn was remembered. An inscription said that, at the foot of the statue to the Great Spirit King, the guardian of the Buddha Hall, Kanishka had buried a treasure to be used to repair the building. Spirits summoned to guard the treasure, appearing as lions, or snakes, or savage beasts, show their rage to anyone daring to steal it. Thus not long before, a petty king of covetous mind and wicked and cruel disposition, having heard of the quantity of jewels and precious substances concealed in this convent, drove away the monks and began digging for them. The King of the Spirits had on his head the figure of a parrot, which now began to flap its wings and to utter screams. The earth shook and quaked, the king and his army were thrown prostrate on the ground; after a while, arising from the earth, he confessed his fault and left.

Tripitaka, the monastery's first Chinese visitor, was greeted with especial warmth by the monks and they related the circumstances of its founding and its subsequent history. Seeing how badly dilapidated the building was, Tripitaka suggested to the monks that the time had come to use the treasure for the purpose for which it had been buried and offered to supervise the excavation. In his presence they dug down seven or eight feet and actually found a copper vessel containing several pounds of gold and scores of pearls. Soon after this agreeable event, the king invited Tripitaka to take part in an impressive gathering of Buddhist philosophers. Only Tripitaka, Hui-li proudly wrote, proved himself proficient in all the systems of doctrine and all those present acknowledged his pre-eminence. Soon the time came when Prajnakara and Tripitaka had to separate: Prajnakara to return to Balkh and Tripitaka to take the road for India.

Once Tripitaka had descended a mountain and crossed the Kabul River he was in a country sacred to events associated with Buddha. At Nagarahara [near Jalalabad] the three-hundred-foot stupa erected by the Emperor Asoka marked the very spot where hundreds of thousands of years ago, in a previous life, the Sakyamuni Buddha met Dipamkara, the former Buddha, and to keep the Buddha's feet from the mud, the Sakyamuni spread his deerskin, and then, loosening his long hair, cushioned the ground. By this deed he was assured that he would achieve Buddhahood. The district abounded in monasteries, but Tripitaka noticed that there were few monks and that numerous stupas were desolate and in ruins. At that place in close succession were sacred relics, each of which he adored with reverence. Thus, a nearby town had a two-storied tower enshrining the Buddha's skull bone and an eyeball, one of his robes woven of fine, silky cotton, and his walking stick. And after he had finished scattering his flowers and prostrating himself in worship before each of the shrines, he figured that to worship the relics he had paid out in gifts and gratuities fifty gold pieces, one thousand silver pieces, four silken banners, two lengths of brocade, and two fine cassocks.

Thus he began giving away the gold and silver, the silks and religious vestments which he had received as a charitable donation from the king of Turfan.

Having made the full tour, he rejoined his companions and took the road for the country of Gandhara. Its capital, Peshawar, held the ruins of its former greatness; its one thousand monasteries, deserted and in ruins, were overgrown with shrubs, and its many stupas were badly decayed. The great monastery built by Kanishka—its double towers, connecting terraces, storied structures, and recessed chambers—stood almost empty. Here many noted philosophers had written works that gained them wide renown; Tripitaka walked carefully through this scene of desolation, and he saw it as it was in its glory and greatness, its pristine splendor and religious importance.

Going northward some six hundred *li* through a succession of mountains and valleys, he came to the country of Uddyana, in the Swat Valley. Here again silence and desolation reigned where once nearly 20,000 monks studied and meditated and wrote. Yet for Tripitaka, each site was hallowed by its holy associations. Continuing over a mountain, he came to the Indus River and headed upstream into a wild, mountainous land. The roads were rocky and steep, and the sunless valleys were gloomy. They crossed gorges on footbridges of ropes or iron chains that were strung from side to side and were suspended perilously in the air; and they lifted themselves up sheer cliffs on wooden steps that were somehow fastened to the rock. They crossed the Indus, clear and pure, flowing with a strong, turbulent current. Once this region had been subject to Kapisi; now it was under the rule of Kashmir. Tripitaka noted its fertility as he went through a region hallowed by its association with the Buddha's life and teachings. Everywhere there were streams and springs; the land had produced rich harvests, and flowers and fruits had been abundant; numerous ruins of religious establishments bore silent witness to the population that had flourished there. Legends still abounded. A stone stupa Tripitaka visited marked where the Buddha had pierced his body with a bamboo splinter so as to nourish an exhausted tiger with his blood. And because of this, he related, the earth and all the plants have the color of blood, and when men dig the earth there they find things like prickly spikes. And having told the legend he wrote, "Without asking whether we believe the tale or not, it is a piteous one."

Still following the difficult road that led across mountains, along precipices, and over gorges spanned by chain bridges, the party came to the borders of Kashmir. At that time it was a kingdom controlling a large region. "Kashmir," Tripitaka wrote, "is enclosed by very high mountains. Although the mountains have passes through them, these are very narrow and difficult. The neighboring states that have attacked it have never succeeded in subduing it. Srinagar, the capital of the country, on the west side is bordered by a great river. The soil is fit for producing cereals, and abounds with fruits and flowers. Here also are dragon-horses, the fragrant turmeric, and medicinal plants.

"The climate is cold and stern. There is much snow but little wind. The people wear leather doublets and clothes of white linen. They are light and frivolous, and of a weak, pusillanimous disposition. As the country is protected by a dragon, it has always assumed superiority among neighboring people. The people are handsome in appearance, but they are given to cunning. They love learning and are well instructed. There are about one hundred monasteries, and five thousand monks. There are four stupas of wonderful height built by Asoka. Each of these has about a pint measure of relics. The history of the country says: This country was once a dragon lake. In old times the Lord Buddha was returning to India after subduing a wicked spirit in Uddyana, and when in mid-air, just over this country, he addressed Ananda thus: 'After my nirvana the Arhat [Saint] Madhyantika will found a kingdom in this land, civilize the people, and by his own effort spread abroad the law of Buddha.'

"In the fiftieth year after the nirvana, the disciple of Ananda,

Madhyantika the Arhat, heard of the prediction of Buddha. His heart was overjoyed, and he hastened to this country. He was sitting tranquilly in a wood on the top of a high mountain crag, and exhibited great spiritual changes. The dragon beholding it was filled with a deep faith, and requested to know what he desired. The Arhat said, 'I request you to give me a spot in the middle of the lake just big enough for my knees.'

"So the dragon withdrew the water just so far, and gave him the spot. Then by his spiritual power the Arhat increased the size of his body, whilst the dragon king kept back the waters with all his might. So the lake became dry, and the waters exhausted.

"Then the Arhat, having obtained this land by the exercise of his great spiritual power, purchased from surrounding countries a number of poor people who might act as servitors to the monks. When Madhyantika died, these poor people constituted themselves rulers over the neighboring countries. The people of surrounding countries despised these low-born men, and would not associate with them."

Kashmir gave Tripitaka a magnificent reception. The night before his arrival, the monks in Srinagar were told in a dream that a stranger-monk from Great China had come to their land to study the Sacred Books and adore the holy sites. Thus, when Tripitaka was close to the city, the king with his ministers and a thousand monks advanced to meet him and escort him, mounted on a royal elephant, into the capital. The procession was resplendent with jeweled banners and honorific umbrellas; it moved through a thick smoke of incense, on a carpet of strewn flowers. Learning that Tripitaka lacked texts for study, the king gave him twenty scribes to copy the sacred books and treatises; he invited him to dine at the palace so that he could meet an eminent Buddhist philosopher, renowned for his spiritual powers, and nine monks, each one learned in various aspects of the Great Vehicle. And there, with teachers and texts, Tripitaka remained for two years.

In the spring of 633, Tripitaka left Kashmir to visit other important Buddhist centers. Leaving Sakala [the present-day Sialkot in eastern Punjab] he had a grim encounter. Traversing a great forest, the party was stopped by a band of robbers, fifty sword-wielding desperados, who stripped them of their clothes and goods and then drove them at sword's point into a dried-up pond. The pond, enclosed by a wall of thickly matted, prickly vines, was an ideal pen where the robbers could kill their victims. One of the young monks noticed a small break in the thorny wall. Quickly he showed it to Tripitaka; together they forced their way through the barbed hedge, and once on the other side ran for help. They had to go almost a mile before they found a Brahman plowing his field. When he heard what had happened, he instantly unyoked his oxen and led them to the village, where he summoned the villagers by blowing on a conch and beating a drum. Eighty men answered the call. They grabbed whatever weapons they could, and ran to the pond. The robbers, seeing so large a crowd, quickly dispersed and disappeared into the forest. Tripitaka and the villagers freed the men who had been trussed up, and, with makeshift garments given by the villagers, they went to the village to spend the night. Shaken by the terrifying experience, their narrow escape from death, and the losses they had suffered, the men wept. Tripitaka was the only one who seemed utterly unaffected. "The greatest gift living creatures possess is life," he said to explain his equanimity. "In one of my country's books it is said 'Heaven and earth's greatest treasure is life.' We are alive; let us rejoice that we have our greatest treasure; why lament the few garments and possessions we have lost?"

On the morrow, another great forest brought them another

and very different adventure. In a grove of mango trees at the border of the Takka country, Tripitaka's party met a Brahman, eminent for his deep knowledge of diverse philosophies and remarkable for his age. He claimed to be seven hundred years old—he said he had been a disciple of the great Nagarjuna [lived about A.D. 100]—though his mind and body were those of a man in his thirties. He was served by two followers, each of whom was 100 years old. He and Tripitaka conversed awhile to their mutual delight and edification. When the Brahman heard of their encounter with the robbers, he invited Tripitaka to stay with him and sent one of his servingmen to the nearby town to get food for so large a party. The inhabitants, mostly Hindus [and therefore not too friendly to Buddhists] heard the Brahman's messenger: "The monk from China, whose fame has come to us from Kashmir, has arrived in our neighborhood. He has been robbed of everything, even to his clothes." Forgotten were all animosities, and three hundred of their leading townsmen, shocked at this news, in a body set out to welcome Tripitaka, each one bringing a length of cotton cloth and a contribution of food and drink for the party. Respectfully they offered their presents to Tripitaka. Deeply moved, he thanked them and blessed them, using one of the many formulas of blessing. He might have said, "Peace and security to you who have two feet. Peace and security to yours that have four feet. Peace be to all your goings and peace to your returns. When you plow your fields, may you have your desires, when you sow your seed, may you have your desire."[7] Then Tripitaka spoke to them about the doctrine of rewards and punishments, explaining how men, in whichever of their incarnations, receive the just due for what they have done. After he had spoken, Hui-li said, the townspeople gave up their erroneous Hinduism and accepted the right reason of

[7] Waley, op. cit., p. 35.

Buddhism. With light and joyous hearts they then returned home. Tripitaka stayed a full month to have the Brahman expound the philosophical system of his master, Nagarjuna.

After a leisurely route arranged to see the places where Buddha had walked and preached the Law, he came to Cinabhukhti [probably near the present-day Ferozepore, just south of the Sutlej River]. This fertile region, whose climate was hot and humid and its people timid and listless, was where the Chinese prince had spent the winters while a hostage to King Kanishka; its name remembers the hostage's residence there. And Tripitaka further explains that there existed neither pear nor peach in this kingdom and throughout the Indies until the hostage planted them, and therefore the peach is called Chinani, and the pear is called Chinarajaputra. [Cina, according to Waley, can be equated with Serindia, as the region between the Pamirs and China is called, and thus with Han, when the Han Empire controlled this vast area of Central Asia.] Tripitaka went there to study under Vinitaprabha, a monk renowned for his commentaries on Mahayana doctrines. [In one of his works of thirty verses, this North Indian prince turned monk summed up "the doctrine of the extreme Idealists. An immense body of literature had grown up around these verses, and a summary of this literature made under Tripitaka's direction in the winter of 659 became the standard textbook of Idealism in China and Japan."][8] After a year, Tripitaka felt that he had mastered Vinitaprabha's treatise and furthered his studies in the New Logic under this eminent authority; he continued his search, going from place to place to meet and study under other well-known scholars.

In the Kulu Valley, set in the foothills of the Himalayas, he noted besides the rich vegetation and fertile crops that the country produced many medicinal roots of value; that gold,

[8] Waley, op. cit., p. 36.

silver, and copper were found there; and that the people were much afflicted with goiter and tumors. He saw the stone chambers that had been hollowed out of the high cliffs and were used by ascetics and holy men. His road led in and out of kingdoms connected with the Mahabharata, the "holy land" of the Sanskrit epic, and its heroes of antiquity. Here, Tripitaka commented, the families were rich, given to excessive luxuries, and addicted to the use of magical arts, honoring those adept in its different branches.

Finally his party came to the upper Ganges, whose water is blue like the ocean, and whose waves are wide-rolling as the sea. "The taste of the water is sweet and pleasant, and sands of extreme fineness border its course. In their books this is the River of Religious Merit which can wash away countless sins. Those who are weary of life, if they end their days in it, are borne to heaven and receive happiness. If a man dies and his bones are cast into the river, he cannot fall into an evil way; whilst he is carried by its waters and forgotten by men, his soul is preserved in safety in the other world. In this belief men and women swarm to the banks of the river." Tripitaka did not discuss the merits of this Hindu practice; he was more interested in relating the fate of Vimalamitra, a Master of the Lesser Vehicle, who dropped straight into hell. He investigated the exact spot near Matipura [thought to be the modern Bijnor], where at a stupa beside a grove of mango trees, Vimalamitra, a master of established name and fame, vowed to write a treatise which would make scholars forget the principles of the Great Vehicle and of Idealism. His would be an immortal work, the fruit of his long-meditated design. No sooner had he spoken the vow than his mind became confused and wild, his boastful tongue, multiplied five times, protruded, while his hot blood gushed out. Realizing that his blasphemy had brought him to the edge of death, he tore up his notes, recanted of his foolishness, and vowed never to attack the doctrines of the Greater Vehicle. The earth shook as he expired. Where he died it split wide open; below was the abyss of hell. ["Long afterwards the same story was told of a monk who had the audacity to suggest that Tripitaka sometimes talked nonsense. He can little have foreseen, when he heard the story of Vimalamitra at Matipura, that his own every saying would become as inviolate as the Mahayana itself."][9]

The next important place to be visited was Kanyakubja [now called Kanauji, located about fifty miles northwest of Cawnpore], one of the kingdoms ruled by the extraordinary King Harsha [*c.* 610–650]. Himself the hero of a famous Sanskrit poem, he was dramatist and poet, and a notable patron of Buddhism. Hui-li says there were 10,000 monks in the capital studying the Great and Lesser Vehicle promiscuously. Tripitaka stayed there three months furthering his education under the direction of Viryasena, a Master of the Lesser Vehicle. He related how Kanyakubja got its name. There once was a king who was widely reverenced and feared. He had 1000 sons famed for wisdom and courage and 100 daughters of singular grace and beauty. At this time there was a Rishi [ascetic] who, having entered a condition of ecstasy, by his spiritual power passed several myriads of years in this condition, until his form became like a decayed tree. Now it happened that a wandering bird let a seed drop on his shoulder which grew up and afforded him a welcome protection and shade. After a succession of years he awoke from his ecstasy. He arose and desired to get rid of the tree, but feared to injure the nests of the birds in it. The men of the time, extolling his virtue, called him "The Great-Tree Rishi." The Rishi saw the daughters of the king gamboling together. Then the world of desire which pollutes the mind was engendered in him. Im-

[9] Waley, op. cit., p. 37.

mediately he went to pay his salutations to the king and ask for one of his daughters.

The king, hearing of the Rishi's arrival, went himself to meet him, and addressed him graciously. "Great Rishi! you were reposing in peace—what has disturbed you?" The Rishi answered, "On awaking from my trance, I saw the king's daughters; a lustful heart was produced in me, and I have come to request one in marriage." The king hearing this, and seeing no way to escape, said to the Rishi, "Go back and rest, and await the happy period." The Rishi, hearing the mandate, returned to the forest. The king then asked his daughters in succession, but none of them consented to be given in marriage. The king, fearing the power of the Rishi, was much grieved. And now the youngest daughter said, "The king, my father, has his thousand sons. Why, then, are you sad as if you were afraid of something?"

The king replied, "The Great-Tree Rishi has been pleased to seek a marriage with one of you. If he is thwarted he will destroy my kingdom."

The girl replied, "Dismiss your heavy grief. Let me, I pray, in my poor person promote the prosperity of the country." At her words the king was overjoyed, and ordered his chariot to accompany her with gifts to her marriage. At the hermitage of the Rishi, he offered his respectful greetings and said, "Great Rishi! since you condescended to fix your mind on external things, I venture to offer you my young daughter." The Rishi, looking at her, was displeased, and said to the king, "You despise my old age, surely, in offering me this ungainly thing." The king said, "I asked all my daughters in succession, but they were unwilling to comply with your request; this little one alone offered to serve you." The Rishi, extremely angered, uttered this curse. "Let the ninety-nine girls become humpbacked; being thus deformed, they will find no one to marry them in all the world." From this time the town had this name: Kanyakubja, *i.e.*, "city of the humpbacked women."

Tripitaka's party boarded a vessel carrying some eighty other passengers to go down the Ganges to Cawnpore. At a place where the river flowed between banks covered with thick foliage, ten pirate boats suddenly darted out from their hiding places and closed in on them. Some of the passengers threw themselves into the river. The pirates took the vessel in tow, brought it to the shore, and then ordered the men to strip so that they could be searched for gold and precious stones. The pirates worshiped the goddess Durga; to ensure good fortune it was their yearly custom to sacrifice a handsome young man. That year still was without a suitable victim. Tripitaka caught their attention. "This young monk is of noble form and pleasing features; he will bring us good luck. Let us kill him." Tripitaka coolly answered them, "I don't grudge your using my poor miserable body, but I think it will bring you bad luck, not good. I came from a far distant country to worship the image of Buddha under the bodhi tree, to visit the Vulture Peak where he preached, and to study the Sacred Books and Law. Since I have not yet accomplished this, bad luck will surely come." His logic did not convince the pirates; when one of Tripitaka's companions offered himself, they refused to accept a substitute and went ahead with their preparations. They built an altar in the woods, plastered it neatly with mud, and at the point of their knives forced Tripitaka to mount it. There they bound him. Even then Tripitaka showed no fear. He made one request. "Give me a little time to compose my thoughts so that with joyous spirit I can enter into extinction." Concentrating on his deepest religious desires his mind was composed and his whole being was fixed on Maitreya; in his meditation his body and soul were ravished with such joy that he forgot that he was on an altar and that pirates were waiting to kill him. Then a miracle happened. Suddenly a cyclone swept a path through the forest. It sent the sand swirling and whipped the river into waves; it lifted the boats moored along the shore and then smashed them down. The pirates were terrified. "Whence comes this young monk? What is his name?" they asked. Tripitaka's companions said, "He is the famous monk from China come to search for Buddha's Law. If you kill him your guilt will be unparalleled. Behold how the winds and waves have risen. These are but small samples of heaven's rage. Hasten to repent!" More frightened than before, the pirates begged to be forgiven, and prostrated themselves before Tripitaka. He was still in a trance when a pirate accidently touched his hand. At that, he opened his eyes and asked, "Has the hour come?" But the pirate answered, "We dare not hurt you; we pray you accept our repentance." Tripitaka accepted their confession of sins, and then preached to them about the punishment they would suffer in the Avici Hell, the lowest of the Buddhist hells, if they pursued their pagan ways and persisted in an evil life of robbery and murder. His words encouraged them to make amends. Not only did they throw their pirate gear into the river, they also restored everything they had taken. Then and there they took the Five Vows to become lay members of the Buddhist community. By that time the wind and the waves subsided.

Continuing southward down the river, Tripitaka came to Prayaga [the modern Allahabad] where the Jumna flows into the Ganges. At the confluence of the sacred rivers, Tripitaka saw the Holy Ganges cult in its most extreme forms. "Every day many hundreds drowned themselves in ritual suicide in the belief that whoever wishes to be born in heaven ought to fast down to a grain of rice, and then drown himself in the waters. By bathing in this water they say all the pollution of sin is washed away. From various quarters and distant regions people come here. During seven days they abstain from food, and afterwards end their lives. And even the monkeys and mountain stags assemble here in the neighborhood of the river, and some of them bathe and depart, others fast and die. On one occasion, a monkey who lived by the riverside under a tree also abstained from food, and after some days died from starvation.

"Ascetics have raised a high column in the river; when the sun is about to go down they immediately climb up the pillar; then clinging with one hand and one foot, they hold out one foot and one arm; and so they stay stretched out in the air with their eyes fixed on the sun, and their heads turning with it as it sets. When the evening has darkened, they come down. There are dozens of ascetics who practice this rite. They hope by these means to escape from birth and death, and many continue to practice this ordeal through several decades."

Journeying about five hundred *li* to the northeast, the party reached Sravasti. Here began many kingdoms which because of their association with the daily occurrences and significant events in Buddha's life formed the heart of the Holy Land of Buddhism. "Sacred buildings follow one another in succession," Tripitaka wrote of the memorials erected as pious markers, "and the woods and lakes reflecting their shadows are seen everywhere." Among the places he visited reverentially were the stupa erected over the old foundations of the Great Hall of Law where Buddha preached; a bottomless pit into which a Brahman woman who had slandered Buddha went down alive into hell; a statue of Buddha sitting where he had sat when arguing with the Hindu heretics; and a relic-filled tower built upon the spot where Buddha first saw his father after having attained Perfect Enlightenment. About eight hundred *li* to the southeast, they came to the country of Buddha's birth, the kingdom of Kapilavastu. Faithfully, eagerly, adoringly, Tripitaka walked in the footsteps of the Buddha.

Within the walls of the ancient capital, he found a plentitude of hallowed sites. A monastery rose above the old foundation of what had been the sleeping room of Buddha's mother, Queen Maya. Close to this are four stupas to denote the place where the four heavenly kings received Buddha in their arms when he was born from the right side of his mother. The four kings wrapped him in a golden-colored cotton vestment, placed him on a golden bench, and, bringing him to his mother, they said, "The Queen may rejoice indeed at having given birth to such a fortunate child!" And Tripitaka adds, "If the Heavenly Ones rejoiced at the event, how much more should men!"

By the side of the queen's chamber is another monastery with a figure of a pupil receiving his lessons; this indicates the old foundation of the schoolhouse of the royal prince. Another monastery has the figure of the royal prince riding a white and high-prancing horse; this was the place where he left the city; and outside each of the four gates of the city is a monastery in which there are, respectively, figures of an old man, a diseased man, a dead man, and a shaman. Each in turn gave the royal prince an increase of religious feeling and a deeper disgust at the world and its pleasures until, filled with this conviction, he ordered his coachman to return and go home again.

Guided by the footsteps of the historical Buddha, Tripitaka went not far off to a great forest in which was a stupa erected by the Emperor Asoka. It honored the place where the prince royal, having fled from the palace in the middle of the night, took off his precious robes, loosed his necklace, bade farewell to his horse, and taking the Mani gem from his crown, commanded his equerry thus: "Take this gem, and, returning, say to my father the king, now I am going away, not in inconsiderate disobedience, but to banish lust, and to destroy the power of impermanence, and to stop all the leaks of existence."

The emotions Tripitaka felt when reverencing such momentous sites can be measured by what he wrote of a simple well where Buddha drew water for his personal use: "A mysterious sense of awe surrounds the spot; many miracles occur. Sometimes heavenly music is heard, at other times divine odors are perceived—the happy omens of good acts would be difficult to recount at length." Or again, when he tells the story associated with the stupa placed where Asita, the soothsayer, came from afar to announce the horoscope of the newborn prince. "Asita requested to see the king, who, overjoyed, went forth to meet him and do him honor. Seating him on a precious chair, he addressed him. 'It is not without an object that the Great Asita has condescended to visit me today.' And Asita spoke. 'I was quietly resting when I suddenly saw a multitude of celestial spirits dancing together for joy. And when I asked them why they rejoiced in this extravagant way, they said that they wanted me to know that of Maya, the First Queen of the King, was born a royal son who would attain perfect enlightenment and become all-wise, all-excellent. And when I had heard this I came to behold the child. Alas for me! my age will prevent me from awaiting the holy flowering.' "

And again: Tripitaka told of Buddha's return after his Enlightenment. His father, the king, knowing that his son had defeated the Great Temptress and was traveling about leading people to the true way of life, was moved by a strong wish to see him. He sent a messenger to remind his son of his promise to return to his native country when he had become Buddha. Buddha told the messenger that he would return in seven days. On hearing this the king ordered the road watered and swept, and adorned with incense and flowers. He and his ministers of state rode in their chariots beyond the palace gates; there they waited. Soon they saw a great multitude approaching; four heavenly kings came first and then hundreds of celestial beings and behind them *bhikku* [wandering ascetics], and last came Buddha by himself, as the full moon is amidst the stars. His supreme spiritual presence shook the Three Worlds, the brightness of his person exceeded that of the sun, moon, and five planets; and thus winging through the air he approached his native land. After the king and his ministers had reverenced him, they returned to the palace while Buddha and his divine escort stayed in the grove, which henceforth was sacred. Not far off was a *tank* [a man-made pond] to which herds of wild elephants had regularly come to gather flowers and scatter them in the water. Some mysterious power from the beginning of the world had impelled them to offer this homage.

The trail then led through a great forest, where wild oxen and herds of elephants, robbers, and hunters harassed travelers, to the kingdom of Kusinagara [near the modern village of Kasia, thirty-five miles east of Gorakhpur]. Its villages were waste and desolate. In a grove of salt trees [*Shorea robusta*], whose bark is greenish-white and smooth and whose leaves glisten, were four trees of extraordinary height; they marked the spot where Buddha died. Next to them, a huge brick monastery had a figure of Buddha lying with his head to the north, as if asleep. According to tradition, Buddha was eighty years old when he entered nirvana [c. 480 B.C.]. When Buddha died, a legend tells how mortals and immortals lovingly formed a coffin of the seven precious substances, swathed his body in a thousand cloths, spread flowers and incense, draped it with canopies and coverings and carried the bier to the river. They filled the coffin with scented oil, and piled aromatic wood around it and set it afire. But it would not burn. The beholders were filled with fear, but Aniruddha said, "We must await Buddha's chief disciple, Kasyapa." Even as he spoke the disciple arrived. He asked Ananda, Buddha's devoted attendant, "Can I behold Buddha's body?" Ananda was explaining that this was impossible, that the body was ready to be burned, when behold! Buddha stuck his feet out. At this compassionate gesture, Kasyapa, chanting Buddha's praises, worshiped him and circumambulated the coffin. When he finished his devotions, the wood caught fire of its own accord; everything burned in a mighty blaze. Where Buddha showed his feet, they erected a stone pillar to relate the miraculous incident. After the cremation the kings of eight countries divided the relics equally so that all countries could worship them.

Traveling more than five hundred *li* through densely wooded country, the party came to Benares [Varanasi: the Sanskrit form comes from the city's position between two streams, the Varana and the Asi]. Sprawled out along the Ganges, Tripitaka likens its inner gates to a small-toothed comb. He notes that its families are very rich and their dwellings filled with rare and costly objects. Most of the people are Hindus; only a few follow the Law of Buddha. Some cut their hair off, others tie their hair in a knot and go naked, smearing their bodies with ashes, and, by the practice of every kind of austerity, seek to escape from rebirth and death. Not far off is a large monastery where 1500 monks study the Lesser Vehicle. It is divided in eight sections connected by a surrounding wall, and in one large courtyard a two-hundred-foot tower has rows of niches on each of its four sides with a golden figure of Buddha in each niche.

Sravasti, Kapilavastu, Vaisali, Benares, Rajagriha are names of places made holy by Buddha's birth and death, his preaching and his miracle-working.

Rajagriha had been the capital of the Magadha kingdom in Buddha's lifetime. Later Asoka made Pataliputra the center of his empire. When Asoka ascended the throne, and before he was converted to Buddhism, he was a cruel tyrant. Tripitaka relates how he tortured men. Inside high walls were huge cauldrons filled with molten metal, sharp scythes, and every possible instrument for torture—a hell ruled over by a vicious man he had appointed. At first anyone who committed a crime, large or small, was consigned to this place of calamity and outrage; afterwards all those who passed by the place were seized and destroyed. It so happened that a young monk, while begging food, came to the hell-gate, and the keeper seized him. The novice, filled with fear, asked for a respite to perform an act of worship and confession. Just then he saw a man bound with cords enter the prison. In a moment they cut off his hands and feet, and pounded his body in a mortar until it was a pulp. The novice, his fear forgotten, deeply moved by pity, arrived at the conviction of the impermanence of all earthly things, and reached the fruit of "exemption from learning" [arhatship]. Then the keeper said, "Now you must die." The novice, transformed into an arhat, freed in heart from the power of birth and death, though cast into a boiling caldron, felt it as a cool lake. On its surface a lotus flower appeared, whereon he took his seat. The terrified keeper sent a messenger to the king to tell him what had happened. The king came, beheld the sight, and raised his voice in loud praise of the miracle.

The keeper, addressing the king, said, "Maharaja, you too must die." "And why so?" said the king. "Because you decreed that all who came to the walls of the hell should be killed; it was not said that the king might enter and escape death." Asoka said, "The decree was established, and cannot be altered. But when were you excepted? You have long destroyed life. I will put an end to it." At his order, the attendants seized the keeper and cast him into a boiling caldron. With his death the king departed. The walls were leveled and the ditches filled up;

he put an end to the infliction of such horrible punishments. Soon after, Asoka met Upagupta, known as the "Buddha without marks," who converted him. The king became Buddhism's first royal patron: he made Buddhism the official religion; he sent missionaries abroad and built, as Tripitaka noted, 84,000 stupas. Magadha, though a country whose glory had long since died, abounded with precious sites. Here was the Bodhgaya, where under the pipal tree Buddha achieved Enlightenment. Hui-li gives the meaning of the tree protected by its high brick wall: "In the center of the enclosure is the diamond throne, which was perfected at the beginning and rose up from the ground when the world was formed. It is the central point of the universe and goes down to the golden wheel. In using the word *diamond*, we mean that it is firm and indestructible. If it were not for its support the earth could not remain." And he explains that as Buddha reached perfect wisdom [*anuttara bodhi*] while sitting under the pipal tree, it is called the bodhi tree. The tree, Tripitaka was told, which had been two hundred feet high in Buddha's time, had been continually cut down by wicked kings, and even though its roots had been bathed with scented water and perfumed milk, it was only fifty feet high.

When Tripitaka had gazed on the bodhi tree and thought of that moment of Perfect Enlightenment, he threw himself face down at the holy site. Aware of his own shortcomings, he wept. To him it was inescapably clear that, had he not been sinful in a previous existence, he might have won the right to have lived in the golden days when Buddha walked the earth and would have not been condemned to this present baser age. "I wonder," he thought, "in what troubled whirl of birth and death I was caught when Buddha achieved Enlightenment."

Not far off was a great stone house set in a bamboo garden.

Tripitaka was told that there Buddha's disciple Kasyapa held the convocation of arhats [saints]. It happened thus. The great Kasyapa had been meditating in a desert when the earth shook, and, thus prepared for a miracle, he saw the Lord Buddha between two trees, entering nirvana. Immediately he hurried to Buddha, saying to his followers, "The Sun of Wisdom has quenched his light. The world is now in darkness. Our good guide has left us. And gone, all creatures of flesh must fall into calamity." While he was bemoaning, he overheard some shiftless monks talking amongst themselves, saying with satisfaction, "How lucky this is for us. Now that Buddha is in nirvana we will not be plagued by constantly being told what to do and what not to do." This troubled Kasyapa deeply. He realized that it was important to set rules and regulations for monks and enforce them by supervision. But first he went to behold the dead Buddha and worship him. Then he ascended Mount Sumeru and sounded the great gong. He announced a religious assembly: "Let all who have attained arhatship hasten to the spot". A multitude hastened to the convocation. Kasyapa dismissed all of limited saintliness, sending them back to their homes. This left 999 men. Ananda was desolate when Kasyapa, reminding him that he was not yet free from defects, said, "You must leave the holy assembly." "During all the years I followed Buddha as his attendent," Ananda said, "I was part of every assembly which met to consider the Law; now that you are going to hold an assembly after his death, I find myself excluded. Since the King of the Law is gone, I am without my protector." Kasyapa said, "Do not be sad. True, you were Buddha's personal attendant, and though you heard him whenever he preached you still persisted in falling in love. The binding habits of love still chain you." [Ananda, says Waley, "was very good-looking, and women were constantly falling in love with him, and, alas! he with them."][10] Ananda, meekly admitting his failing, retired to a nearby spot where unceasingly he tried to attain the condition of an arhat. All his efforts were in vain. At length, utterly exhausted, he longed only for sleep. Scarcely had his head touched the pillow, when lo! he became an arhat. He rushed back to the assembly and knocked on the door. From the inside, Kasyapa said, "If you have rid yourself of all your bonds, you need but to exercise your arhat power and enter without my opening the door." No sooner had he spoken when Ananda entered through the keyhole. [The monastic rules set up by the conference disillusioned the monks who imagined that they could henceforward do as they pleased. Drawn up by the venerable Upali, formerly a hairdresser, the "writing down of the Scriptures was entrusted to Ananda, who despite his lapses had been Buddha's favorite companion for thirty years."][11]

For eight or nine days Tripitaka stayed near the bodhi tree worshiping at each sacred spot. While he was there four monks from the famous Nalanda monastery, some sixty miles away, came to escort him back with them. The welcome took on impressive proportions when, at one of the monastery's farms, they were joined by two hundred monks and a thousand lay patrons of Buddhism. With such an escort, with banners and with parasols, flowers and incense, Tripitaka made his entrance into Nalanda, where the entire community of ten thousand monks awaited him. He was conducted to a special seat beside that of the presiding monk, who invited him to be seated. Only then did the others sit down. Then the great gong was sounded, and the presiding monk announced, "While the Master of the Law dwells in the monastery everything is to be at his disposal." After that he was entrusted

[10] Op. cit., p. 43.
[11] Waley, op. cit., p. 43.

to twenty middle-aged monks well versed in the proper etiquette, to be prepared and coached before being led into the presence of the elderly Silabhadra, Nalanda's greatest scholar. Observing the approach he had been taught for a would-be disciple, Tripitaka advanced on his hands and knees, kissed the aged monk's foot, and touched his head to the ground before him. After the usual greetings and compliments, when Tripitaka was invited to be seated, he told Silabhadra that he had journeyed from China to study the principles of a certain doctrine (the Yoga-sastra) under him. At these words the aged monk turned to his disciple Buddhabhadra, a man over seventy, and with tears in his eyes bade him recount the dream. It had happened three years ago when he was suffering intense, protracted pain. While he dozed, three celestial visitors told him that he should desire to live so that he might proclaim to those who have not yet heard it the truth of the Yoga-sastra Doctrine. Having exhorted him, they announced that "a monk of the country of China, eager to understand the Great Law and desirous to study with you, will arrive in due time; instruct him carefully." All those present were filled with wonder at hearing the miraculous event. And when Silabhadra asked Tripitaka how many years he had been on his journey, Tripitaka, forgetful of everything but the awe and excitement of the tremendous moment, answered, "During three years." [Both men were enchanted that the prophecy was confirmed; the only flaw is that Tripitaka had been journeying a good five years.] They rejoiced in their divinely heralded relationship of master and disciple.

Nalanda was a notable institution of learning. Tripitaka proudly described its extraordinary standing and its profound contributions to Buddhist philosophy and doctrine. "The monks, to the number of several thousands, are men of the highest ability and talent. Their distinction is very great at the present time, and there are many hundreds whose fame has rapidly spread through distant regions. The rules of this monastery are severe, and all monks are bound to observe them. The day is not sufficient for asking and answering profound questions. From morning till night they engage in discussion; the old and the young mutually help one another. Learned men from different cities, who desire to acquire a renown in discussion quickly, come here, and then their wisdom spreads far and wide. For this reason some style themselves Nalanda students, and are honored as a consequence. If outsiders desire to take part in the discussions, the keeper of the gate proposes some hard questions; many are unable to answer, and retire. One must have studied deeply both old and new books before admission. Men of conspicuous talent, of solid learning, great ability, and illustrious virtue, add their names to the succession of celebrities who have belonged to the college and who have composed many treatises and commentaries which, widely diffused and known for their perspicuity, endure to the present time." Tripitaka spent five years there [633–637].

The Chinese visitors were impressed with Nalanda, which stood, foursquare, like a city precinct. It was the only monastery which by imperial decree was permitted to keep a water clock to determine the exact time. [Its vast ruins testify to its former size and grandeur.] Originally, Hui-li says, the area was a nobleman's garden which five hundred merchants bought for ten *lakhs* of gold [a *lakh* equals 100,000] and presented to Buddha. He preached the Law there for three months and most of the merchants thus attained arhatship. After Buddha's nirvana, a former king built the monastery, which six successive rulers enlarged. The vast establishment, surrounded by a wall having a single gate, had richly decorated towers and fairy-like turrets grouped around a central hall; on all sides were cool groves shaded by mango trees and deep, clear ponds. The dormitories, four-storied buildings located on the outside courts, were brightly ornamented with carved porches, colored eaves, and pearl-red pillars, carved and painted and joined by beautifully adorned balustrades. Roofs of shining tiles added to the beauty of the scene. Of all the monasteries of India, Nalanda is remarkable for its grandiose size and its towering structures. Its 10,000 monks and visitors were studying the Great Vehicle, which, because of the nature of the Buddhist dialectic, also required mastery of the writings of the eighteen branches of the Lesser Vehicle, and proficiency in Indian subjects—in the Vedas, logic, grammar, medicine, mathematics, astronomy, and so forth. Out of the whole student body, a mere dozen, including Tripitaka, were considered to have mastered fifty books; but only Silabhadra, so the Nalanda students thought, had read and digested everything ever written. The schedule offered daily lectures in about a hundred classrooms, and the students attended them with great punctuality—"not even an inch of shadow on the dial late" is Hui-li's expression. In the monastic university's seven hundred years there had never been a single case meriting disciplinary action.

This avid pursuit of learning was subsidized. The king had endowed the university with more than a hundred villages each of which had two hundred households whose duty required a daily delivery of a stated number of pounds of ordinary rice, *ghee* [purified butter], and milk. It was to this largesse that the presiding monk had welcomed his distinguished visitor and Tripitaka was thus admitted to his allotment of the commodities furnished the monks and all the facilities for study. He took up his residence in the large establishment of Buddhabhadra, Silabhadra's disciple. Every day he received 120 betel leaves for chewing, twenty areca nuts and the same number of cardamoms, an ounce of camphor, and a *sheng* (about one and a half pounds) of Mahasali rice. He recalled that the grains of this unusual rice, grown only in Magadha, were as large as black beans, were scented, and of an exquisite flavor and shining color; it was called "the rice for the use of the great." His daily ration also supplied him with *ghee* and other staples. Each month he received a *sheng* of oil. To relieve the monks of domestic chores, two lay servants attended the wants of each monk—a convenience also extended to visiting students, for Tripitaka was one of many such studying at Nalanda. In addition he had the use of an elephant for his excursions outside the university. Freed from every want during their residence at Nalanda, the students were expected to apply their minds and energies to an inner development. [Small wonder "that Nalanda was the headquarters of Idealism—of the doctrine that mental happenings alone are real."][12]

On his elephant, Tripitaka made a brief pilgrimage to the holy places near the monastery—Rajaghriha, the capital where the king lived during Buddha's lifetime, and Vulture Peak, a bold solitary rock where Buddha preached the Lotus Scripture; in the opposite direction, but also close by, was the Bamboo Garden, the first piece of land presented to Buddha and his followers, where Kasyapa convoked the assembly of arhats after Buddha's death. When Tripitaka had visited all the holy sites nearby he returned to Nalanda to begin five years of intensive study in Buddhist writings and in Sanskrit, a language whose structure and vocabulary differed radically from his native Chinese.

When he had completed his studies he continued his tour of India. Heading eastward through a dark forest he came to a monastery in which there was a miracle-working sandal-

[12] Waley, op. cit., p. 46.

wood image of the Bodhisattva Avalokitesvara. So great was the shrine's reputation that its guardian had had to erect an iron-tipped wooden fence to protect the statue. The crowds of worshipers who flocked there were forced to throw their floral offerings from a distance and they believed that if a flower lodged in the Bodhisattva's hands or attached itself to his arm, it was a sign that their prayers would be answered. Forewarned of this, Tripitaka was forearmed; that his requests would be surely heard, he strung a large assortment of flowers into garlands before going to the image. He fell on his hands and knees before the statue and made three prayers. First, that when all his studies were finished he might return peacefully and quietly to China; second, that he might be worthy of being born again in the Tusita Heaven where he could worship Maitreya; and, third, a sign to know whether he possessed some portion of "the nature of Buddha." If his flowers fell on the statue's hands, the first prayer would be answered; if on the arms, the second would be; and if around the neck, then he would know that he had some part of the nature of Buddha. Having uttered his prayers, Tripitaka threw three garlands; one came to rest on the statue's hands, another on the arms, and the third ringed the neck. He stood overpowered with joy while the pilgrims and custodians clapped their hands and stamped their feet at the miracle they had seen. "When you arrive at Perfect Wisdom and become a Buddha, remember this day, and make us the first to whom you bring salvation," they implored him.

Southeast his travels took him; he crossed Bengal, punctuating his progress with lengthy halts at monasteries and sacred sites, through what Tripitaka called the seventeen countries. Among them was Mongir, a kingdom no larger than the hill it sat upon, but a kingdom because the hill commanded the land route as well as traffic on the Ganges. At Champa [a kingdom of Southeast Asia], whose fields were level and fat, the temperature was warm, and the people simple in their habits. At Pundra [near Rangpur], Tripitaka admired the jack, or breadfruit tree, whose pumpkin-sized fruit had dozens of seeds, each the size of a pigeon's egg, that yield a yellowish-red juice of delicious flavor. So he came to Kamarupa [western Assam] whose inhabitants were small and of a dark yellow complexion, their language differing from that of Central India. This kingdom, he learned, bordered on the barbarian tribes of southwest China whose customs resembled those of the Man tribes. He further learned that it was but a two months' journey to the western edge of the province of Szechuan. But mountains and rivers presented obstacles, pestilential mists, poisonous snakes, and choking vegetation marked this route. South of this, he reached Samatata, which bordered on the Great Sea. There he heard of six kingdoms lying to the east—among them the Burmese Dynasty, whose capital, on the Irawaddi, was near Prome, and the kingdom that controlled the Irawaddi delta [possibly Siam], but hemmed in by mountains and rivers.

So Tripitaka turned to the southwest toward Udra, or Orissa. He was delighted with the strange shrubs and all the lovely flowers that bloomed there. The people, tall and of a yellowish-black complexion, were uncivilized though they loved learning and applied themselves to it continuously. He came to a port from which merchants sailed for distant countries and to which strange vessels put in when passing. He noticed rare and valuable cowrie shells and pearls used as currency, and dark-colored elephants, native to the region, that were harnessed to wagons in which they made lengthy trips. Beyond Orissa was a belt of jungle forest whose mighty trees blotted out the sun; the climate was burning. The people of Kalinga [near, it is thought, the present Cuttuck] were vehement and impetuous, the men rough and uncivilized, "though still they keep their word and are trustworthy." Their language sounded light and tripping and their pronunciation distinct and correct. But both words and sounds were very different from those of Central India. In the old days, he heard, Kalinga had so dense a population that their shoulders rubbed one with the other, and the axles of their chariot wheels ground together, and when they raised their arm sleeves a perfect tent was formed. But a rishi possessed of supernatural powers, who lived on a high precipice, being put to shame because he had gradually lost his magic powers, cursed the people. He caused young and old to perish; wise and ignorant alike died, and the population disappeared. After many ages the country was gradually repeopled by emigrants, but it is not yet properly inhabited. This is why at the present time there are so few who dwell here.

In the seaports he passed through, Tripitaka learned that in the middle of the ocean was Simhala [Ceylon], a country distinguished for scholars who expounded primitive Buddhism and Idealist doctrines. To reach Simhala meant a voyage of "over 4000 miles" unless—so it was explained by a monk from southern India—he went overland to India's southernmost tip from where it could be reached in a three days' voyage. Furthermore, the monk suggested, along the overland route he would find sacred sites to visit and scholars to talk with. [Though on his way he stayed several months in the neighborhood of the Amaravati stupa, he does not give any details, possibly because it was not a wonder-working site, but only a stupa whose exquisite carvings has made it one of the most famous names in early Indian sculpture.] At last he arrived at Kancipura, the capital of the kingdom of Dravidia. From here a three days' voyage away was Simhala. While he had been traveling to Kancipura, the king of Simhala had died and the country was in the grip of famine and great disorders. Three hundred monks who had fled from Simhala were in Kancipura, among them two of their most eminent scholars. The arrival of these refugees brought the very men Tripitaka had been planning to visit. Discussing passages of the Yoga-sastra with them, he found they added nothing to what he had learned from Silabhadra, nor could they equal that master in the depth of their understanding and the clarity of their explanation.

In the company of seventy Simhalese monks, Tripitaka headed northwest from Dravidia. He was interested in all he saw and heard. He noted that the king of Maharashtra was fond of military affairs and boasted of his strength. His troops and cavalry were well equipped and discipline was strict. If a general suffered defeat he was not punished; instead he was given women's clothes, and thus shamed he would take his own life. The army was made up of several thousand men and hundreds of savage elephants. When the army was drawn up in battle array, the soldiers were given a drink which intoxicated them so that they rushed into battle excited and unafraid. His military prowess had made the Maharashtra king contemptuous of anyone who might try to conquer him. Utterly different was the kingdom of Ujjain, whose people were cultivated, polite, and most agreeable, where the arts were highly appreciated and an elegance in diction and conversation was valued. Tripitaka was told of Siladitya, their king who had lived some sixty years before. A man of great learning and unique disposition, he was humane, affectionate, generous, considerate of his people, and to avoid hurting even a fly or an ant, he had the water given to his horses and elephants strained lest he destroy an insect. So deeply had he impressed his people with the need to avoid taking life that the wild beasts became tame and the wolves ceased preying on cattle.

In a country far in the northwest, lying close to the Great

Sea, Tripitaka heard of the country of Persia, beyond the boundaries of India, a land abounding in pearls and precious goods, in silken brocades and woolens, in sheep, horses and camels. He heard, too, of Hormuz, a city on its eastern border, and to its west, the country of Fo-lin [probably Babylon]. Also of an island to the southwest called the Land of the Western Women, where the women have no male children among them. The country, rich in precious products, is tributary to Fo-lin, whose king every year sends men to cohabit with the women; but whenever male children are born, they do not rear them.

Going eastward [the southern Punjab or northern Rajasthian] he reached a large monastery whose one hundred monks were studying the Great Vehicle. Among them were three outstanding scholars, men of real attainment, with whom he spent two years in study. [One of the books on which he received instruction "was a Hinayana treatise which disproves on moral grounds of the usual Buddhist theory that neither I nor other people have any real existence. Murder, they said, then becomes merely a fable about one phantom who slays another."][13]

After this long tour of holy sites and study with outstanding teachers, Tripitaka returned to Nalanda, paid his respects to the aged Silabhadra, and went on to a neighboring monastery to work under the renowned Prajnabhadra, an authority on grammar and logic. From there he went to the Walking-stick Forest [Yashtivana] where Jayasena, a native of Surat of the warrior caste, taught the secular disciplines of astronomy and geography, medicine, mathematics, grammar, and logic. Jayasena's accomplishments made him the admiration of his time. First one king of Magadha and then his successor invited the distinguished sage to serve as State Philosopher, of-

[13] Waley, op. cit., p. 49.

fering him the revenue of twenty large towns. To titles as to money, he turned a deaf ear. He also declined an offer from Harsha, overlord of Orissa, to receive all the revenues from eighty large estates! To so mighty a king and so munificent an offer, Jayasena replied, "My urgent object is to learn how to free myself from the bonds of life and death. How could I possibly find the leisure to become familiar with king's concerns?" And, bowing respectfully, he went away. Nor could the mighty king detain him. [Jayasena, then close to one hundred, spent his time modeling little mud stupas into which he inserted snippets from the Scriptures. When he had enough little ones, he enclosed them in a larger one with a larger piece of text. At night he read or sat quietly meditating. "It would certainly have infuriated King Harsha if he had found a man who claimed to be too busy to take on any extra work spending most of his day playing with toy pagodas. But Jayasena was at any rate harmlessly employed whereas Harsha's 'business' consisted in carrying war into almost every corner of India."][14]

While living and studying with Jayasena, Tripitaka had an unusual strange, and frightening dream. He saw the cells of Nalanda deserted and filthy, and, looking, he saw that they were inhabited not by monks but by water buffalos. He also saw on the top of the four-storied monastery towers a man of gold, of a grave and imposing face, whose glorious radiance lighted the whole scene. Tripitaka wished to ascend to the top, but he saw no stairway and begged the figure to reach down and lift him up. "I am the Bodhisattva Manjusri," the figure replied. "Your past actions do not yet admit of such a privilege. Look there," and the figure pointed outside the monastery where a conflagration was devouring the towns and villages of Magadha. "Leave soon," Manjusri said. "Ten

[14] Waley, op. cit., p. 50.

years from now King Harsha will be dead; India will be torn by rebellions, wicked men will struggle and slaughter. Remember what I have said." And with these words the golden figure vanished. Tripitaka awoke troubled and related his dream to Jayasena. The old philosopher, having listened, said, "It is quite possible that it may be as you heard in your dream. We know that in the world of matter, mind, and feeling there is no rest or peace. As you had the warning, the responsibility is yours; you must do as you think best." [Harsha died before the time prophesied, probably in 647. However, Waley wryly remarks that in Chinese ten and seven look very similar—in the T'ang texts they are often confused—"so perhaps the prophecy was exact."][15]

That same month was the time when the relics at Bodhgaya were taken out and displayed. Together Tripitaka and Jayasena joined the crowds that went to see the relic bones. Whether large or small, they were bright and glistening; the flesh relics, large as a bean, were shining red. At night, Tripitaka and Jayasena, talking over what they had seen, agreed that compared with other relics at other places, which were the size of rice grains, these at Bodhgaya were unusually large. Doubts troubled both men. Suddenly the lights of the lamps were eclipsed by a celestial illumination. The relic tower was as radiant as the sun, rays of different colors filled the sky. Heaven and earth were flooded with a light that dimmed the moon and the stars; and a subtle perfume filled the temple. When the heaven and earth were again filled with darkness and the stars had reappeared, those who had beheld the miracle no longer were troubled with doubts.

Shortly thereafter a messenger came from King Harsha asking Nalanda to send four monks well versed in the different branches of Mahayana Scriptures to Orissa to debate with a

[15] Op. cit., p. 52.

group of Hinayana monks. Among the four, Silabhadra named Tripitaka. As the time approached the other three grew increasingly anxious about their ability to defend their doctrines before the great king. Tripitaka, calm and unafraid, said, "In China and later in Kashmir I was well schooled in all the Hinayana texts; there was never a Little Vehicle argument that I was not able to refute. No matter how slender my ability and how ordinary my wisdom, I will be more than a match for them. But you should not worry. If I am defeated it will not affect the outcome; it will simply mean that henceforth a monk from China will not have a very high reputation." But before it was time to start for Orissa, Harsha changed his mind and sent another messenger, postponing the debate. During this time a noted Hindu philosopher, eager for a religious debate, hung forty theses on the Nalanda gate and defiantly wrote at the end, "If anyone can refute these principles, I will give my head as proof of his victory." Tripitaka answered the challenge, discoursing until the Hindu was silent and unable to reply. At last, rising, the Hindu said, "I am vanquished. I am ready to abide by my compact." The least bloodthirsty of men, Tripitaka bade him stay, serve, and follow his teachings. It was in friendly conversations with this learned Hindu that the Master of the Law became sufficiently informed to be able to write his refutation, "The Destruction of Heresy," which point by point maintained the Mahayana doctrine over Hindu arguments. When he had completed this, he told the Brahman he was free to go where ever he wished. Soon thereafter the Brahman, filled with joy at his meeting with Tripitaka, went to Assam and told King Kumara of the extraordinary qualities of the Chinese monk. The king lost no time in sending a messenger inviting Tripitaka to his court.

The day before Kumara's messenger arrived, a naked Jain of the Sky-clad sect unexpectedly walked into Tripitaka's cell. Knowing that such Jains were skilled diviners, he bade him welcome. When the stranger was seated, he opened his doubts to him. "I am a monk from China who has been in India studying and traveling to holy sites for many years. I wish to return home. Cast my horoscope and tell me whether I shall get back safely, whether it is better for me to wait awhile or start at once. Can you tell me whether I shall live a long or short time?" With a piece of chalk the Jain drew a figure on the ground, and after casting lots, he replied, "The signs are good for your remaining, and if you do you will gain profound respect among the religious and laymen all over India. If you leave, you will have a safe return and continue to be respected by all here, but not as much as if you remain. Your span of years will end ten years from now. It is impossible for me to know if there might not be a continuation of your good fortune." Then Tripitaka said, "I intend to return, but I have collected a great number of images and sacred books and I do not know how to get them back to China with me." To this the Jain replied, "Do not be anxious about that. King Harsha and King Kumara will provide you with an escort. You will return without an accident." "But this is preposterous," Tripitaka answered. "I have never seen these two kings. Why would they show me such kindness?" The Jain continued, "Kumara has already sent messengers to invite you; they will be here in two or three days. After Kumara you will also meet Harsha." And with these words he left. His mind made up to return, Tripitaka began arranging his collection of statues and books.

When the monks learned of Tripitaka's decision they pleaded with him to stay. "India is the place of Buddha's birth. What greater happiness can you have than spending the rest of your life visiting the holy sites? Moreover, China is a land of barbarians and so the Buddhas are never born there." Tripitaka answered with a patriotic discourse on the government, culture, and excellence of his own land. "Just because Buddha did not go to China," he concluded, "does not mean that it is an insignificant kingdom." He finally silenced their arguments by reminding them that the Scripture related that Vimilakirti once asked a disciple why the sun travels to the Rose Apple Tree [the world of men]. "And he was properly answered, 'So that it might dispel the darkness.' This is the reason I intend to return to my own country." When Silabhadra asked him why he had come to his decision, Tripitaka answered with great respect, "Since my arrival at Nalanda you, sir, have condescended to explain the difficulties I encountered in the Yoga-sastra. In India I have visited the sacred sites and learned the hidden meanings of the different schools. I desire now to go back and translate the texts and explain them to others so they will know what I have heard. This will cause others to be as grateful as I am for your kindness in helping me understand. This is the only reason I am unwilling to delay my return and remain here." When his aged teacher heard these words, he gave him his consent and blessing.

Two days later, as the Jain had foretold, Kumara's invitation arrived. With it began the fantastic finale to Tripitaka's stay in India.

Silabhadra recognized the awkwardness of the situation. Suppose Harsha should renew his invitation to hold the great debate with the Hinayanists and Tripitaka were not there to support the Nalanda doctrines? Unwilling to risk defeat or offend Harsha, the aged monk respectfully declined Kumara's invitation, pleading that Tripitaka was about to start for home. Kumara replied that Tripitaka could return by way of Assam. Again Silabhadra declined for his disciple. Then Kumara, his imperial will thwarted, threatened to let the evil part of his nature prevail. "If necessary," his letter continued, "I will equip my army and elephants and sweep down on Nalanda and trample it to dust." How much better it would be, he suggested, if Tripitaka came and converted the king, who would lead his country to join the Great Vehicle. The aged monk saw the logic of the king's arguments; he urged Tripitaka not to shrink from the slight trouble of visiting Assam. The Master of the Law, leaving his teacher, went with the envoy and arrived there.

Kumara's capital, Gauhati, on the Brahmaputra River, was six hundred miles east of Nalanda. There the king, attended by his principal ministers, met Tripitaka and with great honor and reverence conducted him to the palace, where he received the vows at Tripitaka's hands. Every day he arranged music and banquets as well as religious offerings of flowers and incense. Thus a pleasant month had gone by when King Harsha, returning from a military expedition, was annoyed to learn that Tripitaka was the guest of Kumara. Peremptorily, he sent a messenger bidding Kumara send the monk from China to him. Kumara impetuously replied that he would rather send Harsha his head than his revered guest; and then, frightened at his folly, he mobilized an impressive escort to conduct Tripitaka to Harsha. Twenty thousand elephants marched as 30,000 boats went up the Ganges to Kajangala [just south of the Ganges and 280 miles east of Benares]. Kumara left Tripitaka in a pavilion-of-travel erected on the north side of the river, and crossed the river to apologize to Harsha. The latter, overjoyed and placated, asked the whereabouts of the monk from China. Why had Tripitaka been left behind at the pavilion? Kumara replied with suave grace, "Your Majesty is known for his respect for men of virtue and wisdom and his love of religion; therefore I thought he would prefer to go to meet Tripitaka instead of having him brought to you." The king agreed, "It is well. You can go now and tomorrow I myself will come there to him." But when Kumara had returned to Tripitaka he told him, "Though the king says he will come tomorrow, I suspect he will arrive tonight. Be prepared; if he comes, don't be alarmed." "That would be against my understanding of the Laws of Buddhism," Tripitaka reassured him.

About the first watch of the night, some men announced that several thousand lighted torches could be seen on the river, and that they heard the sound of ceremonial drums. It was the king. [When Harsha marched, he and he alone was always accompanied by several hundred men with golden drums who beat one stroke for every step taken, the "music-paced drums."] Kumara ordered everyone to carry torches and to go out to meet him. King Harsha threw himself at Tripitaka's feet, scattered flowers over them, and then, looking up at him with ardent respect, sang his praises in flowing words. Then he asked the monk why did he not comply with the royal invitation made long before. Calmly, Tripitaka explained that when his first invitation came he was still intent on finishing his studies and could not leave. Harsha's next question was unexpected. "You come from China. I have heard that you have a song and a dance called 'The Prince of Ch'in Breaks the Ranks.' Who is this prince and what deed of his made him so distinguished?" Tripitaka related that that song and dance, performed in temples and village fairs, reenacted the great event that occurred in the summer of the year 620, when the Emperor T'ai Tsung, then the prince of Ch'in, defeated the last opponents of the T'ang Dynasty. After his victory, "the sun and moon and stars shone out again, and the world was filled with gratitude for his care. For this reason we sing his praises."

["In 641 the King of Tibet had married a Chinese princess

who was brought from China by six hundred followers. As the 'Breaking of the Ranks' had become a sort of Chinese national dance anthem, it is extremely likely that some of the Chinese followers danced it at the wedding festivities. Probably an account of the dance was brought back by Assamese envoys who represented their country at the wedding."][16]

After the formal and elaborate entry, Harsha entertained the monk at a great banquet. He mentioned that he would like to read Tripitaka's treatise, "The Destruction of Heresy."

"Here it is," said Tripitaka, giving the king a copy. The king was pleased with what he read and said to his priests, "I have heard that the rising sun puts out the glowworm's light and that the voice of the thunder silences the sound of hammer and chisel. Just so Tripitaka's doctrines have annihilated your preachments about salvation. Not one of you has stepped forward to refute him. Even your abbot, who claimed he was superior to all his rivals and boasted that he had mastered every science, always opposed the Great Vehicle. And yet when he heard that this foreign monk had arrived, he immediately decided to go on a pilgrimage. From his action I guess none of you would be willing to stand up to a debate." The king addressed Tripitaka, "This treatise is good, very good; quite enough to convince me and those present. But there are those in other parts of the country who will still cling to and defend their foolish doctrine of the Lesser Vehicle. Let us have a great assembly in Kanyakubja [modern Kanauj], and invite all the monks and Brahmans, too, from all India. I want them to hear the subtleties of the Great Vehicle. This will stop their slanders. It will give you the opportunity to demolish, once and for all time, their arrogant beliefs." And that same day the king sent an order for all disciples of all schools to gather at his capital, Kanauj, there to examine the

[16] Waley, op. cit., p. 61.

treatise of the Chinese Master of the Law. Tripitaka, in the king's company, went to Kanauj; the year 642 was ending. Already present were the kings of eighteen vassal countries, three thousand monks versed in the literature of the Lesser and the Great Vehicle, and some three thousand Hindus and Jains. A thousand monks from Nalanda attended. Each of these thousands of celebrated visitors was accompanied by a retinue of servants; some came on elephants, some in chariots, some were carried in palanquins, and some were distinguished by their show of standards and parasols. The vast conclave spread over many miles. "Without exaggeration," said Hui-li, "they were as numerous as the drops of rain which fall from the skies."

Now Harsha, the empire builder, whose deeds were celebrated in the Sanskrit poem the *Harshacarita*, was a dramatist and poet in his own right; with an eye for the dramatic, he staged the great public debates. He arranged the arena carefully. About a mile from the palace two thatched halls were built, the one for the Buddha images, the other to house the vast assemblage. At dawn of the day the debates were to begin, a huge elephant, richly and elaborately caprisoned, carried a splendid howdah in which was a large gold statue of Buddha flanked by the two kings, Harsha holding the white chowry [whisk], the symbol of the Lord Indra, and Kumara, holding the precious parasol of the Lord Brahma. Both were crowned like celestial beings and were wreathed with flowers and streamers of jeweled ribbons. Two other large elephants walked solemnly behind, from which flowers were strewn behind the Buddha statue, and behind them was an elephant carrying Tripitaka and the king's principal officers. The great procession had some three hundred more elephants, also picked for their outstanding size, carrying the vassal kings and distinguished visitors from abroad. The principal monks brought together from the entire kingdom rode in a double file on each side of the procession, chanting their praises as they moved. When they approached the Buddha Hall, elephants and men knelt while the golden image was carefully lifted down and installed inside, and then the kings with Tripitaka advanced to make their reverential offerings. When the sacred nature of the convocation had been established, Harsha gave a state banquet for the vassal princes, for the most renowned scholars—a thousand monks from all the Buddhist sects—for five hundred famous Brahmans and Jains, and for about two hundred foreign officials. His lavish hospitality included presenting the guests with golden dishes and bowls, purses filled with coins, and the finest cotton cloths. Food was liberally provided for those outside the hall.

When the ceremonial gift-giving was over, Harsha had a special chair brought in for Tripitaka to sit in while he presided over the assembly. First, the Master of the Law presented the case for the Mahayanists, directing his argument against the doctrines of the Hinayanists; as he was speaking, a Nalanda monk read Tripitaka's speech aloud for the thousands gathered outside, beyond the reach of his voice. In addition, a copy of Tripitaka's argument was posted where it could be read and studied by all present. So true and unanswerable did Tripitaka feel his position to be that he ordered a placard placed under the text: "If anyone can find a single word in the text contrary to reason or a single argument that can be refuted, I will forfeit my head." And so the debate got under way.

For five days the assembly met, each beginning with the elaborate procession and offerings to Buddha; for those five days not a single opponent spoke out to refute Tripitaka. Whether Harsha would have recognized the Hinayanist arguments or permitted any criticism of Tripitaka is dubious; but many of them who had traveled far to attend the debate were ignored, and scorned. They seethed with fury; Hui-li says that they plotted to kill Tripitaka.

The eighteen days of the assembly's duration passed. On the last evening, Harsha, elated and filled with enthusiasm, showered gifts on Tripitaka—10,000 pieces of gold, 30,000 pieces of silver, and 100 garments of exquisite cotton—and each of the vassal kings presented him with precious jewels. But he declined everything. Then the king wanted Tripitaka—as was customary for the winner of a public debate—to ride through the city in the howdah of a great elephant so that the people could see and applaud him. This, too, Tripitaka refused. He finally agreed to let one of his garments be carried in a procession that proclaimed his victory in establishing the doctrine of the Great Vehicle.

Tripitaka said farewell to the Nalanda monks who had brought him his books and statues; then he went to the king to pay his respects before starting on his homeward journey. The king's reply was to urge Tripitaka to delay his departure briefly so that he might witness the King's Great Almsgiving, a ceremony to which Harsha was deeply committed. Held every five years—this would be the sixth in his thirty-year reign—the *Pancavarsha* took place at the Arena of Charitable Offerings, a large field, flat and smooth as a mirror, located at the junction of the Ganges and Jumna rivers. It attracted all the monks and Brahmans of his kingdom, and from far and wide the orphaned and the destitute, ordinary beggars and religious mendicants. There is a tradition that it is more advantageous to give one mite in charity in that spot than a thousand in any other. Tripitaka accompanied the king there. The arena, a square a thousand paces to a side, was hedged in by bamboo. Within were many thatched buildings, each one to hold one kind of treasure to be distributed—one for gold, for silver, fine pearls, red glass, mother-of-pearl, silk and cotton garments, gold and silver coins, and so forth. Outside the hedge were booths for eating and covered sheds where the throngs could rest. When Harsha's entourage arrived in an impressive procession of elephants and a flotilla of barges, he found half a million persons gathered, an unusually large number, for many of the people who had traveled to attend the Great Debate went on to attend the Great Almsgiving. It lasted seventy-five days. On the first day, the image of Buddha was installed in a building inside the field of charity. They distributed precious articles and the finest clothing; they offered delicacies while they scattered flowers to the sound of music. On the second day they installed the image of the Hindu Sun God, the traditional divine protector of Harsha's family, and offered the same kind of articles as before but only half the amount.

On the third day, Siva, the mighty Hindu deity, was installed; he, too, received only half the amount that Buddha had.

On the fourth day, the royal largesse was distributed to 10,000 monks; each one received 100 pieces of gold, one pearl, one cotton garment, drink and meat, flowers and incense.

On the fifth day began a similar bestowal of gifts on the Brahmans—this took twenty days to accomplish.

After the Brahmans, it was the turn of the Jains; they took ten days. The next category was those who came from distant regions to ask for charity; this lasted ten days. Finally, it was the turn of the poor, the orphans, and the destitute; this went on for a month.

When this was over, the treasure and goods accumulated in five years had been exhausted. Except for horses, elephants, and the military stores—Harsha's striking power—nothing remained. In addition, the king gave away his own gems and goods, his personal adornments—necklaces, earrings, bracelets, chaplets—and his entire wardrobe, until he had to beg his sister for a second-hand, patched-up garment. Clothed in this, he stood before the Buddha and reverentially addressed the image: "In amassing all this wealth and treasure, I lived in fear that it would be stolen; but now, having given it all in the field of religious merit, I can safely say it is well distributed. May I, in all my future births, continue always to give thus, so that thus I may attain salvation."

But this was not the end of the Great Almsgiving. Then came the turn of the eighteen vassal kings; they were expected to reverse the flow of wealth. The vassal kings distributed among the people their money and treasure for the purpose of redeeming the royal necklaces, hair jewels, court vestments, and so forth, and then, taking them, restored them to Harsha. When they had finished their task, Harsha was as rich as he had been. [There must have been, as Waley suggests, an immense organization to care for so large a number of people and to arrange the system by which each vassal knew what he was to redeem, how much he would have to pay, and so forth.]

The Great Almsgiving over, Tripitaka again asked Harsha for permission to depart. He asked Tripitaka to stay another ten days, so that they could discuss how best to promote Mahayana doctrines throughout his realm. At the same time Kumara offered to found a hundred monasteries in his kingdom if Tripitaka would live there. Finally, when it became clear that on one pretext or another Harsha and Kumara would continue to delay his homecoming, Tripitaka admonished them by quoting from the Scriptures: "Whoever hinders men from receiving knowledge of the Law, will generation after generation be born blind." Thus he made them understand the terrible punishment they could incur by detaining him from his task of bringing the Law to China. This finally won him his release. Harsha asked Tripitaka to choose the route he desired and offered, if he wanted the southern sea route from the Bengal coast to Canton, to provide him with ships and attendants. "I will return by the northern road," Tripitaka said, relating the king of Turfan's generosity in making his outward journey safe and easy, and his promise to visit him on his return. [By 640, Turfan had been engulfed in the Chinese emperor's "forward policy" to the West and had become part of the Chinese Empire. The king of Turfan, harassed and powerless, had died just before the arrival of the Chinese army.]

Harsha, acquiescent to the will and wishes of his guest, asked what provisions he would require. Tripitaka replied, "I require nothing." But Harsha was not to be denied his feelings of generosity. "It is impossible to permit you to go thus." But even though Harsha and Kumara offered Tripitaka gifts of money and every kind of valuable, he would only allow them to furnish him with a coat of pressed buffalo down which he thought would protect him from the rain while on the road. At last, when he bade farewell to the kings they could not keep back their tears and expressions of grief. His books and images were entrusted to the care of a homeward-bound North Indian king. To speed his journey Harsha sent a great elephant that could carry his entire precious cargo as well as 3000 gold pieces and 10,000 pieces of silver given to defray his expenses along the way. ["A large elephant," Waley remarks, "like a big car, is expensive to run. This one consumed over forty bundles of hay a day and over twenty pounds of buns."]

Three days after the tearful parting, Harsha and Kumara, attended by several hundred light cavalrymen, galloped after Tripitaka to see him once again. And once again the final leave-taking was repeated. This time Harsha delegated four chamberlains [*mahattaras*] to accompany Tripitaka. Written on fine white cotton stuff and sealed with red wax were letters that commanded the rulers of the countries through which Tripitaka would pass to furnish him with carriages and relays of escorts. As far as it lay within his power, he tendered his help to the western borders of China.

Keeping a path toward the northwest, Tripitaka reached a monastery where he met two fellow students from Nalanda whose doctrinal beliefs he had attacked. Despite their disagreements, they were delighted to meet again, and Tripitaka stayed with them for two months, studying and discoursing. Passing through various countries he arrived at Jalandhara, the royal city of North India [Punjab]. There the king with whom he had traveled left him, but Tripitaka's party was augmented by a hundred monks, who, homeward bound, also laden with texts and statues, sought the protection of Tripitaka's escort through the robber-infested mountain passes. To safeguard the holy treasures from hurt or theft, Tripitaka regularly sent a monk on ahead who was told to say, if he was held up, "We have traveled a great distance to seek the Law. Our baggage contains only Scriptures, images, and holy relics. We pray you protect us and do not do us violence." Hui-li was convinced that this prevented their being harmed by the brigands they encountered. When they came to the borders of Kashmir, the king sent messengers inviting Tripitaka to visit his capital. Unavoidable delays and the slow pace set by their heavily laden elephants made it inadvisable to accept the cordial invitation.

Pushing on, they came to the fast-flowing, mile-wide Indus River. Tripitaka bravely forded it in the back of his elephant. The large party of monks with their books and statues and Tripitaka's collection of Indian flower seeds were ferried over by boat; one of the men was told to look after the precious cargo. As the boat was in midstream, it was caught in a sudden, violent storm; the water was whipped into high waves and the boat, pitching and rolling, was tossed helplessly about. The guardian of the books and flower seeds, paralyzed by fear, was thrown into the swirling water. While the passengers were hauling him aboard, fifty manuscripts and the flower seeds were washed overboard and swept away. Safe on the other shore, they congratulated themselves that everything else was saved. The king of Kapisi had come from his winter capital to pay his respects. His first words were, "You say that you lost many sacred books in the river. Did you happen to be bringing flower seeds from India?" "I did," said Tripitaka. "Ah," said the king, "that is the cause of your misfortune. Whoever tries to cross the river with flower seeds suffers the same accident." Tripitaka went with the king to his city. To replace some lost manuscripts, Tripitaka sent to Uddyana for new copies. After two months they arrived. While he was waiting, the king of Kashmir made the long journey to visit him. When he left, the king of Kapisi personally escorted him as far as the Hindukush, and then provided him with an official to guide him and oversee the one hundred porters needed to transport the provisions for the men and hay for the elephant. Thus they began the difficult passage over the Snowy Mountains.

They climbed toward a high mountain along a trail that led over pointed peaks and around dangerous cliffs, mounting by giant rocky steps to an occasional level space before ascending once again. And after seven arduous days when, fatigued, they attained this summit, before them stretched still more difficult, loftier mountains to be crossed. Riding was no longer possible; they walked staff in hand, the going ever harder. Another seven days brought them to the foot of a high ridge where there was a village of about one hundred houses. The people, Hui-li noted, kept sheep that were as large as asses. That day they stopped there and at midnight, when the bitter cold had crusted the snow, they advanced up the ridge guided by a native riding a mountain camel. They floundered in deep snowdrifts and crossed crevasses trusting to snow bridges. Anyone who did not follow in the guide's footsteps would have fallen and perished. The entire party of seven monks, twenty porters, one elephant, ten asses, and four horses struggled up the pass. Only as the sun was setting were they safely over and down the other side. Taking up the march the next day over a winding path that led toward a distant snow-covered ridge, they found when they reached it that it was shining white stone. The ridge was very high. In the rarified air they did not get to the top until late in the afternoon; a freezing wind blew so hard they could not stand upright. There was not a trace of vegetation, only a mass of crazily piled rock on rock and everywhere slender stone pinnacles looking like a forest of trees without leaves. "The mountain is so high," Hui-li said, "and the gusts of wind so strong that birds cannot fly across it. In the whole world of mountains, there is no higher one than this." From the south side of the ridge to the north side was but several hundred paces; once this was passed they found a little ease. And some miles farther on they found a small level place where they could pitch a tent and rest. The next six days they spent going down the other side of the pass to reach Anderab, where there were three monasteries and a few dozen monks. Here they rested for five days, and then, still descending and keeping to the north for several hundred miles, they reached the Oxus. Tripitaka was welcomed in the encampment of the Turkish khan, where he and his party rested for a month. [It is thought that early in the fifth century, Central Asia, Afghanistan, and the Punjab were overrun by the Hephthal, more commonly known as the White Huns, an Iranian-speaking people. About a century and a half later, they were attacked simultaneously by the Indians, the Turks, and the Persians, who broke their power. When Tripitaka crossed this region, shattered Hephthal remnants lived on in mountain pockets where they had taken refuge. Their customs resembled those of the Turks, except for one difference—the characteristic headdress of the married women with its three-foot wooden horn. "The upper branch of the horn symbolizes the husband's father and the lower his mother. When either dies, the corresponding branch is removed; when both are dead they discard the headdress."][17]

Though it was midsummer, snowstorms to the east held them up for over a month. They made their way up the Penj Valley, a mountainous and precipitous country, to a district that bred excellent horses, small in size but very strong. Hui-li described the inhabitants as rude and uncivil, of violent nature, and an unseemly appearance: "Most of them have gray-green eyes different from all other people." In a monastery built by a former king, they saw a miraculous statue whose action no one could explain: a copper circlet set with gems above a statue of Buddha turned as the worshipers circumambulated, and stopped when they stopped. One old man told them that it was the result of the prayers of a saint; others explain it as being mechanically operated. "Since the hall in which it stands is of a towering height, it is hard to determine which account is correct."

Continuing up the Penj Valley they were in a kind of corridor through which tempests and blizzards born in the mighty Pamirs raged during the spring and summer months; its soil is always frozen, its vegetation is scrawny and rare, and no seeds sown there ripen—it is desolate and without inhabitants. In the middle of the valley [at an altitude of 15,600 feet] is

[17] Waley, op. cit., p. 73.

the Great Dragon Lake [Lake Victoria], two hundred *li* from east to west and fifty *li* from north to south. Frogs of infinite variety live there and the noise of their ten thousand cries is like the racket of a hundred workshops. They saw birds about ten feet high and eggs as large as a water pitcher; Tripitaka thought that, like the "big eggs of T'iao-chio" [ostrich eggs], about which old books speak, they must have been laid by this bird. [His conjecture is not as fanciful as it sounds. The *Encyclopaedia Britannica*, 1911, mentions the possibility that ostriches still exist on the lower Oxus.][18]

So they came to the kingdom of Sarikol. In the old palace was a monastery associated with Kumarajiva, a man of great spiritual discernment and of a brilliant reputation. Hui-li wrote that each day Kumarajiva repeated 32,000 words and also wrote others down. He delighted in pursuing religious studies; elegant in composition, he was the author of a score of scriptures which gained wide renown.

["Tripitaka's most formidable predecessor was Kumarajiva, 344–413. He was the son of an Indian of high birth who settled in Kucha, in Central Asia, and married the sister of the king of Kucha. Kumarajiva spent part of his childhood in Afghanistan where he indulged in precocious debates with his teacher Bandhudatta and various Hindu philosophers. He afterwards returned to Central Asia and in 401 arrived at Ch'ang-an and devoted himself to translation. No one had ever been so well equipped for the task. He was as much at home in Chinese as in Sanskrit and also possessed very high literary gifts."][19]

They stayed twenty days in this monastery. After five days on the trail, the party was attacked by robbers. Merchants who had accompanied them for safety ran, panic-stricken, for the mountains; the elephant, frightened by the pursuing brig-

[18] Waley, op. cit., p. 74.
[19] Waley, op. cit.

ands, plunged into the deep, swift river and perished. It was a lightning attack; the robbers soon went away, the merchants reappeared, and slowly they continued toward the Pamirs. Through the intense cold they laboriously made their way over jagged boulders and crept around perpendicular mountain gorges toward the kingdom of Kashgar. So they reached the kingdom of Och. At a great mountain, not far from the capital, a stupa crowned the top of the sheer peak. According to the old story, many hundred years ago a thunderstorm made the mountain shiver and revealed an ascetic of extraordinary size who sat with closed eyes, his matted hair hanging over his face and shoulders. Some woodcutters spied him, and told the king, who went to look and do homage. The news spread, people came from far and near to bring their floral offerings and soon there was a high mound. The king asked who he was. A monk who had seen him replied, "This is a saint who entered the state of Utter Extinction. Since this occurred, many years have passed, and that is why his hair has grown so long." Then the king asked, "Is there a way we could bring him out of his trance and cause him to rise from where he sits?" "When one has gone so long without mortal food [spiritual beings feed on incense] and is suddenly wakened from a trance, the body decays. It is necessary first to sprinkle him with milk so that it can trickle through the pores of his skin and lubricate him; then we can sound the gong. If it is possible to restore him to consciousness perhaps he will rise." "Well spoken," said the king, and ordered the saint to be sprinkled with milk and then to have the gong sounded. At this, the saint opened his eyes and looked around. "What kind of men are you," he asked, "who wear the robes of religion?" They replied, "We are monks." "Where is my master, the Buddha Kasyapa?" he asked. "He entered nirvana long ago," they answered gently. The saint uttered a cry, and again asked, "Has Sakyamuni Buddha achieved the unequaled condition of Perfect Enlightenment?" "Yes," they told him, "yes, he, too, long ago passed into the Peace of Extinction." When the saint heard this he closed his eyes and meditated for a while. Then he quickly raised his hand to his hair, tossed it back from his face, and rose straight up into the air where his body was consumed by celestial flames. His bones, Hui-li related, which fell to the ground as his bequeathed relics, were piously collected by the king and all the people, who raised a stupa over them—the very stupa they now saw.

From this southern part of Kashgar, far from where the capital was situated, their route went southeast toward Khotan. They heard of a cliff pocked with niches in which were many Indians who by their immense spiritual power had flown there to meditate in peace. Many achieved the Peace of Extinction and three saints were there at that time who had passed into the trance of Utter Extinction; as their hair and nails continued to grow, these were trimmed from time to time by monks from a nearby monastery. Such news gladdened their hearts for it demonstrated that people were absorbed in the study of the Great Vehicle. Passing through Karghalik, they came to Khotan. Khotan was famous for its jade market, for it was here that the highly prized stone was mined—both the white and dark kinds—and it was the source for all Chinese jade. Hui-li noted that the soil though sandy and stony was very productive; and that the people also wove wool rugs and fine woolen goods and silken cloth. The people themselves—and in this they differed from all other Tartar tribes—were polite and honorable in their transactions, and they valued learning and greatly enjoyed music. Their writing resembled that of India with slight differences. The king of Khotan, as soon as he learned that the Master of the Law was within his borders, went forward to where Tripitaka was resting outside the city so as to escort him into his capital. The king himself led the ceremonial entry and was followed by ranks of monks and laymen; the procession, advancing to the sound of music, the color of flowers, and the scent of incense, came to a large Lesser Vehicle monastery where Tripitaka was to reside for seven or eight months. His long sojourn pleased the king, who valued his presence there; but Tripitaka remained there to await the messengers he had sent back to Kucha and Kashgar where he hoped to be able to replace the manuscripts lost when crossing the Indus. He had hardly settled down when the unexpected appearance of a young Turfanese traveling to China with a caravan of merchants made it possible for Tripitaka to send a letter announcing his impending return. In his letter he outlined his search for Buddhist learning—the marvelous words of the three Pitakas, which are able to liberate us from the delusions of the world, and the extent of his travels, over 50,000 *li*. He ended by mentioning that "since the mighty elephant was drowned, I have not succeeded in obtaining suitable transport for the many texts which I am bringing back. But despite this difficulty, I propose at once to go forward and visit Your Majesty."

Tripitaka might well be apprehensive about his reception in China; he had done worse than absenting himself without permission: he had gone in defiance of an edict forbidding him! The emperor's reply [which he received some seven months later], gracious and to the point, reassured him: "When I heard that you who had gone to distant lands to study Buddhism and to seek for religious texts were now returning, I was delighted. I pray you come quickly so that I may personally hear your report. I have already instructed Khotan [then subject to China] and the other places along the route to furnish you with their best guides and all the transport you may require. The officials at Tun-huang are to go out to meet you so as to guide you through the desert of shifting sands, and I have desired the Shan-shan [Charkhlik] officials likewise to go to Cherchen to meet you." [When the T'ang Dynasty took power in 618, China for three hundred years had been constantly subjected to invasions. As their capital was in the northwest on the road to Central Asia and India, it was imperative to protect it from attacks mounted in Turkestan. So Turfan was annexed in 640, Kucha in 648, and that same year Khotan yielded to propaganda pressure about the "majesty and magic" of the T'ang, and submitted.]

As soon as Tripitaka received this welcome, he started. Well mounted and amply provisioned by the king of Khotan, the party covered the long desert route, their journey eased by help furnished at every oasis along the way. Without incident or accident they reached Tun-huang, at the western border. Tripitaka contrasted his homeward passage, free from fears and ordeals, with what he had suffered when, all alone, he had crossed the desert of burning sands where demons ruled over a lifeless, waterless wasteland. From Tun-huang he sent back the horses and camels Khotan had supplied—nor would the guides and porters accept any recompense for their work.

From Tun-huang he again wrote the emperor, and then hurried to Ch'ang-an to report to him in person. But the emperor had left his capital [to "inquire into the misdeeds on the banks of the Liao," as his punitive expedition against Liao-tung in Manchuria was referred to]; before setting out the emperor had ordered a high official to arrange a suitable reception for Tripitaka. With such speed did Tripitaka push forward, he arrived outside the city while the official reception was still in its planning stage. He had come by way of the canal to make time, and news of his homecoming ran before him and the streets were filled with the people, who came to see him and pay their respects. He spent the night on the canal outside the city's walls.

The following day, with flags flying and banners waving, Tripitaka was escorted to the Monastery of Extensive Happiness. Here he deposited the treasures he had brought back with him—relics, one hundred and fifty particles of Buddha's flesh, six statues of Buddha in various holy acts, and 657 distinct volumes carried on twenty horses.

It seems, and it may well be true, that relations between India and China were started by King Harsha soon after his meeting with Tripitaka. Certainly, the Indian monarch made the first overture, sending an envoy to Ch'ang-an. Among the presents he brought was a broad-leafed ilex unknown in China. A return mission went to Magadha in 643. One of its younger members, a fervent Buddhist, erected a commemorative inscription on Vulture Peak and at the Monastery of the Great Enlightenment. There were commercial as well as diplomatic rewards; the Chinese secured the Indian recipe for making sugar, and soon the sugar refined at Yangchow, the sugar-cane center, was said to be superior to that made in India.

CHAPTER FOUR

THE TAOIST CH'ANG-CH'UN GOES TO VISIT CHINGHIZ KHAN

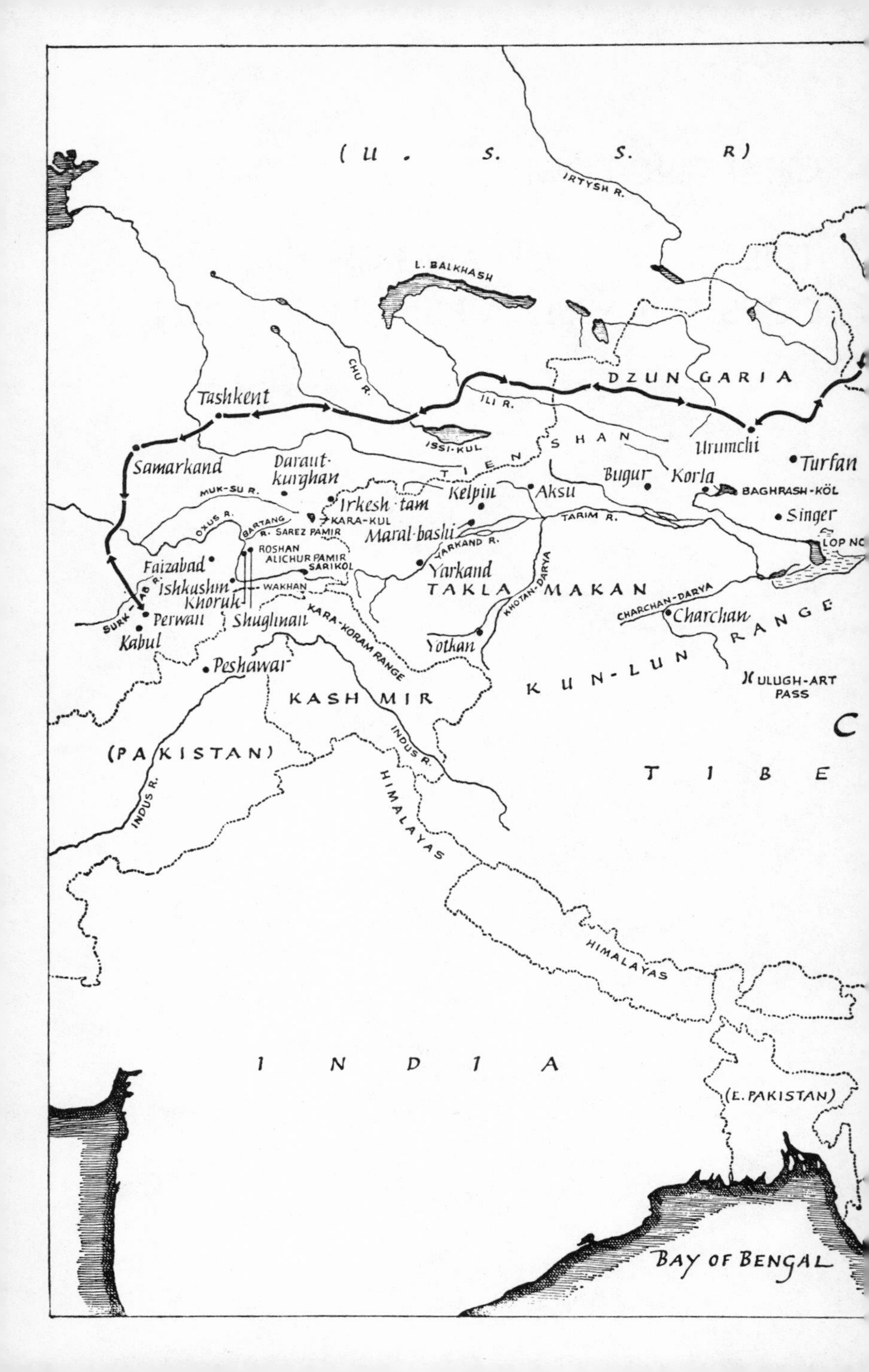

(U. S. S. R)
IRTYSH R.
L. BALKHASH
CHU R.
DZUNGARIA
ILI R.
Tashkent
ISSI-KUL
Urumchi
Turfan
Samarkand
Daraut-kurghan
TIEN SHAN
Bugur
Korla
BAGHRASH-KÖL
MUK-SU R.
Irkesh tam
Kelpin
Aksu
KARA-KUL
TARIM R.
Singer
OXUS R.
BARTANG R.
SAREZ PAMIR
Maral-bashi
LOP NO
ROSHAN
ALICHUR PAMIR
YARKAND R.
Faizabad
SARIKOL
Yarkand
Ishkashim
WAKHAN
TAKLA MAKAN
Khoruk
KHOTAN-DARYA
CHARCHAN-DARYA
SURK-AB R.
Perwan
Shughnan
KARA-KORAM RANGE
Charchan
Kabul
Yotkan
KUN-LUN RANGE
Peshawar
ULUGH-ART PASS
KASHMIR
(PAKISTAN)
INDUS R.
HIMALAYAS
TIBE
INDUS R.
HIMALAYAS
INDIA
(E. PAKISTAN)
BAY OF BENGAL

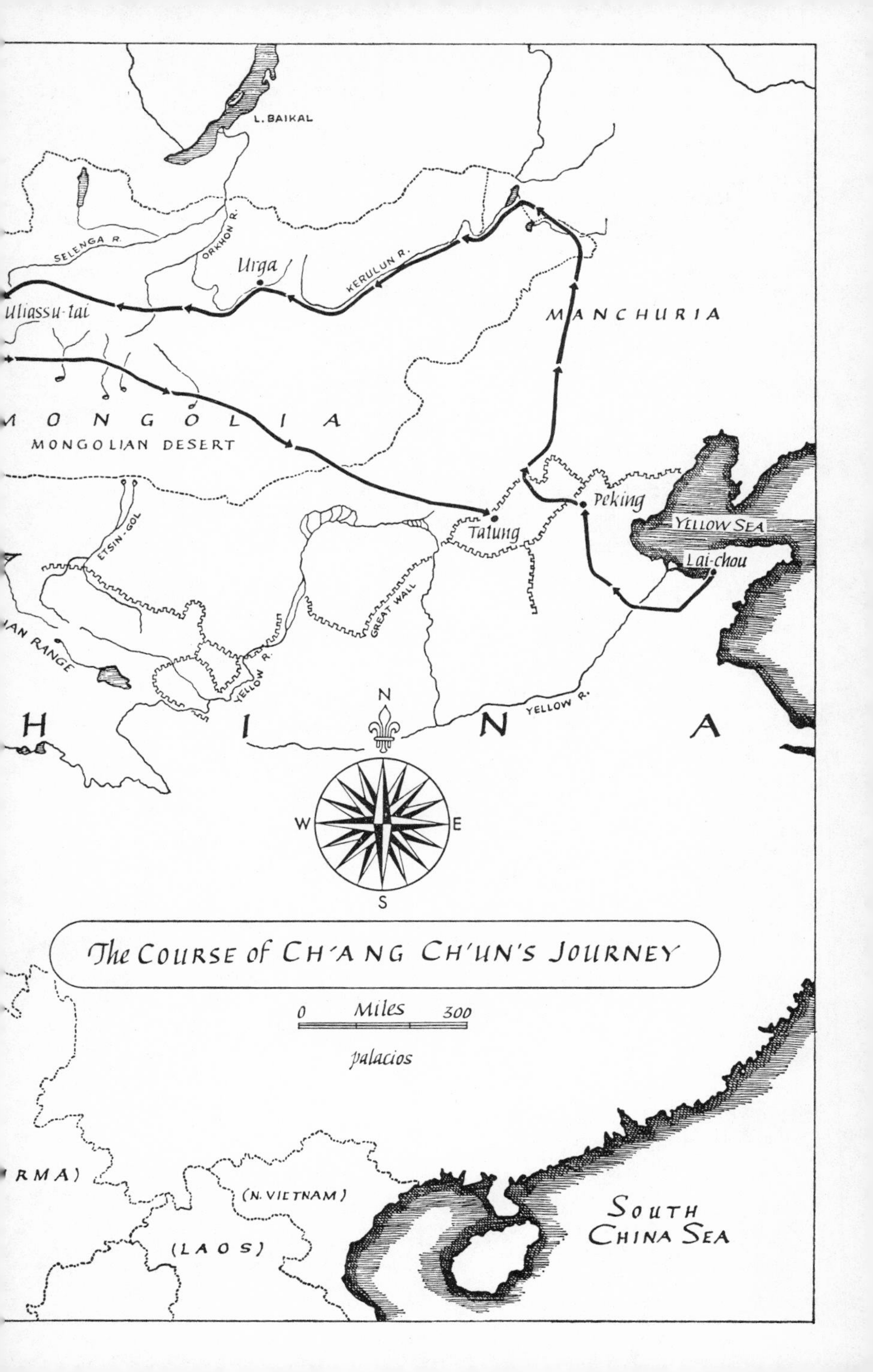

L. BAIKAL
SELENGA R.
ORKHON R.
Urga
KERULUN R.
Uliassu-tai
MANCHURIA
MONGOLIA
MONGOLIAN DESERT
ETSIN-GOL
Tatung
Peking
YELLOW SEA
Lai-chou
GREAT WALL
YELLOW R.
YELLOW R.
AN RANGE
CHINA
N
W
E
S
The Course of Ch'ang Ch'un's Journey
0 Miles 300
palacios
RMA)
(N. VIETNAM)
(LAOS)
South China Sea

THE TAOIST CH'ANG-CH'UN GOES TO VISIT CHINGHIZ KHAN

The Journey of the Taoist Ch'ang-ch'un from China to the Hindukush at the Summons of Chinghiz Khan, as Recorded by His Disciple Li Chih-ch'ang.

INTRODUCTION

The reader is quite free to decide whether this Journey *is a heroic odyssey or high comedy. So preposterous is its plot that it suggests an allegory or political parable. Yet it is a true narrative of an actual journey. Its tempo is as slow and deliberate as the slow, hard,* li*-by-*li *peregrination across the vastness of Central Asia. Through a disciple's eye and pen a little-known moment in time is preserved; we feel the quality of Ch'ang-ch'un, the master, as he leaves the populous cities of the Chinese plains and moves westward to keep a rendezvous with the redoubtable Chinghiz Khan. We have glimpses of the Mongol nomads with their mobile carts and tents, their ordered encampments and lively courier service, of alien clothes, customs, and crops, of turbaned Muslim farmers already entrenched in Central Asia, of life in the fair city of Samarkand, and of dogs barking in the streets of the dead city of Balkh.*

Waley points out that, interesting as is the cultural and geographical material presented, the Journey *has unique importance "as a source for early Mongol history, enabling us as it does to fix with absolute certainty the otherwise obscure and much disputed dates of Chinghiz Khan's movements during his Western campaign.*"[1]

Historical and Tribal:

At the time of the Mongol invasions China was split into three kingdoms: (1) the Sung empire, south of the Yangtze, the only one of the three that was native Chinese; (2) the Tangut kingdom, established in Kansu by a Tibeto-Burman people; (3) the kingdom of the Kin Tartars in northern China; it was their territory that Europeans knew as Cathay. This name, however, does not properly belong to the Kins, but to their predecessors, the Kitai. As this latter, an Eastern Mongol tribe, is frequently mentioned in this book and played an important part in Central Asian history, it will be convenient to give some account of its rise and migration.

THE KITAI [CATHAYANS]

Taking advantage of the confusion that followed the fall of the T'ang Dynasty at the end of the ninth century, these people began to press southward into China. In 938 they made their capital at Peking. The Kitai rapidly absorbed Chinese culture, and in the thirteenth century a member of their ruling family became the most celebrated writer of his time. For more than 180 years the Kitai reigned at Peking; but in 1114 they were attacked by a North Manchurian tribe, the Kin Tartars, who eventually captured Peking in 1123.

A certain number of Kitai refused to submit to the Kins. We know that a band of fugitives, fleeing across the Mongolian Desert, was crushed by the Lion Khan, prince of Kashgar, in

[1] Arthur Waley, *The Real Tripitaka* (London, Allen & Unwin, 1952), p. viii. The following historical and tribal material is excerpted from Waley's "Introduction" to his *Travels of an Alchemist. The Journey of the Taoist Ch'ang-ch'un* (London, 1931), pp. 1–46. For the narrative itself I have used E. Bretschneider, *Medieval Researches from Eastern Asiatic Sources*, 2 vols. (London, 1888), vol. 1, pp. 35–108.

1128 or a little later. Another sortie was destined to have much more important consequences. Yeh-lü Ta-shih, a member of the Kitai royal family, managed to escape with a few hundred followers to seek the protection from the Uighur prince of Beshbalig. Here Ta-shih collected an army and embarked upon a career of conquest as surprising in its way as that of Chinghiz himself. In some half-dozen years (he died in 1135 or 1136) he built up an empire that extended from the Zungarian desert to the confines of India. To the Muslim world his people were known as Kara-Kitai (Black Cathayans).

In 1208 the Black Cathayan king gave shelter to the Turkic prince Küchlük (ruler of the Naiman tribe), who had just been defeated by Chinghiz Khan. Recently a vassal of the Cathayans, Alà-al-din Muhammed (Shah of Khwārizm), had asserted his independence. Küchlük now conspired with Muhammed against the Black Cathayan kingdom. Muhammed captured Samarkand in 1209; the last Cathayan monarch himself was captured by Küchlük in 1211.

THE KIN EMPIRE

We have seen that the Kin Tartars captured Peking in 1123. In 1127 they captured K'ai-feng Fu, the capital of the Sungs, who retired beyond the Yangtze and set up a new capital at Hangchow. The Kins continued to rule from Peking, where their government was supported by such of the Kitai as had remained behind. By a treaty signed in 1141 the Kins were allotted the provinces of Chihli, Shansi, Shantung, most of Honan and Shensi, with a small part of Kiangnan.

THE CONQUESTS OF CHINGHIZ KHAN

It is not necessary to give here a full account of Chinghiz Khan's career. It will be sufficient to remind the reader that he was born in 1155 or 1156. It was not till 1206 (that is to say, in his forty-ninth or fiftieth year) that, by a series of campaigns, he succeeded in uniting under his rule the various Mongol and Turkic tribes. It was on this occasion that he was proclaimed Ocean-great Khan. He then conquered successively the Tangut and the Kin Tartars, his generals capturing Peking in 1215. While the Mongol armies steadily advanced in China, Chinghiz himself turned west and attacked the former empire of the Black Cathayans. By 1218 he was master of Turkestan. He then fell upon Muhammed, who had inherited the more westerly portions of the Cathayan empire. Samarkand fell in May 1220. Already, a year before this, Chinghiz had sent his first summons to the Taoist Ch'ang-ch'un.

CH'ANG-CH'UN

He was born in 1148 and "became a Taoist monk in 1166, studying in the K'un-lun Mountains in Shantung. In 1167 he became a pupil of Wang Ché, the founder of the Completely Sublimated Sect. The sect was distinguished . . . by a fanatical asceticism. Of Ch'ang-ch'un himself we read that he took neither fruit nor tea. His reputation had spread far and wide over northern China. In 1188 he had an audience with Shih-tsung, the Kin Tartar emperor of northern China. In 1191 he returned to Shantung and lived at Ch'i-hsia, near Ning-hai.

LI CHIH-CH'ANG,

the author of the *Hsi Yu Chi,* was born in 1193. He became a pupil of Ch'ang-ch'un in 1218, and soon afterward, as we shall see, accompanied him on his journey to the West. In 1227 when, upon Ch'ang-ch'un's death, Yin Chih-p'ing became head of the sect, Li Chih-ch'ang became the register of the sect and intendant of the Ch'ang-ch'un Temple.

CHINKAI, THE LEADER OF CH'ANG-CH'UN'S ESCORT

seems to have been born in 1171. In 1203 he "drank the waters of the Baljiuna River" with Chinghiz Khan and was present at the assembly on the Onon River in 1206. During the campaign against the Naimans Chinghiz presented him with one of his own horses. During the campaign against the Kara-Kitai he was rewarded for his services by the gift of a banner decorated with marvelous pearls and was allowed to carry the Golden Tiger Tally. He was ordered to found a colony of artisans and craftsmen near the Argun Mountains, and the place was called after him "The City of Chinkai." In 1212 he took part in the campaign against the Kin Tartars and at the siege of Fu-chou went on fighting despite an arrow wound in his left arm. After the capture of Peking in 1215 he climbed the Tower of the Great Compassionate One and shot four arrows, one in each direction. Chinghiz allowed him to keep for his own, within the range of these arrows, whatever houses or lands most took his fancy. The tribe to which Chinkai belonged had been converted to Christianity early in the eleventh century.

LIU CHUNG-LU

Liu Chung-lu, who figures so frequently in this narrative, originally entered the Khan's service as a herbalist. He also was renowned for his skill in making "singing arrows". It was he, apparently, who told Chinghiz that Ch'ang-ch'un was three hundred years old and could teach others to live to a like age.

A-LI-HSIEN

He was a Tangut. The Mongols had, previous to the journey of Ch'ang-ch'un, employed him on numerous missions to the Kin Tartars from 1214 onward.

SUN HSI'S PREFACE

The adept Ch'ang-ch'un was certainly a true possessor of the Secret Way. By the time I reached middle age I made sure that this old man must long ago have flown aloft and in some new guise be communing with the divinities of the clouds or conversing with the Primeval Darkness itself; and it grieved me to think that I had never met him. But in the year *chi-mao* [1219] one winter day a rumor reached me that he was living near the coast and had just received an invitation to make a "comfortable journey." In the spring of the following year he actually arrived in Peking and put up in the monastery of Jade Emptiness. I saw at my first meeting with him—for he sat with the rigidity of a corpse, stood with the stiffness of a tree, moved swift as lightning and walked like a whirlwind—that he was by no means an ordinary person. Conversation with him showed me that his learning was tremendous; there seemed to be no book he had not read. Henceforward my admiration for his genius continually increased. The number of those who wished to do homage to him by formally enrolling themselves as his disciples was prodigious, and their eminence may be judged by the high distinction of several important officials, now in retirement, who delighted to spend their time with him. After awhile he moved to the Lung-yang Temple. Here he was visited by messengers bearing a second invitation, and this time he actually set out for the West. . . . Most men nowadays, when business or public duty calls them abroad, leave their homes with reluctant feet and faces downcast at the prospect of separation. But here was the Master setting out to cover thousands of miles of most difficult country, through regions never mapped, across deserts unwatered by rain or dew, in which, though he was everywhere received with the utmost honor, it was inevitable that he should suffer considerable hardship and fatigue. Yet whenever opportunity arose he was ready to loiter on the way, enjoy the beauties of the scenery in the most natural and leisurely manner, write a poem, talk, or laugh. To him life and death seemed a succession as inevitable as cold and heat, and neither of them occupied in his heart so much as the space of a mustard seed or spike of grass. Such an attitude, it will be readily admitted, is only possible for one who truly possesses the Way.

His pupil Li Chih-ch'ang was with him throughout the whole journey, and kept a record of their experiences, noting with the greatest care the nature and degree of the difficulties —such as mountain passes, river crossings, bad roads, and the like—with which they had to contend; also such differences and peculiarities of climate, clothing, diet, vegetation, bird life, and insect life as they were able to observe. He called this record *A Journey to the West*, and asked me for a preface.

Written on the second day of autumn in the year *mou-tzŭ* [October 31, 1228] by Sun Hsi, the Recluse of the Western Brook.

WHY CH'ANG-CH'UN WAS CALLED AN ALCHEMIST.

The sect of which Ch'ang-ch'un was the recognized head belonged to that part of Taoism which Waley has summarized: "In one branch of study the Taoists were unique. To them alone is due the vast body of alchemical literature, which makes the Chinese sources more important than even the Mohammedan to the historian of this strange subject. The Chinese had inherited from the remote past the belief that certain substances such as jade, pearl, mother-of-pearl, cinnabar, were life-giving, and that if absorbed into the body they would prevent the gradual deteriorations of old age. As they exist in nature, however, these substances, it was thought, are always 'impure.' Only when made artificially can they be safely and efficaciously ingested. In early China gold was not highly valued. When through contact with gold-prizing nomads of the northwest the Chinese, in the three or four centuries before the Christian era, began to accept gold as their highest standard of value; the ideas previously attached to other 'life-giving' and consequently valuable substances became associated also with gold. Thus arose various distinct forms of alchemy: (1) the attempt to produce a liquid gold that could be drunk and so produce longevity; (2) the so-called "gold-cinnabar" alchemy. To the recipes for making artificial cinnabar and thus producing an elixir of life was arbitrarily added the further clause that 'when the cinnabar is made, gold will easily follow.' We thus see the new life-giving substance gold tagged on to the beliefs connected with the older substance, cinnabar; (3) an attempt, parallel to that of the earliest Western alchemy, to produce gold from baser metals such as lead. . . .

"Often in the alchemical literature of the Renaissance and later we have a suspicion that we are reading not about material experiments, but about a spiritual quest allegorically described in terms of the laboratory. In China this suspicion is a certainty. From the tenth century onwards exoteric alchemy (*wai tan*) gives place to esoteric (*nei tan*), which instead of using tangible and material substances as its ingredients, uses only the 'souls' or 'essences' of these substances. These 'souls' are the 'true' or purified mercury, sulphur, lead, etc., and are in the same relation to common metals as is the Taoist Adept or Chem-jen (purified, perfected men) to ordinary mortals. By the end of the eleventh century a fresh step has been made. These transcendental metals are identified with various parts of the human body, and alchemy comes to mean in China not an experimentation with chemicals, blow-pipes, furnace and the like (though these survive in the popular alchemy of itinerant quacks), but a system of mental and physical re-education. It was in this sense that Ch'ang-ch'un, whose travels are here recorded, was an alchemist, and it is a mysticism of this kind that is expounded in his 'Straight Guide to the Mighty Elixir.' "[2]

ALCHEMIST

Chinghiz Khan, who could not write in any language, had Yeh-lü Ch'u-Ts'ai, his able Chinese minister, compose this letter to be sent to the Taoist adept, Ch'ang-ch'un:

"Heaven has abandoned China owing to its haughtiness and extravagant luxury. But I, living in the northern wilderness, have not inordinate passions. I hate luxury and exercise moderation. I have only one coat and one food. I eat the same food and am dressed in the same tatters as my humble herdsmen. I consider the people my children, and take an interest in talented men as if they were my brothers.

". . . In the space of seven years I have succeeded in accomplishing a great work—uniting the whole world in one empire. I have not myself distinguished qualities. But as my calling is high, the obligations incumbent on me are also heavy; and I fear that in my ruling there may be something wanting. To cross a river we make boats and rudders. Likewise we invite sage men, and choose assistants for keeping the empire in good order. Since the time I came to the throne I have always taken to heart the ruling of my people; but I could not find worthy men. I heard that thou, master, hast pentrated the Truth, and that thou walkest in the Path of Right. Deeply learned and much experienced, thou hast much explored the Laws. Thy sanctity is become manifest. Thou hast conserved the rigorous rules of the ancient sages. Thou art endowed with

[2] Waley, *Travels of an Alchemist. The Journey of the Taoist Ch'ang-ch'un*, pp. 11–13.

the eminent talents of celebrated men. For a long time thou hast lived in the caverns of the rocks, and hast retired from the world.

"But what shall I do? We are separated by mountains and plains of great extent, and I cannot meet thee. I have fasted and washed [A Chinese phrase of politeness, meaning that the host has worthily prepared himself to receive the guest]. I have ordered my adjutant, Liu Chung-lu, to prepare an escort and a cart for thee. [In ancient times, in China, the emperor used to send a cart for the sages when inviting them.] I implore thee to move thy sainted steps. Do not think of the extent of the sandy desert. Have pity upon me, and communicate to me the means of preserving life. I shall serve thee myself. I hope that at least thou wilt leave me a trifle of thy wisdom. Say only one word to me and I shall be happy. In this letter I have briefly expressed my thoughts, and hope that thou wilt understand them.

"Given on the 1st day of the 5th month [May 15], 1219."

Ch'ang-ch'un's answer to Chinghiz:

". . . I confess that in worldly matters I am dull, and have not succeeded in investigating the Tao, although I tried hard in every possible way. I have grown old and am not yet dead. My repute has spread over all kingdoms; but as to my sanctity, I am not better than ordinary people, and when I look inwards, I am deeply ashamed of myself. At the first call of the Dragon Court [the Mongol Court] I am ready. Why? I have heard that the emperor has been gifted by Heaven with such valor and wisdom as has never been seen in ancient times or in our own days. Majestic splendor is accompanied by justice. The Chinese people as well as the Barbarians have acknowledged the emperor's supremacy.

"At first I was undecided whether I would hide myself in the mountains or flee to an island in the sea; but I dared not oppose the order. I decided to brave frost and snow in order to be once presented to the emperor. I am old and infirm, and fear that I shall be unable to endure the pains of such a long journey, and that perhaps I cannot reach Your Majesty; and even should I reach You, I would not be good for anything. Public affairs and affairs of war are not within my capacity. The Doctrine of the Tao teaches to restrain the passions; but that is very difficult. Considering these reasons, I asked Liu Chung-lu that I might wait in Peking or Te-hsing the return of Your Majesty. He would not agree to that. Wherefore I solicit the decision to start or wait. We were four who at the same time became ordained monks. Three have attained sanctity. Only I have undeservedly the repute of a sainted man. My appearance is parched, my body is weak. I am waiting for Your Majesty's order.

"Written in the 3rd month [April] of 1220."

It was in the year 1220 that the Emperor Chinghiz sent his adjutant, Liu Chung-lu, with an escort of twenty Mongols to the adept Ch'ang-ch'un. Liu Chung-lu transmitted the urgent invitation from the emperor; he wore an imperial golden tablet [*paizah*, see ahead, p. 179] on which it was written to treat the adept as the emperor himself was treated. Chung-lu reported that he had received the order in the fifth month of 1219 from the emperor, who was then at the imperial camp in the country of the Naiman tribe. Ch'ang-ch'un agreed to go with him and chose nineteen disciples to accompany him. In the beginning of 1220 they set out for the north and arrived at Peking, where the master was received with great homage; it was toward the end of the second month [beginning of April] when he wrote his answering letter.

In Peking, the master was informed that Chinghiz had moved to the west. He felt apprehensive that his advanced age (he was about seventy years old) would not permit of his enduring the fatigue of a long journey; he wished to await Chinghiz' return to the east. It was decided to ask permission of the emperor. And there was yet another aspect which distressed Ch'ang-ch'un. Liu Chung-lu had had another order from the emperor: to assemble a number of girls to be brought back for the emperor's harem. The master said: "I am only a savage from the mountains. But I cannot be expected to travel in the company of harem girls." To lay the master's hesitations before the emperor, Liu Chung-lu dispatched a courier with a report, and the master also sent his letter to the emperor.

The first steps of the long journey began. In May the master and his disciples with Liu Chung-lu left Peking, and traveled north through the Chu-yung Pass. At night, at the northern end, we met a band of robbers. When they were told who was in the party, the robbers bowed and said, "We do not harm the master." In the fifth month [June] we arrived at Te-hsing, where we lodged in the Lung-yang Temple. There the master passed the summer. Winter was already approaching when A-li-hsien arrived at the temple from the princely tent of Tämügä ot-Chigin [the emperor's younger brother]; he was soon followed by another envoy. They invited the master to visit the prince on his way to the emperor. He nodded his head to signify that he would. That same month the courier sent to Chinghiz returned with an imperial letter repeating the invitation in the most flattering terms. Chung-lu also received a letter commanding him to take the greatest care of the aged master. Again the master conferred with Chung-lu. "Winter is beginning," he said, "and the route through the desert is bitterly cold and long. We still have not equipped ourselves with those things that are utterly necessary for such a journey. Would it not be better to pass the rest of the winter here and start in the spring?" Liu Chung-lu agreed, and so they passed the winter at the Lung-yung Monastery.

The journey began on a fine day early in March 1221. The master's friends brought presents, and, standing before his horse, shed tears. "Master, you are starting on a journey of several tens of thousand *li;* when shall we have the happiness of again bowing before you?" The master replied, "If you will be strong in the faith, I shall meet you again." Again the friends pressed the question; he said evasively, "Our staying and our going do not depend on our own will." But the friends would not desist; they wanted a decisive answer. Finally the master said, "I will be back in three years—in three years." He repeated it twice.

Two days later we passed the night at Ts'iu-ping K'ou, passing the Yeh-hu [wild fox] Range on the following day. Looking back southward we got a good view of the T'ai-hang and other mountains. A fresh breeze had cleared away the clouds and the air was very agreeable. Northward lay nothing but wintry sands and withered grass. "Here China—its customs and climate—suddenly comes to an end. We saw a battlefield covered with bleached human bones [where in 1211, Chinghiz vanquished the army of the Kin Tartars]."[3] Continuing to the north, we passed through Fu-chou [not far from Kalgan] and proceeding to the northeast arrived at a salt lake called Kai-li-po. On the south shore we saw the first settlements—about twenty houses; the lake stretches away to the northeast. Beyond this to the north there are no rivers, and water can be obtained only from wells dug in the sand. Nor are there any high hills for several thousand *li.* After five days on horse-back, we crossed the Ming-ch'ang boundary—[a fortified line built by the Kin Tartars in 1190–96, the Ming-ch'ang period, which gives the line its name].

In another six or seven days we arrived at the Great Sand Desert. In low places stunted elms trees are found, some as large as an "arm-hug" in circumference; but otherwise for

[3] Ibid., p. 62.

more than ten thousand *li* in a northeasterly direction, no tree is to be seen. We left the sandy desert on the fifth day of the third month [March 30] and arrived at a place called Yü-erh-li [Ta-li-po] where we began to find settlements. The people here are mostly peasants and fishermen. [In Mongol times there was a junction at this point; for the imperial camp at Karakorum, one took the west fork; for the encampment of Prince Tämügä ot-Chigin one took the northeast road.] Though it was fifteen days after the spring equinox, there was no trace of spring nor had the ice began to melt. We rested there four days and then continued in a northeasterly direction. All around we saw black wagons and white tents [probably the tents-on-wheels which Marco Polo describes]. These are the habitations of the nomads, who move constantly in search of water and pasturage. No tree could be seen; and our eyes saw nothing but clouds brown with dust and whitened grass. After moving in the same direction for more than twenty days, we came to a sandy river which flows to the northwest into the Kerulen River. When we crossed the stream the water was just high enough to wash the horses' bellies. Its banks are lined with willow trees. Another three days' travel to the north brought us to the Small Sand Desert. On the first day of the fourth month [April 23] we arrived at Prince Tämügä's encampment.

The ice was just beginning to melt and the grass to green. A wedding was being celebrated and many Mongol chiefs had arrived for the feast with presents of mare's milk. We saw several thousand black carts and felt tents drawn up in rows. On the seventh day the master was presented to the prince, who asked him about the means of prolonging life. As it would have been improper for the prince to hear the precepts of the master before the master had seen the emperor, it was arranged that the master should visit the prince on his return.

On the seventeenth day, the prince presented us with a hundred horses and oxen to expedite the master's journey. We started again to the northeast.

On the twenty-second day [March 15] we arrived at the Kerulen where it becomes a lake several hundred *li* in circumference. A wind had whipped the lake into waves; huge fish were thrown onto the shore, where the Mongols caught them easily. Keeping to the southern bank of the Kerulen we moved through a luxuriant growth of wild garlic. On the first day of the fifth month [May 23] there was an eclipse of the sun. It became so dark that the stars could be seen, but it soon brightened again. In this country it is cold in the morning and warm in the evening. We saw many plants bearing yellow flowers. The river flows to the northeast between banks on which tall willows grow. The Mongols use them to make the framework for their felt tents. After traveling sixteen days along the same bank of the Kerulen, we came to where the river, winding around hills, changes its direction and flows to the northwest. We could not follow it to its source but turned toward the post road that leads to Yü-erh-li. The Mongols here were very glad to see the master and said that they had been waiting for him for a year. They brought him millet; he made them a present of dates, something they had never seen before. We continued on for another ten days. At midday on the summer solstice the shadow of the gnomon measured three foot six or seven inches. [Since the exact length of the gnomon used is not known, it is impossible to determine their location.] Here we noticed the peaks of the mountains; and as we continued to the west the country became hilly and populated.

The people live in black carts and white tents; they breed cattle and hunt, dress in furs and leather, and live upon fermented milk and meat. The men and unmarried young women wear their hair in two braids that hang down over their ears. The married women wear a headdress made out of birch bark; it is two feet high and sometimes is covered with a woolen cloth or, if the woman is rich, with red silk. Attached to the headdress is a long, goose-shaped tail which they call a *ku-ku* [from which the word "queue" comes]. The women are always apprehensive that someone will knock into it accidentally and this makes them cautious when they enter a tent; they usually back in and lower their heads. These people have no writing. [Chinghiz introduced Uighur script a few years after the master's journey.] Their agreements are all verbal and contracts are recorded by marks cut in wood. They are never disobedient to orders nor do they ever break their word once it is given. They have preserved the values of earlier ages.

Four stations farther on, to the northwest, we crossed a river [the Karuha?] and came to a grassy, well-watered plain surrounded by hills and picturesque valleys. To the east and west of the road we saw the ruins of an ancient city and could make out the arrangement of its streets. Tradition says that this city was built by the Kitai; and indeed we found on the ground a tile with Kitai letters. [Kitai writing, Waley said, was ". . . made by mutilating and rearranging Chinese characters; it was concocted by order of the Kitai ruler Yeh-lü I in 920."][4] Most probably the city had been founded by those Kitai warriors who, unwilling to submit to the new rule of the Kin Tartars, emigrated to the west. We were also told that the capital of the Kitai, Samarkand, more than 10,000 *li* to the southwest, was the loveliest city in the entire vast Hui-ho [Muslim] Empire, and that seven of their emperors had reigned there. [The Kitai held Samarkand from 1141 to 1209, but it was never their capital. There seems to be a confusion between . . . the Chinese name for Samarkand, and . . . the

[4] Ibid., p. 68, fn. 2.

name of the encampment in the Chu valley, south of Lake Balkash, where the Kitai monarchs resided. . . . It is possible, however, that Samarkand had the status of a Western capital, though this is not recorded."][5]

On the thirteenth day of the sixth month [July 4] we crossed the High Pine Road and stopped for the night on the other side. The stands of the pines and firs were so lofty that they reached the clouds and so dense that they blotted out the sun. They are found principally on the northern slopes of the mountains and only scantily on the southern slopes. The next day we crossed a mountain and a shallow river and camped for the night in meadows. It was frightfully cold and in the morning we found a thin coat of ice on the water. The natives said that snow usually begins to fall in the fifth and sixth months and that happily this year the cold was not as intense as in others years. The master renamed them the Hugely Cold Mountains. Rain here always turns to hail. From there we went along toward the southwest, a winding, twisting mountain trail more than a hundred *li* long; and then for another fifty *li* we followed a rock-strewn river where it flowed through steep banks at least one hundred feet high on which grew a huge kind of leek three or four feet high. The river was clear and icy cold and sounded with the bell-like note of jade. The valleys were splendid with high pine trees and the pine-clad mountains stretched to the west in an unbroken line. Five or six days we spent in those mountains, our road turning in and around the peaks. The scenery was magnificent—noble tree-clad slopes, with the river gliding through pines and birches in the plains below. Then we climbed along a rocky ridge arched like a rainbow that hung over the abyss. It was awful to look straight down onto a lake almost a mile below.

On the twenty-eighth day of the sixth month [July 18] we

[5] Ibid., p. 68, fn. 3.

stopped just east of the *ordo* of the empress. [*Ordo* is the Mongol word for the encampment of a chief. Chinghiz's four *ordos* were under the charge of one of his four empresses.] One of the Mongol officials went ahead to announce our arrival. The empress immediately sent an invitation to the master; we crossed a shallow river whose water reached the axle of the cart, and entered the encampment. There were hundreds and thousands of carts and tents. We received daily presents of melted butter and fermented milk. Both the Chinese princess [actually a Kin Tartar princess who had been surrendered to Chinghiz in 1214] and the Tangut princess [handed over to Chinghiz by her father in 1210] "sent us warm clothing and other comforts; also a peck of millet and ten pounds [*liang*] of silver. Eighty catties of flour here cost as much as fifty pounds of silver, for it is brought on the backs of camels from beyond the Yin Shan [the T'ien Shan], some two thousand *li* away, by foreign traders from the Western lands. It was now the period of the Second Subdual [hot spell], but there were no flies in the tents. *Ordo* is the Mongol for temporary palace, and the palanquins, pavilions, and other splendors of this camp would certainly have astonished the khans of the ancient Huns."[6]

On the ninth day of the seventh month [July 29] we left the *ordo*, going to the southwest for five or six days. Several times we saw snow on the summits of the mountains and, lower down, we often noticed grave mounds. We investigated a high hill and found traces of sacrifices made to the mountain spirits. Two or three days later we crossed a mountain thickly covered with pines and firs, with a high, razor-sharp peak; nearby was a lake. We threaded our way southward through a vast defile and so came to a westward flowing river. [A modern traveler on the same route identifies this as the Ulias-

[6] Ibid., p. 71.

sutai River that has its source in the Argun Moutains.] Its northern bank is thickly covered with a variety of trees; our trail led for many *li* through a lush growth of wild onion and sweet-scented grasses. North of this are the ruins of a city called Ho-lo-hsiao [near the modern city of Uliassutai]. Continuing to the southwest, we crossed a belt, some twenty *li* wide, of sandy desert where water and grass were scarce. There we saw the first Hui-ho [Muslim]; he was irrigating his fields by means of ditches. Another five or six days' travel brought us to a ridge which we crossed and, on its southern side, to a Mongol encampment. We passed the night in a tent and at daybreak continued on the arduous path through the mountains, some of which were still covered with snow. At the encampment we had been told that to the north of these snowy mountains there is a military colony called Chinkai Belagasun, or City of Chinkai, to which a colony of skilled silk and wool weavers had been moved; also there are huge storehouses of grain—for which reason it is also known as the Granary.

On the twenty-fifth day of the seventh month [August 14] a body of the transplanted Chinese artisans and workmen from there came to see the master, greeting him with joyful reverence, bowing before him, and accompanying him with colorful pennants and bright, fragrant bouquets of flowers. There were also two concubines of the late Emperor Chang-tsung [who died in 1208]; one was the mother of the Tangut princess whose *ordo* had just been visited. The two ladies greeted the master, mixing their tears with cries of joy, and the older one said, "I have heard of your holy reputation and virtues for a long time and always grieved at never having seen you. And now, unexpectedly, I meet you in this country." The next day Chinkai himself arrived from the northern side of the Argun Mountains; the master told him how surprised he was to see the prince's people engaged in agriculture; it contrasted sharply with the arid country where crops were a rarity. He also proposed to the prince the advisability of his remaining there for the winter to await the emperor's return. But Chinkai told the master that he had just received orders from Chinghiz to expedite the master's journey and that he himself would be held accountable if he detained him any length of time. Chinkai further said that he would accompany the master and that he hoped the master would agree to push forward to where the emperor awaited him. The prince ended by saying, "The country through which we will have to pass is a region of precipitous mountains and vast bogs which cannot be crossed by heavy wagons. It would be best if you, master, will travel on horseback and cut down on the size of your party." The master agreed and left nine of the disciples behind. A monastery was built for them—everyone worked in its construction, the rich gave money, and the workmen their labor; in less than a month the different parts—the monks' cells, the kitchens at the east end, and the cloisters on the west end, the cloud chambers on the sides and the Hall of Saints—were completed. It was named, after the master's birthplace, the Ch'i-hsia Monastery.

On the eight day of the eighth month [August 26], with only ten disciples, the master took the trail. The caravan consisted of but two carts and twenty Mongols from the encampment. Liu Chung-lu still accompanied him; but now he also had an additional escort of Prince Chinkai with a hundred mounted men. The way led westward toward the lofty mountains. One of Chinkai's men related to us that the mountains were know for their evil demons—once a demon had pulled him by his hair. Chinkai added a tale of how the khan of the Naiman tribe had been bewitched by a mountain goblin who persuaded him to offer his choicest goods. The master made no comment on these tales.

After traveling about three days to the southwest, the trail veered to the southeast, crossed a mighty mountain, threaded a deep, large defile and on the fifteenth day of the eighth month [September 2] came out on the northern slopes of the Altai Mountains. After a short rest, we went southward. These mountains are mighty and very high, cut by deep gorges and with steep sides. No road for a wagon exists. The trail through this difficult terrain was planned and built by the Great Khan's third son, Ögödei, at the time the Mongol Army proceeded to the West [1219]. When we came to steep ascents, the hundred riders who were escorting us hauled the wagons up by ropes and by ropes lowered them when the descent started. In three days we crossed three mountain ridges and finally camped on the southern side of the range near a river [the Ulungu]. The tents were pitched in a pasture, rich in water and grass, where we waited the arrival of fresh oxen and horses.

After several days we again proceeded southward, passing over a hill made up of different-colored rock bare of even a trace of trees or grass. In the space of seventy *li* we saw two red-colored hills and, thirty *li* further on, came to a well that furnished water fresh enough for cooking though it was dug in a salt desert. The grass around the well was badly trampled by sheep and horses. At this point, the most difficult part of the journey, Liu Chung-lu conferred with Prince Chinkai, asking his advice about the route ahead. Replying, Chinkai addressed the master, "I have known these places well for a long time. Before us is the Field of White Bones, where the ground is strewn with black stones. It will be two hundred *li* before we will reach the northern end of the desert where there is abundant water and grass. Then we will have another hundred *li* across a desert whose length from east to west is so vast that it has never been measured. Not until we reach the south side of that desert where the Muslims have a town will we find water and grass again." When the master asked why Chinkai had called it the Field of White Bones, the prince answered, "It is an old battlefield—a field of death. Once an entire army perished there of exhaustion; not a single man escaped. More recently [1208] the whole Namian army was defeated there by Chinghiz. To attempt to cross in the daytime when the sun is shining means exhaustion and death for man and horse. But by starting in the evening and traveling during the night it is possible to reach water and grass by noon the next day."

We rested during that day and started late in the afternoon. Our way led us across a hundred large sand hills over which we seemed to swim like ships in the midst of waves. The next morning, between eight and ten o'clock, we came to the water and grass Chinkai had mentioned. By traveling during the dark we did not get tired, but we were afraid of being bewitched by spirits of the night. To prevent this we smeared our horses' heads with blood. When the master saw what we were doing, he smiled and said, "Evil spirits and ghosts fly when they see a good man. We all know that to be true for it is written so in books. It certainly does not become a Taoist to have such fears." When, at sunset, we started again, we had to leave our exhausted oxen behind and harness six horses to the wagons; henceforward we used no more oxen. While we were still at the northern side of the great desert, we saw far off on the southern horizon a sliver of silver light. We asked our Mongol escorts, but none of them knew what it was. "That must be the T'ien Shan Range," the master said. The next day, after we had crossed the desert, we met some charcoal burners and asked them; they told us that it was as the master had said. Yet we did not reach the foot of the range until the twenty-seventh day of the eighth month [September 15]; there we found the small town Chinkai had mentioned. Some Uighurs came to meet the master and the chief of the town presented him with grape wine, excellent fruits, huge onions, and pieces of Persian linen. The local leader told us that, on the other side of the range, about three hundred *li* away, was the city of Huo-chou where the climate was very hot and people produced wine plentiful and famous.

The next day we proceeded westward along a river and passed two small towns. At this season the grain was just beginning to ripen. The fields were irrigated by spring water brought from the mountains, for rain is rare. Further west is the large town of Beshbaliq ["Five Castles," near modern Kuchen] whose Uighur ruler attended by his high officials and with many inhabitants, and Buddhist and Taoist monks, came a long way out of the city to greet the master. "The Buddhist priests were all dressed in brown. The headdresses and robes of the Taoists were quite different from those worn in China." [Waley suggests that they may not have been Taoists but Manichaean priests, since between the two religions there were similarities to make such confusion possible. The Manichaean Electi wore tall white cylindrical hats.][7] Our tents were pitched in a vineyard to the west of the city; the relatives of the ruler brought us grape wine and all kinds of fruits. The attention the people showered on the master grew from day to day; he was visited by the Buddhist and Taoist priests, as well as Confucians. From them he asked about the history of the country and its customs. They told us that in T'ang times [618–907] this city was the northern court, or residence, of the Chinese governor-general and that the [western] frontier towns established by the T'ang still exist.

When the master asked how far they estimated it to be to the place where the Emperor Chinghiz then was, all agreed that

[7] Ibid., p. 80–81.

it was another 10,000 *li* to the southwest.

That night there was a storm. Just outside our vineyard stood a huge tree. It was on this occasion that the Master composed and handed around the poem:

> At night I lodged at the foot of Yin-shan;
> A silent night, with no sound or stir.
> Suddenly in the sky heavy clouds massed,
> And a tempest shook the leaves of the great tree.
> You speak of voyages of ten thousand *li;*
> Already we are come where the winter knows no chill.
> Whether I live or die, what matters it now?
> Like thistledown, I will go where I am blown."

On the second day of the ninth month [September 19] we started again and after four days' journey to the west stopped just short of the city of Lun-t'ai where we were greeted by the chief of the Tarsa [literally, "Quakers," a term used by Muslim Persians to non-Muslims, probably Nestorian Christians, but also to Zoroastrians, or fire worshipers]. To the south, toward the T'ien Shan Range, we saw three rugged peaks outlined against the sky; the master wrote a long poem dedicated to them. After passing two towns we arrived at Chambaliq [City of Chang]. Its ruler, a Uighur and an old friend of Chinkai, at the head of his relatives and a number of Muslim priests came far outside the city to meet us. Once within the city we were entertained with a dinner upon a terrace, and the ruler's wife gave us grape wine and watermelons, enormous and very heavy, and also sweet melons. The master was visited by a Buddhist priest and through an interpreter he conversed with him. It must be observed that from this city eastward the country belonged to China at the time of the T'ang Dynasty, which is why he was a Buddhist. West of this place there are neither Buddhists nor Taoists, only Muslims, people who worship the west [they prayed toward Mecca; from here it was to the west of them].

The next day we proceeded westward along the northern slope of the T'ien Shan for about ten marches. Then we crossed a desert where the loose sand, tossed by the wind, now was swept up into hillocks and now was leveled, seemingly rather like ocean waves. It was utterly without any vegetation. The wagons sank deep into the sand and even the horses plodded through it—it took a long day to cross this barren place. This is probably that part of the great desert Chinkai had called the field of the White Bones. It reaches right up to the southern edge of the T'ien Shan. For five more days the ground was sandy until we came to the northern side of the T'ien Shan. The next day, after an early start, the road sloped down for seventy or eighty *li;* at evening we stopped to rest but the night was bitterly cold and we found no water. We started early in the morning and, going in a southwesterly direction for some twenty *li*, suddenly saw a splendid lake [Sairam] about two hundred *li* in circumference encircled by snow-capped peaks that were mirrored in the tranquil water. The master named it the Heavenly Lake. Following the lake to the south, we found ourselves in a deep ravine [the Pine Tree Pass] whose perpendicular cliffs and rugged peaks closed in on us so that we could see nothing but the dense forests of birches and mighty pines that clothed the mountains up to their very summits and the river that rushes through the winding gorge for some sixty or seventy *li* in a turbulent current, with waterfalls every so often. The Great Khan Chinghiz' second son, Chagatai, who was with the emperor when he went on his western campaign (1219), first constructed a road through this gorge; he hacked a way through the rocks and built forty-eight bridges from wood cut on the mountains, bridges wide enough to accommodate two wagons side by side.

We passed the night in the canyon and emerged later the

next morning into a broad valley running east to west; it was well watered, had abundant grass, and was dotted here and there with mulberry and jujube trees. The next city we came to was Almaliq [northwest of Kulja; *alma* is the Turkic for apple] on the twenty-seventh day of the ninth month [October 14]. The Muslim ruler and the Mongol *darugachi* [governor] came out to welcome the master. [The ruler, son of a highwayman, had married the Great Khan's granddaughter.] They set aside a fruit orchard in the western part of the city for our party. The native word for fruit is *a-li-ma* and, as the place is renowned for the abundance and variety of fruits, this gave the city its name. Here, too, they have a kind of cloth called the *tu-lu-ma* woven, the people here say, from "vegetable wool." [The Chinese at that time had very little knowledge of cotton and could not believe that the boll came from a plant. And so, they imagined that a lamb was buried like a seed and bore a crop of fresh lambs. The idea of such a vegetable lamb goes back in Chinese literature to the sixth century. Europe took over the idea; there it was known as the Tartary lamb.] We obtained seven pieces of this cloth to be made into winter clothes. The hair of this stuff resembles the down in which willow seeds are wrapped; it is very clean, fine, and soft, and it is used for making thread, ropes, cloth, and wadding. The people use canals to irrigate their fields, but the only method they have for drawing water is by means of a jar which they then carry on the head. Our Chinese buckets delighted them hugely; they said, "You Y'ao-hua-shih"—for so they call the Chinese—"are very clever men."

We continued journeying to the west. After four days we reached the T'a-la-ssu Mu-nien [an approximation of *mürân*, the Mongol word for river; they had reached the Ili]. It is deep and broad and cuts through the T'ien Shan in a northwestern direction. South of it are more snow-covered mountains. On the second day of the tenth month [October 18] we crossed it in a boat; continuing to the south we came to a mighty mountain on whose southern side a small town rested. Then we traveled to the west for another five days. As the master was journeying by imperial order and as we were now approaching Chinghiz's encampment, Liu Chung-lu went on ahead to announce his arrival to the emperor while Chinkai remained with the escort. Another seven days of travel in the same direction brought us to a mountain pass where we encountered an ambassador from the Kin Tartars on his way back to China. The envoy bowed in reverence before the master's tent. "When did you leave?" the master asked. "I left Chinghiz on the twelfth day of the seventh month [August 1]. The emperor is pursuing the Sultan Khan [of Khwarizm] into India."

Next day in a heavy snow we came to a small Muslim town; the snow was a foot deep but when the sun came out it melted quickly. On the sixteenth of the tenth month [November 1] we crossed a river [the Chu] over a wooden bridge and by evening had come to the foot of the Nan Shan. Here was the former capital [Belāsgūn] of the Ta-shih Lin-ya* whose rulers were descendants of the Liao [Kitai] Dynasty. When the Kin armies conquered the Liao, Ta-shih, with several thousand men, retreated to the northwest and after wandering for ten years found this country. Its climate is quite different from the regions north of the Chin Shan [Altai]; much of it is flat and the people are farmers who raise mulberry trees for the breeding of silkworms. They make wine from the grape and have the same fruits as are grown in China. No rain falls during the summer and autumn and so the fields are irrigated by water brought in canals from the rivers. Their harvests are rich.

* Lin-ya, meaning "Grand Scribe," was the title Ta-shih had held in the Kitai empire before founding his Kara-Kitai state.

There are mountains to the northeast and to the southwest stretching for ten thousand *li.* Ta-shih's kingdom [Kara-Kitai] lasted about a hundred years [1124–1211]. When the Naiman tribe was defeated [1206–1208 by Chinghiz], the survivors fled to the Ta-shih, and, when they again became strong, they ousted the tribe that had offered them refuge. Later the Khwarizm shah conquered the western part of their land; then Chinghiz appeared and the Naiman were totally destroyed and also the shah [1218].

The people there warned us that the way ahead would be hard; we abandoned one of our carts which was broken. On the eighteenth of the tenth month [November 3], we traveled westward following the mountains for some seven or eight days until they turned sharply to the south. Before us was a city [Talas, near the modern Dzhambul] constructed of red stone still showing traces of an ancient military encampment. To the west were great grave mounds arranged as the stars are in the Polar Constellation. We went over a stone bridge. Another five days' journey to the southwest over the hills brought us to the city of Sairam. It has a high stupa. The Muslim ruler came out to meet us and direct us to the official guest house. During the first days of the eleventh month much rain fell.

On the fourth day of the same month [November 20], 1221, the people here celebrated their New Year [it was the Little Festival after the end of Ramadan], walking about in groups, greeting one another. On the same day one of the master's disciples said to a companion, "When I was in Hsüan-te and resolved to follow the master, I had a presentiment that I would never return and during the journey my heart has been sad. But I have adhered to our master's teachings that thoughts of death and life should not concern a man of Tao and that the heart should be indifferent to joy or sorrow. Whatever happens in life is good. I feel now that my death is near. Do you, my friends, serve the master faithfully." In a few days he was dead: it was the fifth of the eleventh month.

Very soon after this, we proceeded, still to the southwest, and three days later reached a city whose ruler, also a Muslim, welcomed and regaled us. The next day we passed another city [Tashkent] from where in another two days we reached the Khojand Müràn [Syr Darya] which we crossed on a floating bridge [pontoons]. We camped on its west bank. The bridge guard presented Chinkai with a large fish that had an enormous mouth and no scales [a sheath-fish]. This river rises in the southeast between two snow-covered mountains; its waters are muddy and swift-flowing, its depth is several tens of feet. It flows northward for no one knows how many thousand *li;* on the southwest it is bordered by a desert some two hundred *li* wide and because it has neither water nor grass we traveled by night. We went southward to the foot of high mountains and then turned to the west. This range connects with that south of Samarkand.

We came to a town [Zarafshan] where we found grass and water, and then to another whose chief, a Muslim, came out to meet us and entertained us with dinner and wine at a place just south of the town. He ordered boys to entertain us with a sword dance and acrobatics on high poles. Beyond that we passed two more cities, and then, traveling for half a day among the mountains, emerged at a valley [Zarafshan]. Under a splendid mulberry tree whose branches could shelter a hundred men we spent the night. Approaching another city we passed a well that was a hundred feet deep situated by the side of the road. An old native drove a bullock to turn a windlass that drew water for anyone in need of a drink. When the Emperor Chinghiz passed along this route on his way to conquer the West, he had been so moved by this old man's task that he ordered him henceforth to be exempt from taxes and forced labor.

We reached the great city of Samarkand on the eighteenth of the eleventh month [December 3], 1221, after crossing a mighty river [the Zarafshan]. Coming in from the northern side we were met in the outskirts by the civil governor, His Excellency I-la, [the Chinese rendering of his Kitai name Yeh-lü; he was the Chinese secretary who wrote the emperor's letter to the master, the eminent statesman Yeh-lü Ch'u-ts'ai]. With him came high Mongol military leaders and Muslim officials; they brought us wine and set up a number of tents for our use. Here we stayed and rested. Chung-lu left immediately, going ahead to inform the emperor. He soon returned, having found the road blocked. "About a thousand *li* from here," he reported to the master, "is a great river [the Amu Darya, known to the Greeks as the Oxus]. I have been told that bandits have destroyed the floating bridge and the boats. Since we are now in the middle of winter, I think it would be advisable for you to stay here and start out in the spring." The master agreed; then we entered the city by the northeast gate.

Samarkand is a city of canals. As it never rains in the summer and autumn the people have diverted two rivers to the city and distributed the waters through all the streets so that every house has an ample supply. Before the Khwarizm Shah was defeated, Samarkand had a population of more than 100,000 families, but now only a quarter of this number remain. Most of the fields and gardens belong to the Muslims, but they have been forced to recruit Chinese, Kitai, and Tanguts to handle the work and manage the properties. The homes of the Chinese workmen are scattered throughout the city. The new palace of the shah was built within the city on a hundred-foot high hill where before the Mongol governor had resided; but because this section of the city was terrorized by robbers—famine had made people desperate—the palace had been abandoned; the Shah's new residence was in a safer part of the city. The master occupied the deserted palace with his disciples: "The man of Tao lets fate lead him whither it will and measure his days as it may choose. Even when a naked sword is at his throat, he does not blench. How then should he be in panic at a rising that has not yet even taken place?"[8] The governor provided for the master's needs and comfort and daily his respect for the sage increased. In Samarkand we saw peacocks and huge elephants which had been brought there from India, a country several thousand *li* to the southeast.

While the master remained in Samarkand for the winter, Liu Chung-lu, with several hundred soldiers, went forward to reconnoiter the road. The Chinese inhabitants came often to pay their respects to the master. He also was visited by an astronomer. The master asked him about the eclipse we had witnessed on the first of the fifth month. The astronomer told him, "Here between seven and nine o'clock in the morning, the eclipse was at its greatest—three fifths of the sun was covered." The master then remarked that we had observed the same spectacle by the Kerulen River, where at midday it has been a total eclipse; that while we were west of the Altai, there the people told him seven tenths of the sun had been covered at its height at ten o'clock in the morning. "Thus the same eclipse was seen at different places in different aspects. He remarked that K'ung Ying-ta [A.D. 574–648, a descendant of Confucius and a distinguished scholar himself] in his commentary on the *Springs and Autumns* explained that when the moon comes between us and the sun, we have an eclipse of the sun; but it is only those who are

[8] Ibid., p. 93.

in a straight line with the sun and the moon who have a total eclipse. Those who are not in a straight line, however, see the eclipse differently; the amount of the eclipse is noticeable every thousand *li*. It is as if, for instance, a fan were put in front of a light—in the direct shadow of the fan there is no light but the further one moves to the sides, the greater the light gradually becomes."

At the end of the twelfth intercalary month [beginning of February 1222], Liu Chung-lu and his escort returned to report to the master that the emperor's second son [Chagatai] had moved out with his army and had repaired the bridge and boats. He also said that when he sent word to the prince in his encampment that the master was on the way to the emperor, the prince had informed him that his faher was southeast of the Great Snowy Mountains [Hindukush] and that about a hundred *li* of the pass leading there was covered by very deep snow. In view of this, the prince invited the master to his encampment where he could wait for more favorable conditions. He also offered a special escort of Mongol soldiers. The master declined the invitation. He excused himself, "I have heard that the country south of the river [Amu Darya] is completely lacking in vegetables; and I eat only rice, meal, and vegetables. Please convey my apology to the prince."

In the first month [February 13–March 15, 1222] the almond trees blossomed. Their fruit is as small as peaches and tastes like walnuts; it is gathered and eaten in the fall. On the second day of the second month, the time of the equinox, the blossoms of the apricot trees began to fall. The astronomer and others invited the master to take a little excursion to the west of the city. Chung-lu and some officers came along bringing wine. The day was fine and the air delicious, the flowers and the trees were fresh and full; everywhere we looked there were delightful views of lakes and orchards, pagodas, terraces, and tents. We lay on the grass and all were very happy. The mysteries of Tao were discussed and from time to time wine was handed around. The sun was already setting when we returned.

The fifteenth of the second month [March 29] was a holiday honoring Lao Tzu, the Great High Pure Original One [regarded as the founder of Taoism]. The officials begged the master to take another walk with them. In whatever direction they walked there was nothing but gardens and shaded groves for more than a hundred *li*. Even Chinese gardens do not compare with them; but here the rustic scene is silent; no birds sing.

In the first ten days of the month [mid-April] A-li-hsien [who had brought the message from Prince Tämügä] arrived from the emperor's encampment with the following message: "Adept! You have come from the land where the sun rises; you have met with hardships crossing mountains and plains. I am now about to return but I am impatient to have you explain the doctrine of the Tao. Hasten to meet me." Chung-lu, the envoy, also received an imperial order: "Persuade him to come. If you successfully carry out my wishes, I shall reward you with rich lands." And Chinkai as well was exhorted: "Accompany and protect the master on his journey and you will experience my benevolence." And finally the Commander-in-Chief Bŏ'ŏrju [one of the three leaders of the Mongol Army] was told to take a thousand men to escort the master through the Iron Gates Pass. When A-li-hsien delivered the emperor's message, the master asked him about the route: He replied, "I left Samarkand on the thirteenth day of the first month [February 25] and after traveling three days to the southeast passed through the Iron Gates; five days later I crossed a great river [Amu Darya]; on the first day of the second month [March 15] still heading to the southeast, I crossed the Great Snowy Mountains [Hindukush]. The snow was very deep—I pushed my whip into the snow but did not get near the bottom of it; even where the path was trodden down the snow was five feet deep. Proceeding southward, after three days I arrived at the khan's encampment. When I announced your arrival, the emperor was delighted. He ordered me to rest for a few days and then return to Samarkand."

The final lap of this journey [from Samarkand toward Kabul] began on the fifteenth of the third month [April 28]. The master left three disciples in the old palace; he was accompanied by five or six disciples, Liu Chung-lu, and the small body of Mongols. Four days later they passed the city of Chieh-shih [formerly Kesh, now Shahr-i-sabz], where they were joined by Commander Bȯ'o̊rju at the head of a thousand Mongols and native Muslim soldiers, who, as ordered, was to conduct the master through the Iron Gates. [The Buzgala Defile, fifty-five miles south of Kesh, is a deep, knife-thin canyon about a mile and a half long; its rocky walls are straight, smoothly polished, and are iron-colored. At its narrowest point it was once closed by heavy wooden gates re-enforced with iron and hung with massive iron bells, which literally made it the gate through which passed all trade and traffic between the Indus and the Oxus. See Tripitaka's description, p. 54.

Going in a southeasterly direction we crossed some mountains; we found them very high and the path so strewn with great boulders that the escort worked hard to help us get the wagons across. After two days spent in getting over this pass we came to a valley and followed its south-flowing stream while the soldiers made a sortie into the mountains to the north in pursuit of brigands. Five days later we were ferried across a small river that flowed through a thick forest and seven days after that boats again ferried us over the mighty A-mu Mu-nien [the Amu Darya]. On its other side we kept to the southeast; that evening we camped near an ancient aqueduct whose banks were thick with reeds of a kind not found in China. The larger ones keep their green leaves all winter and are so strong that some we cut for walking sticks did not break when we used them to prop up the wagon shafts at night. The smaller plants lose their leaves in the winter and get new ones in the spring. A large bamboo with a pith inside grows in the hills to the south. We also saw lizards at least three feet long and darkish in color.

We were now at the twenty-ninth of the third month [May 11] and six days later arrived at the emperor's encampment. He sent one of his high officials out to meet the master.

No sooner had the master installed himself in his lodgings than he presented himself to the emperor. Chinghiz greeted him, "You were invited by rulers of other courts, but you refused. Yet you journeyed ten thousand *li* to see me. I am deeply gratified." The master answered, "That I, a hermit of the mountains, responded to Your Majesty's request was the will of Heaven." Delighted, Chinghiz graciously invited him to be seated and ordered food to be served. Then he asked, "Adept, what medicine of immortality have you brought me from your distant home?" To which the master replied, "I have means for protecting life but no elixir for immortality." The emperor praised him for his sincerity and candor. He ordered the master's two tents pitched to the east of the royal tent and conferred on him the title Heavenly Eternal Man.

When the days started to get hot, the master accompanied the emperor to a valley high in the Snowy Mountains where it remained cool; the fourteenth of the fourth month [June 24] was appointed as the day when he would explain the doctrine of the Way. Shortly before that date word was received that some mountain bands were rebelling. Chinghiz decided to attack them himself and this forced the postponement of the master's appointment until the first of the tenth month [November 5] an auspicious day according to the signs. When the master heard this, he asked to return to Samarkand. "But," said the emperor, "will it not be too fatiguing for you to have to make the journey a second time?" The master said it meant a mere twenty days on the road between Samarkand and the encampment. Still the emperor objected, saying that there was no one he could assign as an escort. But the master reminded him that he had already ordered Yang A-kou to attend to the master's wants. And so Chinghiz finally granted the master his wish. Three days later he issued orders for Yang A-kou to take a thousand horsemen and escort the master back to Samarkand by a different route.

The new route led us across a high mountain that has a "stone gate," whose rocks seen from a distance look like pointed candles. We found that a gigantic stone slab, lying across the rock pinnacles, formed a bridge over a raging stream. Several pack asses fell and were drowned as they were being driven across the bridge and on the banks below were carcasses of other animals killed while trying to cross. This pass had been captured by the emperor's troops only a short time before. On the trail we met men returning from the west with a big load of coral. Some of the officers in the escort bought about fifty coral branches for two-pound bars of silver. The biggest branch was more than a foot long, but it was broken into small pieces by being jolted in the officer's saddlebag. We traveled by night, when it was cool, and five or six days later arrived at Samarkand. The officials came out to meet the master and accompany him to his lodging in the deserted palace.

The palace had been built in a cliff on the north side of

the Zarafshan River, which, rising in the Snow Mountains, was icy cold and so clear that it held the reflection of the palace above. In the fifth month, during the hot season, the master was in the habit of sitting by a north window to enjoy the breeze and sleeping, as was the custom there, on the terrace-roof of the building. In the sixth month when the heat was most intense, he bathed in the lake. Thus agreeably the master spent his time in the far west.

The arable land in Samarkand is suitable for all kinds of grain; only buckwheat and soya-bean are not grown there. In the fourth month wheat ripens, and, when it is harvested, it is stacked in piles and used bit by bit as the family needs it. In the sixth month the intendant of the governor [Yeh-lü A-hai] presented the master with a large field of watermelons. They are deliciously sweet and fragrant and enormous. We have none like them in China. When, in the sixth month the second prince [Chagatai] returned to the city, Liu Chung-lu asked the master for some of these melons to present them to the prince. Samarkand is very rich in all kinds of fruits and vegetables; only colocasia [elephants' ear] and chestnut are not found. The eggplant are shaped like monstrous fingers, deep purple in color.

Men and women braid their hair. The caps of the men resemble our "distant mountain caps," and are decorated with embroidery and hung about with tassels. All officials wear such elaborate headgear; the men of the lower classes merely wrap a six-yard piece of white muslin about their heads. The wives of the rich or of important officials cover their heads with a piece of black or dark red gauze from five to six feet long. Sometimes they embroider it with flowers or leaves or other figures. Their hair is always worn hanging down; some put padding under it. The women of the lower classes do not braid their hair into a queue on top of the head but cover their heads with linen or other stuff; they resemble our Buddhist nuns. As to their dress, men as well as women generally put on a white woolen shirt which looks like a bag, narrow at the top and wide at the bottom, with sleeves attached. If a man becomes poor, his wife takes another husband; when a husband goes off on a journey and does not return within three months, his wife can marry another man. But there is one thing very strange about these people; some of the women have beards and mustaches. The wagons, boats, and agricultural equipment are made quite differently from ours in China. Their weapons are made of steel. Most of their vessels are made of copper but they also have porcelain ones as in China. For holding wine, they use only glass. Their currency is made out of gold; the coins have no holes but do have native letters written on both sides.

The people are very strong and tall. They carry heavy loads on their backs without a carrying beam. There are certain men well versed in books who spend all their time writing and are in charge of records and correspondence; they are called *dashman* [from the Persian *dānishmand*, a learned man]. At the end of the winter the people fast for a whole month. Every night the head of the family kills a sheep and they all sit around, cross-legged, and spend the whole night eating. In addition, they have six fastings during the other months. They have very high buildings with rafters on the top that extend out about ten feet all around; these rafters support a pavilion bare except for *tassles* [minarets with wooden galleries]. Every morning and evening the leading man goes up and bows to the west; they call this "addressing Heaven," for they do not pray either to the Buddhist or Taoist divinities. The leading man sings in a loud voice and the men and women hearing it run to that place and bow down. This custom is found throughout the whole country. Whoever neglects these religious duties is executed. The leading man is dressed like the others, only he wears a turban of white muslin made very large by being wound over a frame of bamboo.

In the seventh month at the first appearance of the new moon [August 8], the master sent A-li-hsien to the emperor reminding him of the date set for the explanation of the Way. A reply, confirming this, was received on the seventh day of the eighth month [September 13]; the very next day we started for the imperial encampment. The governor was accompanying the master some tens of *li* on his way when the master said to him, "To the east of the native city two thousand households have lately broken into revolt. Every night the city is lit up with flames and there is great anxiety among the people. I would rather you went back and calmed them." "But if by some unlikely chance something should happen to you on the road," said the governor, "what then?" "That," the master reminded him, "is not your business," and persuaded him to return.[9]

On the twelfth we passed the city of Kesh and the next day were joined by an escort of a thousand foot soldiers and three hundred cavalrymen; thus guarded we entered the high mountains along a route that circled the Iron Gates Pass. We crossed a river whose waters were red and followed it to the southeast through a gorge whose rocky walls must have been several *li* high. At the foot of these cliffs is a salt spring whose waters, as they evaporate in the hot sun, form a white salt. We took a large amount of it for use on our journey. Still going to the southeast, we climbed a high ridge, and, looking to the west, saw a deep valley which seemed to be filled with ice; it was not ice, but salt. On the top of the ridge were reddish stones; these, too, were salt, which the master tasted. [The famous rose-colored rock salt used widely in Central Asia.] He ob-

[9] Ibid., p. 109.

served that in eastern countries [China, Mongolia] salt is found only on low ground while here, in the western parts, it is present in the mountains. The Muslims eat cakes which they sprinkle heavily with salt; when they become thirsty, they drink only water—even in winter they drink only water. [This was remarkable to a Chinese, who preferred hot tea even in the heat of summer.] Everywhere poor people are found selling water from jars.

On the fourteenth of the eighth month [September 20] we reached the foot of the mountains southwest of the Iron Gates; the last part of the pass is through high, sheer rock walls. A heavy landslide on the left-hand side had cascaded boulders down on the stream, burying it for several *li*. The next day we arrived at the river [Amu Darya] which reminded us of the Yellow River. It flows to the northwest. We were ferried across in a boat and camped for the night on its southern bank. West of here is a frontier fortress called T'uan-pa-la; it commands a strong position. On the road we met Lord Cheng, physician to the third prince [Ögödei], and after this encounter we proceeded upstream in a boat. After thirty *li* the water became so shallow we went ashore and did our traveling by night. It was dark when we passed the city of Balkh [captured in 1220, destroyed in 1222 just prior to Ch'ang-ch'un's arrival. A very large city whose inhabitants had revolted just a little while before; they were "removed" and put to the sword]. We heard dogs barking in the city streets.

At daybreak, after breakfast, we went eastward for more than twenty *li* to reach a river flowing northward. This could be forded on horseback and once on the other side we camped for the night. On the twenty-second [September 28] Chinkai came to meet the master and escort him to the imperial encampment. When we arrived there, Chinkai asked the master whether he wished to be presented immediately or to rest first. The master begged to be presented. It must be said here, the chronicler noted, Taoists were never required when coming to an imperial interview to kneel or bow their heads to the ground; they merely made a slight obeisance while pressing their palms together on entering the emperor's tent. And so the master was presented to the emperor, who ordered *kumiss** to be set before him; but the master refused to drink it. The emperor inquired if we had been properly provided for during our sojourn in Samarkand and the master reassured him that everything had been satisfactory. The audience was over and we took our leave. When, the next day, the emperor's personal officers come to invite the master to dine daily with the emperor, he replied, "I am a hermit of the mountains, I cultivate the true doctrine and prefer my privacy." The emperor permitted the master to live as he liked.

On the twenty-seventh day Chinghiz started northward with the master accompanying him. On the way we often received presents of grape wine, watermelons, and other delicacies. On the first of the ninth month we crossed the Amu Darya on a floating bridge and continued to the north. On the fifteenth the master suggested that, since the time set for the discourse had come, they prepare to hold it. Chinghiz then ordered a pavilion set up in which he would hear the explanation of the Way. Chinkai and Liu Chung-lu were detailed to guard the entrance and the Governor A-hai was summoned to act as interpreter; everyone else, the emperor's women and all the officers of his retinue, were sent away. The master entered in the company of the Governor A-hai and A-li-hsien. When he was seated he pointed out that both Liu Chung-lu and Prince Chinkai had made immense journeys

* *Kumiss*, fermented mare's milk, was and still is the favorite drink of the Mongols.

on his behalf and he asked that they might be allowed inside the tent to hear his discourse. This request was granted. The emperor was delighted with his presentation of the doctrine. On the nineteenth, when there was a bright moon, he again sent for the master and again was pleasantly edified by what he heard, and four days later summoned the master to his tent once more. The master was always treated with deference and heard with obvious satisfaction. The emperor commanded that the master's words be recorded and was especially eager to have them written down in Chinese characters so that they might be saved from oblivion. Chinghiz then addressed the four men present. "Three times you have heard the holy immortal discourse on the art of nurturing the vital spirit. I count on you not to disclose what you have heard." During the weeks when the emperor traveled to the east, the master repeatedly discoursed to him on the mysteries of Tao.

Part of the sermon preached on November 19 by the master Ch'ang-ch'un, setting forth the tenets of his sect, was recorded. "Tao is the producer of heaven and the nurturer of earth. The sun and moon, the stars and planets, demons and spirits, men and things all grow out of Tao. Most men only know the greatness of heaven; they do not understand the greatness of Tao. My sole object in living all my life separated from my family and in the monastic state has been to study this question.

"When Tao produced heaven and earth, they in turn opened up and produced man. When man was first born he shone with a holy radiance of his own and his step was so light that it was as if he flew. The earth bore fungoids that were moist and sweet-tasting. Without waiting to roast or cook them, man ate them all raw; at this time nothing was cooked for eating. The fungoids were all sweet-smelling. Man with his nose smelt their scent and with his mouth tasted their taste.

Gradually his body grew heavy and his holy light grew dim. This was because his appetite and longing were so keen. Those who study Tao must learn not to desire the things that other men desire, not to live in the places where other men live. They must do without pleasant sounds and sights, and get their pleasure only out of purity and quiet. They must reject luscious tastes and use foods that are fresh and light as their only delicacy. If there is any attachment [to concrete things] the follower of Tao will fail to understand it or its operations. If the eye sees pleasant sights or the ear hears pleasant sounds, if the mouth enjoys pleasant tastes or the natural state is perturbed by emotions, then the Original Spirit is scattered and lost. . . .

"The male we call Yang; his element is fire. The female we call Yin; her element is water. But Yin [the imperfect] can quench Yang [the perfect]; water conquers fire. Therefore, the Taoist must above all abstain from lust. It is true that in providing himself with food and clothing a man expends a good deal of worry and fret, which leads to a loss of Original Spirit. But the loss in this case is quite small; whereas a licentious life wastes the fine particles of the soul and leads to a considerable loss of original spirit . . . If common people, who possess only one wife can ruin themselves by excessive indulgence, what must happen to monarchs, whose palaces are filled with concubines? . . .

"Now all people from the emperors and princes down to the lowest classes, however different their lives may be in other ways, are alike in this, that they possess a 'natural state.' All emperors and monarchs are heavenly beings who have been exiled from heaven. If they are virtuous on earth they will, on their return to heaven, be allotted a higher place than before. Try [Ch'ang-ch'un urges Chinghiz] sleeping alone for one month. You will be surprised what an improvement there will be in your spirits and energy. The ancients said, 'To take medicine for a thousand days does less good than to lie alone for a single night.' " His sermons also included astute political advice.

The master accompanied the Imperial Progress back to Samarkand; we halted twenty *li* to the west of the great city. On the first day of the tenth month [November 5] the master asked to be permitted to return to his former lodging. His wish was granted. After many delays, the emperor set up his Imperial Camp thirty *li* east of the city and on the sixth day of the same month the master appeared before him with the interpreter, Governor A-hai. Chinghiz asked if the master wanted a private audience, and the master replied that there was no need of secrecy in what he had to say. Then through the interpreter he explained his coming. "The hermit of the mountains has for many years devoted himself to the investigation of Tao and likes quiet. When I am with Your Majesty I am constantly disturbed by the noise of your soldiers and cannot think. I would like henceforth to have permission to travel either in advance or in back of the Imperial Army." The emperor granted his wish.

This was the season when the first rain began to fall and the grass again became green. Later, after the middle of the eleventh month, the rain becomes more frequent, heavier and sometimes turns to snow. The master, as had been his habit from his first coming to Samarkand, distributed all the grain we could spare to the many poor and hungry people. On the twenty-sixth [December 30], 1222, we set out. On the twenty-third of the twelfth month [January 26, 1223] heavy snow fell and the cold was so intense that many oxen and horses perished on the road. Proceeding to the east, three days later we crossed the Khojand-müran [Syr Darya] and reached the emperor's camp. We were told that the very next night after we had crossed over the bridge of boats, they had broken loose and had been swept away by the current. This prompted the emperor to ask the master the reason for calamities such as earthquakes, thunder and so on. The master replied, "I have heard that in order to avoid the wrath of heaven, you forbid your countrymen during the summer to bathe in rivers, wash their clothes, make fresh felt or gather mushrooms in the fields. This is not the way to serve heaven." [This prohibition was based on a desire to avoid offending the water spirits. Summer was the season of the thunder, that is, God's wrath. The prohibition against making felt was limited to the summer months; but that against washing clothes was continuous and absolute; clothes had to be worn until they were in rags.] And the master continued, "It is said that of the three thousand sins the worst is ill-treatment of one's father and mother. Now in this respect I believe your subjects to be gravely at fault and it would be well if Your Majesty would use your influence to reform them."

The master's words pleased the emperor. To a gathering of all the princes including his sons, his princes' ministers and high officials, he announced, "The Chinese reverence this Holy Immortal just as you revere heaven; and I am more than ever convinced that he is indeed a being from heaven." To all of them he repeated what the master had taught during his many discourses, adding, "Heaven sent this Holy Immortal to tell me these things. Do you engrave them upon your hearts." Then the master returned to his own lodgings.

On the first day of the New Year [February 2, 1223] the commander-in-chief, the chief physician, and the chief diviner called on the master to pay the compliments of the season. On the eleventh we continued eastward; we could look back toward Samarkand, already a thousand *li* behind us. The next place we stayed was at a wide valley where water and grass were plentiful; we rested awhile to restore our tired horses and oxen. From there to Sairam is a three-day journey to the northeast. On the seventh of the second month, the master again asked an audience with the emperor; he said, "Your Majesty, at the time the hermit of the mountains left, he gave his word to return in three years. After my three years' absence I long to see my mountains." "I myself am returning to the east," the emperor replied. "Will you not travel with me?" "I have explained all Your Majesty wished to hear," the master said, "and I would prefer going on ahead." And though he begged to be allowed to return to his home, the emperor refused. "Wait a little," he said. "My sons are soon arriving and there are still some points in your doctrine that are not quite clear to me. When I understand it completely, I will not object to your leaving."

The next day the emperor went out hunting in the mountains. Just as he shot a boar his horse stumbled and threw him. The wounded boar stood perfectly still; it did not rush on the fallen khan; it seemed afraid to approach. A moment later his followers brought the emperor a horse; the hunt was over and they headed back for the camp. When the master heard what had happened, he first scolded the emperor—for as a Taoist he considered all life precious and hunting a sin—and then cautioned him to hunt as little as possible since he was well advanced in years. He went on to explain that the fall from the horse was a warning, gravely emphasized by the boar's failure to gore him; together they showed that the emperor had been saved by the intervention of heaven. "Your advice is wise and good," Chinghiz said, "but it is hard not to hunt. We Mongols are brought up to ride and shoot arrows—a habit not easily given up. But I will take your advice to heart and from now on do as the Holy Immortal advises."

On the twenty-fourth day the master again tried to get

permission to return. "I must think over what I will give you on your departure," the emperor said, asking him to wait a little longer. Again, on the seventh of the third month, the master renewed his request. This time the emperor said he had decided on a gift of horses and oxen; but the master would not accept them, saying that he required only ordinary post horses. Then, through A-li-hsien, the interpreter, the emperor asked whether the master had many disciples in China. But A-li-hsien himself answered that he knew the master had a great many. "When I was conducting him to you from China, we halted at the Lung-yang Temple where, on the tax collector's list, I counted the large number of disciples." When he heard this the emperor decreed and issued an edict exempting all the master's pupils from taxation. He also ordered A-li-hsien to accompany the master on his homeward journey and take two Mongol officials as his assistants. On the tenth day of the third month, the master had his final interview with the emperor and took his leave.

When we started all the high-ranking officers of the camp went with us for some tens of *li*, each one carrying a present of grape wine and choice fruits; when the parting came they were all moved to tears.

Three days later we reached Sairam. We were told that in the mountains south of this large town there are serpents two-headed and about two feet long. They are frequently seen by the natives. It was on the day of the full moon when the disciples visited the tomb of their companion who had died there on the journey out. We spoke to the master about taking his remains back to China with us, but the master said, "The body, a temporary compound of the Five Elements, decays and has no value; but the soul, formed of spiritual essence, is free and cannot be held." We argued no more; the next day we started again.

We were joined by the imperial envoy, Yang A-kou, who had been sent to accompany the master along the southern bank of the Chu. Ten days later when we were still a hundred *li* west of Almalig we crossed a large river [Ili] and by the fifth of the fourth month [May 6] were in the orchards east of that city. It was here that Chang, the chief architect of the second prince, Chagatai—he had constructed the bridge of boats over the Amu Darya—came with an urgent request. Would the master cross the river to honor three altars which morning and evening drew hundreds of people to prayer and worship? If the master would instruct the crowds, he would confer a supreme benefit on the devout worshipers. But the master declined, saying that fate had something in store for him and he could not change his course. But when Chang again pressed his request, he promised he would do as asked unless something prevented his going to the Shrine. It was the very next day that heaven spoke—the horse the master was riding bolted and carried him off before his followers could stop the horse.

In the evening we arrived at the foot of the Yin Shan, spent the night there, and the next morning crossed the Forty-eight Bridges and proceeded fifty *li* up the lively stream to the Heavenly Lake [Sairam]. Crossing the Yin Shan [range] in a northeasterly direction, we traveled for twenty days until we came to the same post-road we had taken on our journey where it follows the course of a large river to the south of the Chin Shan [Altai range]. Passing over these mountains from south to north we arrived on its eastern slopes. On the twenty-eighth day of the fourth month [May 29] there was a heavy snowfall and the next day the mountains around us were white. Continuing in a northeasterly direction along the mountains for three days brought us to the A-pu-han Mountains. Here the disciples whom we had left in the newly built monastery and many others came a long way out to meet the master and escort him to the temple. Just as the master got out of his wagon it started to rain. This pleased everyone for, as the people explained, "In this region it seldom rains in the summer, though thundershowers occur frequently in the mountains to the north and to the south. For this abundant summer rain we are indebted to the master's holy power."

In ordinary years the people of this country have to irrigate their fields and gardens, for wheat ripens in the eighth month when there is no rain and the grains must be irrigated. The ripening grain is damaged by mice, mice that are all white. Because it is cold in this region, the fruits ripen late in the year; even in the fifth month [June] we could see along the banks of the river that under about a foot of soil the ground was solidly frozen—every day we sent servants to the river bank to hack out some ice for our use. To the south a high mountain range is covered with snow that does not melt even in the hottest weather. [The travelers appear to be at this time in the high semiarid plateau between the Altai and Khangai ranges.] There are many remarkable things about this country. A little distance to the west, by the side of a lake, there is a "wind tomb" whose top consists of white clay streaked by cracks. In the second and third months [March, April], the season when the wind is about to start blowing in the southern mountains, these cracks emit a howling that warns of an oncoming storm. But this is only the beginning. The wind, emerging from the "tomb," whirls in a kind of spiral like a ram's horn, and gradually many whirls come together to form a cyclone, which sends the sand flying and the rocks rolling; it tears roofs off and uproots trees. In the mountains there is much coal. There are three or four watermills in the river to the southeast, yet when the water reaches the plain it dries up and disappears. To the east are two springs which at wintertime erupt to form rivers or lakes; the water sinks into the ground to reappear in another place with the fish and shrimp intact in the water. Sometimes there is so much water it floods the people's houses; but it recedes in the spring.

Northwest of this, more than a thousand *li* distant, is a country called Chien-chien-chou [the region of the Upper Yenisei] where good iron is found, where squirrels abound, and wheat is cultivated. A great many Chinese live there and carry on the manufacture of silks and fine gauze, brocade and damask. From the monastery, the Chin Shan [Altai] Range is visible. They have a heavy rainfall and much hail. As late as the fifth and sixth months more than ten feet of snow is still on the ground; on its northern slopes are giant hundred-foot pines. Yet deserts are spread throughout the region. In one, the orobanche grows, the local name for it is *söyän* [a succulent plant whose stem is picked and salted to be used for medicinal purposes]. Other local words are water, *wusu*, and grass, *aipusu*. A group of the people said to the master, "This is a remote, barbarous region. The people have never heard of the True Doctrine; they relied on spells and charms for mountain spirits and evil demons. But now, since the master founded the temple, they have celebrated important ceremonies. On the first and fifteenth of every month they have congregated and vowed not to take the life of any living creature. Certainly, this is the power of the True Doctrine; what else could have wrought such a change? At first the Taoists [disciples] suffered deeply from malicious, evil men and were subjected to much unpleasantness. Especially from the physician Lo, who went out of his way to annoy and harass the Taoists. And then once, passing the Taoist temple, he was thrown from his horse and suffered a broken leg. This moved him to repentance: he admitted that he had been punished for his sins and begged the Taoist to pardon him."

Gratified for this Taoist outpost he had been able to plant and for the chance to preach, the master wrote some instructive verses which began, "For ten thousand *li* I have ridden on a government horse, it is three years since I parted from my friends."[10] Then he was ready to take the road to the east.

A-li-hsien and the others told the master, "The southern route is barren, very stony, and grass and water are exceedingly scarce. Our party is too large; the horses will soon get exhausted from insufficient water and fodder; they might slow us down and any delay can prove fatal." The master agreed with their proposal that they should split up into three groups which would follow one another. On the seventh of the fifth month, six disciples started out; the master, with six others, followed a week later, and a week after that the remaining five disciples.

Eastward the road led across a great snow-covered mountain; the cold was intense. We changed horses at a *fu-lu* [from the Tibetan word meaning a crude shelter of stones or skins]. On the seventeenth day the master did not eat, he only sipped rice water from time to time. We continued to the southeast across a great sandy stretch where the grass and trees that managed to live there were infested with gnats and mosquitoes. That night was spent on the east bank of a river; in the morning we went on. From time to time the master dismounted and rode in his wagon. His worried disciples respectfully asked what was wrong. "My illness is not one to be understood by physicians." Likening it to the cutting and polishing of gems that, thus freed from imperfections, shine the more brilliantly, he explained that he was being purified to become holier and wiser. "But do not you be anxious," he concluded. Despite his explanation and reassurance, his disciples continued to be deeply worried. That night one of them had a

[10] Ibid., p. 125.

dream in which a divine spirit appeared and said, "Do not be alarmed by the master's illness. When he arrives in China he will get well again."

For three hundred *li* we followed a track over sand where water and grass were so scarce that we did not stop to camp but kept going through the night until by the end of the second day we had put the sandy waste behind us; we had come to the northern frontier of the Tangut country. Here we began to find huts and tents and had no trouble getting fresh horses; we waited for the third group to catch up with us. On the twenty-second of the sixth month [July 21] we camped at the Yü-yang Barrier [the pass north of Kukukhoto leading over the T'ien Shan Mountains]. The master still did not eat. The next day we traversed the barrier and made another fifty *li* to the east of it to reach Feng-chou [Kukukhoto]. Here the whole town, from the commander to the lowest official, came out to meet the master and invited him to stay at the home of the envoy Yü. When the familiar hot cakes were served, the master immediately ate a quantity of them and after that ate and drank as he always had. This was a confirmation to the disciples of the auspicious dream. They had arrived in late summer and the master found it pleasant to sit at a northern window where he could enjoy the cool breeze.

[The arduous journey was over: the rest of the way was a triumphal return. City after city welcomed him and honored him; princes, dignitaries, officials, and commanders from all over northern China addressed letters to the master inviting him to visit them. The invitations came as fast as the spokes of a rolling wheel; but the master declined them all.] Some of the disciples fulfilled the vow they had taken when, on their outward journey, their hearts had been torn at the sight of the battlefield covered with bleached bones; they performed a service on behalf of the destitute souls who had died there.

This was held at the Lung-yang Temple at Te-hsing and it was just as the service was finished that an officer arrived from the emperor with a letter for the master. "Holy adept, between the spring and summer you have performed no easy journey. I wish to know whether you were properly supplied with provisions and remounts. At Hsüan-te and the other places where you lately stayed, did the officials make satisfactory provision for your board and lodging? Have your appeals to the common people resulted in their coming over to you? I am always thinking of you and I hope you will not forget me."

CHAPTER FIVE

RABBAN SAUMA VISITS EUROPE

RABBAN SAUMA VISITS EUROPE

Sometime after the middle of the thirteenth century, two Uighur monks, Sauma and Mark, left their Chinese homeland to make a pilgrimage to the holy places of Jerusalem. They were Nestorian Christians, members of a church that had been condemned (in 430) and which, excluded from the Roman Empire, spread through Arabia, Syria, and Mesopotamia eastward to Central Asia and China. Neither ever saw Jerusalem.

The religious and political struggles that prevented them from reaching their goal changed the course of their lives. That both men were distinguished by their intelligence as well as their piety is indicated by the success with which they filled the roles they were called on to assume. Mark, the younger, became the Patriarch of the East, the spiritual head of the Nestorians; Rabban Sauma became Visitor-General of the Nestorian congregations in the East and, as ambassador of Arghun, the Mongol Ilkhan of Persia, visited the Pope and the kings of Byzantium, France, and England.

Born into a well-to-do-family, Rabban Sauma while still a boy studied ecclesiastical writings and at twenty renounced the world. He left Peking—his birthplace was then called Khan Balig or Cambulac, the City of the King—and settled down in a mountan cave to a life of stern asceticism. Hs fame spread. Among those attracted by his preaching was the young Mark, already determined to become a monk. After some years spent in isolation and meditation, Rabban Sauma and Mark announced their determination to make a pilgrimage to Jeru-

salem; the Christian community in Peking was appalled, for such a journey was, for that time, a journey to the end of the earth. They started off with nothing but a letter from the Metropolitan of Peking commending them to the Nestorians along their route and a "permit" from Kubilai Khan granting them safe passage through his empire. (Kubilai was tolerant of all religions—Islam and Buddhism and Christianity—but gave special preference to the Nestorians who, learned in medicine and skilled in trade, added both luster and wealth to his vast realm.)

Their journey across the deserts and mountains of Central Asia was filled with the hardships to be expected, but unforeseen dangers were added by the rebellion of a petty chieftain that made the caravan routes unsafe and left the oasis towns shattered and needy. Finally, utterly exhausted, they reached Khorassan and counted themselves lucky to have come there alive. Here were Nestorians to welcome them and monasteries where they could rest; here was wealth and plenty and order. When they were restored and with the blessing of the bishop, they took the road for Baghdad, the seat of the Catholicus, as the Patriarch was called. Traveling through the province of Azerbaijan, they came to Maraghah, its capital (not far from its present capital, Tabriz) and rejoiced to learn that the Catholicus happened to be there. He received them kindly and approved of their pilgrimage. So they came to Baghdad, where they visited churches and monasteries and the tomb of the Prophet Ezekiel who—it was believed—was buried there in the grave of Arphaxad, the son of Shem, the son of Noah. Continuing their leisurely way toward Jerusalem, they stopped at Arbela, a city near the battlefield where Alexander the Great had triumphed over Darius; then at Mosul, the ancient Nineveh. The caravan route brought them to the walled city of Sinjar, whose houses were built up the side of the mountain on whose summit—tradition says—the Ark came to rest; to Nisibis, an important town old enough to be mentioned in cuneiform inscriptions; to the massive fortress of Mardin with its castle, the Falcon, overlooking the town with its famous markets, its khans, or inns, and its colleges. Among the nearby monasteries, the most renowned held the tomb of a saint who, because he had inspired so many disciples, was called the "second Christ." Next they came to the walled town of Jazirat, "the Island," so-called because the Tigris had been led through a ditch to surround it; in this busy and prosperous trading center all the products of Armenia were brought for sale. From there they turned back to the monastery of Mâr Michael, intending to stay there awhile.

They bought a "cell." (Cell is the word used for a building that houses a monk, a bishop, or even the Patriarch; and it was not unusual for the cell of one of the higher orders of the clergy to be a large, comfortable house, while the Patriarch's cell in Baghdad was actually a palace.) From the cell where they had settled down, the Patriarch, Mâr Denha, summoned them to Baghdad to tell them that their remaining at the monastery was a selfish act; he admonished them to spend themselves in the service of the community. Then he sent them on a delicate mission to the court of Abaga, King of Kings. They were uniquely qualified to carry it out because they were familiar with Mongol customs and etiquette and could speak and write Chinese and Persian, and because they were traveling under Kubilai Khan's protection. They asked permission to resume their pilgrimage after they had completed the Patriarch's business.

Again they took the road for Jerusalem. Warned that the direct route through northern Syria was unsafe and, hoping to reach Jerusalem by sea from a Black Sea port, they made the long detour northward through Christian Armenia to

Georgia. But even this roundabout way was barred—murderous robbers infested the mountain country through which the King's Highway passed. Again they returned to Baghdad, and again the Patriarch had an assignment for them. This time they were told to return to China to assist the Patriarch in governing the Nestorian Church. He told them that this meant that Mark would have to be ordained bishop and Rabban Sauma visitor-general. In vain they pleaded to be permitted to remain simple monks and live out their lives in a monastery. The Patriarch decided during the ordination ceremonies to give Mark another name, and writing several possible names on slips of paper, he placed them on the altar thinking to leave the choice to God. The slip chosen had the name Yahbhallâhâ, which means "God gave him," and under this name Mark became Metropolitan of Cathay and Wang, two districts in northern China. The year was 1280; Yahbhallâhâ was about thirty-five and Sauma was more than ten years his senior. They had not gone far on the long road back to China when they were forced to turn back because fighting had broken out on both sides of the Oxus and the caravan routes were cut. They returned to their cell at Mâr Michael.

Two years passed. And then the Patriarch sickened and quickly died. Yahbhallâhâ reached Baghdad only after his death. He attended the burial and sat with the other bishops and notables gathered to elect a successor. They elected him unanimously, not because of his learning or piety, but for the more practical and pressing reason that Yahbhallâhâ knew the customs and languages of the Mongol rulers. He sought to decline the high office, protesting he was unworthy since he did not know Syriac, the holy language of the Church. Rabban Sauma, on the other hand, realized the futility of his refusing and argued that the sensible way was to accept and have his election confirmed by Abaga, King of Kings, as quickly as possible. And so it was. In no time at all, the Patriarch Yahbhallâhâ and Rabban Sauma, visitor-general, escorted by a large party of bishops and monks, journeyed to the royal summer residence. At the foot of Black Mountain in a little town set in the Azerbaijan woods, Mâr Yahbhallâhâ was welcombed by Abaga, who sat him on his throne, placed his cloak about his shoulders, and the great seal of the Catholicus Mâr Denha in his hands, and to show him marked favor, gave him an honorific parasol, a gold paizah, *and a purse of gold to defray the cost of the consecration ceremony on his return to Baghdad.*

(The paizah, *a gold tablet about six inches long and two inches wide, perforated at one end so it could be suspended and inscribed with a formula containing the name of God and the king, conferred great authority and privileges. Originally it seems to have been given by Mongol kings to members of the royal house who were thus deputed to act for the king. The bearer of a gold* paizah *could call on the inhabitants of any settlement to supply him without cost with everything he might require and to treat him as though he were royal. With the* paizah *went the gift of a* yarligh, *a written warrant or patent, which ensured that the holder of the* paizah *was not an imposter or thief. A silver* paizah *which has been found had the number 42 on one side and on the other an inscription in the Mongol language: "By the strength of the eternal heaven! May the name of the Khaghan [King of Kings] be holy! He who doth not pay him reverence shall be slain and must die.")*

The two years (1282–84) between Abaga's death and the beginning of his son Arghun's reign were perilous for the Christian communities. Abaga was succeeded by his brother, who, though baptized in the Nestorian faith, inclined toward Islam. It was not his conversion to Islam that antagonized and alienated the powerful Mongols of his court as much as the treaty he concluded with the sultan at Cairo. A successful revolt placed Abaga's son Arghun on the throne. A historian of the Crusades has described him as being "religiously eclectic" like his father. Arghun's own "sympathies were for Buddhism, but his vizier, Sa'd ad-Daulah, was a Jew, and his best friend was the Nestorian Catholicus, Mâr Yahbhallâhâ."[1]

The two-year period when the Muslims were feeling their power had given the Nestorians a foretaste of the fate they would—and did—suffer if Islam were to triumph. Nor was the lesson lost on Arghun. Besides which, like his father, the young Ilkhan desired to subjugate Syria and Palestine and capture Jerusalem—an ambitious plan that could succeed only if the Western kings could be persuaded to start an offensive in Outremer, as the already threatened Frankish Crusader kingdoms were called. By such concerted action they could destroy the Muslim wedge that separated them and threatened them both. It was to point out the imperatives and possibilities of this alliance that Rabban Sauma went to the West in 1287.

ON THE DEPARTURE OF RABBAN SAUMA TO THE COUNTRY OF THE ROMANS IN THE NAME OF KING ARGHUN AND OF THE CATHOLICUS MÂR YAHBHALLÂHÂ.

King Arghun loved the Christians with his whole heart. And Arghun intended to go into the countries of Palestine and Syria and to subjugate them and take possession of them, but he said to himself, "If the Western kings, who are Christians, will not help me I shall not be able to fulfill my desire." Thereupon he asked the Catholicus to give him a wise man "one who is suitable and is capable of undertaking an embassy, that we may send him to those kings." And when the Catholicus saw that there was no man who knew the language except Rabban

[1] Steven Runciman, *A History of the Crusades* (Cambridge University Press, 1954), Vol. 3, pp. 397–98.

Sauma, and knowing that he was fully capable of this, he commanded him to go on the embassy.

THE JOURNEY OF RABBAN SAUMA TO THE COUNTRY OF THE ROMANS IN THE NAME OF KING ARGHUN AND OF THE CATHOLICUS MÂR YAHBHALLÂHÂ.

Then Rabban Sauma said, "I desire this embassy greatly, and I long to go." Then straightway King Arghun wrote for him "authorities" to the king of the Greeks [Byzantium], and the king of the Franks, that is to say Romans, and *yarlighs* and letters, and gave him gifts for each of the kings addressed by him. And to Rabban Sauma he gave two thousand *mathkâlê* [$2,800] of gold, and thirty good riding animals, and a *paizah*. And Rabban Sauma came to the cell of the Catholicus to obtain a letter from Mâr Yahbhallâhâ, and to say farewell to him. The Catholicus gave him permission to depart. They said farewell to each other, weeping as they did so. And the Catholicus sent with him letters, and gifts which were suitable for presentation to Mâr Pâpâ, the Pope, and gifts according to his ability.

RABBAN SAUMA IN BYZANTIUM.

And Rabban Sauma set out on his journey, and there went with him a number of excellent men from among the priests and deacons of the cell of the Catholicus. And he arrived at the territory of the Romans on the borders of the Black Sea [at Trebizond], and he saw the church that was there, and then he embarked in a ship and his companions were with him. Now there were more than three hundred souls in the ship, and each day he consoled them with [his] discourse on the Faith. Now the greater number of those who dwelt in the ship were Romans [*i.e.* Byzantine Greeks], and because of the savor of his speech they paid him honor in no small degree.

And after [some] days [about Easter] he arrived at the great city of Constantinople, and before they went into it he sent two young men to the Royal Gate [Sublime Porte] to make known there that an ambassador of King Arghun had come. Then the king commanded certain people to go forth to meet them, and to bring them in with pomp and honor. And when Rabban Sauma went into the city, the king allotted to him a house, that is to say, a mansion in which to dwell. And after Rabban Sauma had rested himself, he went to visit the king [Andronicus II] and after he had saluted him, the king asked him, "How art thou after the workings of the sea and the fatigue of the road?" And Rabban Sauma replied, "With the sight of the Christian king fatigue hath vanished and exhaustion hath departed, for I was exceedingly anxious to see your kingdom, the which may our Lord establish!"

And after they had enjoyed food and drink Rabban Sauma asked the king to be allowed to see the churches and the shrines of the fathers, and the relics of the saints that were therein. And the king handed Rabban Sauma over to the nobles of his kingdom and they showed him everything that was there.

First of all he went unto the great church of ἡ Σοφία, [whose name signifies the Church of Divine Wisdom], which has three hundred and sixty pillars all made of marble. As for the dome of the altar it is impossible for a man to describe it [adequately] to one who hath not seen it, and to say how high and how spacious it is. There is in this church a picture of the holy Mary which Luke, the evangelist, painted. He saw there also the hand of Mâr John the Baptist, and portions of the bodies of Lazarus, and Mary Magdalene, and that stone which was laid on the grave of our Lord, when Joseph brought Him down from the cross. Now Mary wept on that stone, and the place whereon her tears fell is wet even at the present time; and however often this moisture is wiped away the place becometh wet again. And he saw also the stone bowl in which our Lord changed the water into wine at Cana of Galilee; and the funerary coffer of one of the holy women which is exposed to public view every year, and every sick person who is laid under it is made whole; and the coffer of Mâr John of the Mouth of Gold [Chrysostom]. And he saw also the stone on which Simon Peter was sitting when the cock crew; and the tomb of King Constantine, the Conqueror, which was made of porphyry; and also the tomb of Justinian, which was [built of] green stone; and also the resting place of the three hundred and eighteen bishops who were all laid in one great church; and their bodies have not suffered corruption because they had confirmed the [True] Faith. And he saw also many shrines of the holy fathers, and many amulets of a magical character [talismans] and images in bodily form made of bronze and stone [icons].

And when Rabban Sauma went [back] to the king he said, "May the king live forever! I give thanks unto our Lord that I have been held worthy to see these things. And now, if the king will permit me, I will go and fulfill the command of King Arghun, for the command to me was to enter the territory of the Franks." Then the king entreated him with great kindness, and gave him gifts of gold and silver.

RABBAN SAUMA IN ITALY AND IN GREAT ROME.

And he departed from Constantinople and embarked on a ship and came to where he saw a mountain from which smoke ascended all the day long, and in the nighttime fire showed itself on it. And no man is able to approach the neighborhood of it because of the stench of sulphur [Vesuvius, or Etna, or Stromboli]. Some people say that there is a great serpent there. This sea is called the "Sea of Italy." Now it is a terrible sea and very many thousands of people have perished therein. And after two months of toil, and weariness, and exhaustion, Rabban Sauma arrived at the seashore, and he landed at the city the name of which was Nâpôlî [Naples]; now the name of its king was Îrîd Shardâlô [Il re Sharl du or, the King Charles II]. And he went to the king and showed him the reason why they had come; and the king welcomed him and paid him honor. Now it happened that there was war between him and another king whose name was Îrîd Arkôn [the king of Aragon, James II]. And the troops of the one had come in many ships, and the troops of the other were ready, and they began to fight each other, and the king of Aragon conquered King Charles II, and slew twelve thousand of his men, and sunk their ships in the sea. [This naval engagement took place in the Bay of Sorrento on St. John's Day, June 24, 1287, and the great eruption of Mount Etna on June 18]. Meanwhile Rabban Sauma and his companions sat upon the roof of the mansion in which they lived, and they admired the way in which the Franks waged war, for they attacked none of the people except those who were actually combatants.

And from that place they traveled inland on horses, and they passed through towns and villages and marveled because they found no land which was destitute of buildings. On the road they heard that Mâr Pâpâ [Honorius IV, who died in 1287] was dead.

After some days they arrived in Great Rome. And Rabban Sauma went into the church of Peter and Paul, for the cell [Vatican] of the throne of Mâr Pâpâ was situated therein. Now after the death of Mâr Pâpâ, twelve men who were called "Kaltûnârê" [not *chartularii*, but cardinals] administered the papal throne. And whilst they were taking counsel together in order to appoint a new Pope, Rabban Sauma sent a message to them saying, "We who are ambassadors of

King Arghun and of the Catholicus of the East have arrived"; and the cardinals ordered them to come in. And the Franks who accompanied Rabban Sauma and his companions informed them that when they were going into the cell [Vatican] of Mâr Pâpâ [they would find] there an altar at which they must bow, and then they must go in and salute the cardinals. And thus they did, and their act was pleasing to those cardinals. And when Rabban Sauma went into their presence no man stood up before him, for by reason of the honorable nature of the throne, the twelve cardinals were not in the habit of doing this. And they made Rabban Sauma sit down with them, and one of them asked him, "How art thou after all the fatigue of the road?" And he made answer to him, "Through your prayers I am well and rested." And the cardinal said unto him, "For what purpose hast thou come hither?" And Rabban Sauma said unto him, "The Mongols and the Catholicus of the East have sent me to Mâr Pâpâ concerning the matter of Jerusalem; and they have sent letters with me." And the cardinals said unto him, "For the present rest thyself, and we will discuss the matter together later"; and they assigned to him a mansion and caused him to be taken down thereto.

Three days later the cardinals sent and summoned Rabban Sauma to their presence. And when he went to them they began to ask him questions, saying, "What is thy quarter of the world, and why hast thou come?" And he replied in the selfsame words he had already spoken to them. And they said unto him, "Where doth the Catholicus live? And which of the apostles taught the Gospel in thy quarter of the world?" And he answered them, saying, "Mâr Thomas, and Mâr Addai, and Mâr Mârî taught the Gospel in our quarter of the world, and we hold at the present time the canons which they delivered unto us." The cardinal said unto him,

"Where is the throne of the Catholicus?" He said to them, "In Baghdad." They answered, "What position hast thou there?" And he replied, "I am a deacon in the cell of the Catholicus, and the director of the disciples, and the visitor-general." The cardinals said, "It is a marvelous thing that thou who art a Christian, and a deacon of the throne of the Patriarch of the East hast come upon an embassy from the king of the Mongols." And Rabban Sauma said unto them, "Know ye, O our Fathers, that many of our fathers have gone into the countries of the Mongols, and Turks, and Chinese and have taught them the Gospel, and at the present time there are many Mongols who are Christians. For many of the sons of the Mongol kings and queens have been baptized and confess Christ. And they have established churches in their military camps, and they pay honor to the Christians, and there are among them many who are believers. Now the king of the Mongols, who is joined in the bond of friendship with the Catholicus, hath the desire to take Palestine, and the countries of Syria, and he demandeth from you help in order to take Jerusalem. He hath chosen me and hath sent me to you because, being a Christian, my word will be believed by you." And the cardinals said unto him, "What is thy confession of faith? To what 'way' art thou attached? Is it that which Mâr Pâpâ holdeth today or some other one?" Rabban Sauma replied, "No man hath come to us Orientals from the Pope. The holy apostles whose names I have mentioned taught us the Gospel, and to what they delivered unto us we have clung to the present day." The cardinals said unto him, "How dost thou believe? Recite thy belief, article by article." Rabban Sauma replied to them, [reciting the Confession of Faith of his church].

Now though the cardinals restrained his speech by means of very many demonstrations, they held him in high esteem because of his power of argument.

Then Rabban Sauma said unto them, "I have come from remote countries neither to discuss, nor to instruct [men] in matter of Faith, but I came that I might receive a blessing from Mâr Pâpâ, and from the shrines of the saints and to make known the words of King [Arghun] and the Catholicus. If it be pleasing in your eyes, let us set aside discussion, and do ye give attention and direct someone to show us the churches here and the shrines of the saints; if ye will do this ye will confer a very great favor on your servant and disciple."

Then the cardinals summoned the amîr of the city and certain monks and commanded them to show him the churches and the holy places that were there; and they went forth straightway and saw the places which we will now mention. First of all they went into the church of Peter and Paul. Beneath the throne is a naos, and in this is laid the body of Saint Peter, and above the throne is an altar. The altar which is in the middle of that great temple has four doorways, and in each of these two folding doors worked with designs in iron. Mâr Pâpâ celebrates the Mass at this altar, and no person besides himself may stand on the bench of that altar. Afterwards they saw the Throne of Mâr Peter whereon they make Mâr Pâpâ to sit when they appoint him. And they also saw the strip of fine linen on which our Lord impressed His image and sent to King Abhgar of Ûrhâi (Edessa). Now the extent of that temple and its splendor cannot be described; it stands on one hundred and eight pillars. In it is another altar at which the king of their kings receives the laying on of hands [*i.e.* is consecrated and crowned], and is proclaimed "Emperor, King of Kings," by the Pope. And they say that after the prayers Mâr Pâpâ takes up the crown with his feet, and clothes the emperor with it, that is to say, places it upon his own head [to show], as they say, that priesthood reigneth over kingship.

And when they had seen all the churches and monasteries

that were in Great Rome, they went outside the city to the church of Mâr Paul the Apostle, where under the altar is his tomb. And there, too, is the chain wherewith Paul was bound when he was dragged to that place. And in that altar there are also a reliquary of gold wherein is the head of Mâr Stephen the Martyr, and the hand of Mâr Khananyâ [Ananias] who baptized Paul. And the staff of Paul the Apostle is also there. And from that place they went to the spot where Paul the Apostle was crowned with martyrdom. They say that when his head was cut off it leaped up thrice into the air, and at each time cried out "Christ! Christ!" And that from each of the three places on which his head fell there came forth waters which were useful for healing purposes, and for giving help to all those who were afflicted. And in that place also there is a great shrine wherein are the bones of martyrs and famous fathers, and they were blessed by them.

And they went also to the Church of My Lady Maryam, and of Mâr John the Baptist, and they saw therein the seamless tunic of our Lord. And there is also in that church the tablet on which our Lord consecrated the Offering and gave it to His disciples. And each year Mâr Pâpâ consecrates on that tablet the Paschal Mysteries. There are in that church four pillars of copper, or brass, each of which is six cubits in thickness; these, they say, the kings brought from Jerusalem. They saw also there the vessel in which Constantine, the victorious king, was baptized; it is made of black stone [basalt], polished. Now that church is very large and broad, and there are in the nave one hundred and forty white marble pillars. They saw also the place where Sîmôn Kîpâ [*i.e.* Simon the Rock] disputed with Sîmôn [Magus], and where the latter fell down and his bones were broken.

From that place they went into the church of Mârt Maryam, and the priests brought out for them reliquaries made of beryl wherein was the apparel of Mârt Maryam, and a piece of wood on which our Lord had lain when a child. They saw also the head of Matthew, the apostle, in a reliquary of silver. And they saw the foot of Philip, the apostle, and the arm of James, the son of Zebedee, in the Church of the Apostles, which was there. And after these sights they saw buildings which it is impossible to describe in words, and as the histories of those buildings would make any description of them very long I abandon the attempt.

After this Rabban Sauma and his companions returned to the cardinals, and thanked them for having held him to be worthy to see these shrines and to receive blessings from them. And Rabban Sauma asked from them permission to go to the king who dwelleth in Rome; and they permitted him to go, and said, "We cannot give thee an answer until the new Pope is elected."

And they went from that place to the country of Tuscany, and were honorably entreated, and thence they went to Genoa. Now the latter country has no king, but the people thereof set up to rule over it some great man with whom they are pleased.

And when the people of Genoa heard that an ambassador of King Arghun had arrived, their chief went forth with a great crowd of people, and they brought him into the city.

And there was there a great church with the name of San Lorenzo, in which was the holy body of Mâr John the Baptist, in a coffer of pure silver. And Rabban Sauma and his companions saw also a six-sided paten, made of emerald, and the people there told them that it was off this paten from which our Lord ate the Passover with His disciples, and that it was brought there when Jerusalem was captured. [Known as the *Sacro Catino*, it had been captured by the Genoese in 1101; in 1809, Napoleon brought it to Paris. This famous vessel was said, according to one tradition, to have been given by the Queen of Sheba to Solomon; according to another, to have been the dish from which Jesus and His Disciples ate the Paschal lamb; and still another identifies it as the dish in which Joseph of Arimathea caught the drops of Jesus's blood when He was crucified. Whatever the tradition all agreed that the receptacle was formed out of a single, flawless emerald. In 1815 it was broken and was then found to have been made of a green opaque glass.] And from that place they went to the country of Lombardy and they saw that the people there did not fast during the first Sabbath of Lent. And when they asked them, "Wherefore do ye do thus, and separate yourselves from all [other] Christians?" they replied, "This is our custom. When we were first taught the Gospel our fathers in the Faith were weakly and were unable to fast. Those who taught them the Gospel commanded them to fast forty days only."

RABBAN SAUMA IN FRANSÂ OR FRANGESTÂN.

Afterwards they went to the country of Paris, to King Fransîs [*i.e.* Philippe IV le Bel]. And the king sent out a large company of men to meet them, and they brought them into the city with great honor and ceremony. Now the territories of the French king were in extent more than a month's journey. And the king of France assigned to Rabban Sauma a place wherein to dwell, and three days later sent one of his amîrs to him and summoned him to his presence. And when he had come the king stood up before him and paid him honor, and said unto him, "Why hast thou come? And who sent thee?" And Rabban Sauma said unto him, "King Arghun and the Catholicus of the East have sent me concerning the matter of Jerusalem." And he showed him all the matters which he knew, and he gave him the letters which he had with him, and the gifts, that is to say, presents which he had brought. And the king of France answered him, saying, "If it be indeed so that the Mongols, though they are not Christians, are going to fight against the Arabs for the capture of Jerusalem, it is meet especially for us that we should fight [with them], and if our Lord willeth, go forth in full strength."

And Rabban Sauma said unto him, "Now that we have seen the glory of thy kingdom, and have looked upon the splendor of your strength with the eye of flesh, we ask you to command the men of the city to show us the churches, and the shrines, and the relics of the saints, and everything else which is found with you, and is not to be seen in any other country, so that when we return we may make known in the [various] countries what we have seen with you." Then the king commanded his amîrs, saying, "Go forth and show them all the wonderful things which we have here, and afterwards I myself will show [them] what I have." And the amîrs went out with them.

And Rabban Sauma and his companions remained for a month of days in this great city of Paris, and they saw everything that was in it. There were in it thirty thousand scholars who were engaged in the study of ecclesiastical books of instruction, that is to say of commentaries and exegesis of all the holy scriptures, and also of profane learning; and they studied wisdom, that is to say philosophy, and rhetoric and healing, geometry, arithmetic, and the science of the planets and the stars; and they engaged constantly in writing theses, and all these pupils received money for subsistence from the king. And they also saw one great church wherein were the funerary coffers of dead kings, and statues of them in gold and in silver were upon their tombs. And five hundred monks were engaged in performing commemoration services in the burial place of the kings, and they all ate and drank at the expense of the king. And they fasted and prayed continually in the burial place of those kings. And the crowns of those kings, and their armor, and their apparel were laid upon their tombs. In short Rabban Sauma and his companions saw everything which was splendid and renowned.

And after this the king sent and summoned them, and they went to him in the church, and they saw him standing by the side of the altar, and they saluted him. And he asked Rabban Sauma, saying, "Have you seen what we have? And doth there not remain anything else for you to see?" Then Rabban Sauma thanked him and said, "There is not." Forthwith he went up with the king into an upper chamber of gold, which the king opened, and he brought forth from it a coffer of beryl wherein was laid the Crown of Thorns which the Jews placed upon the head of our Lord when they crucified Him. Now the crown was visible in the coffer, which, thanks to the transparency of the beryl, remained unopened. And there was also in the coffer a piece of the wood of the cross. And the king said to Rabban Sauma and his companions, "When our fathers took Constantinople [in the Third Crusade, 1204], and sacked Jerusalem, they brought these blessed objects from it. "And we blessed the king and besought him to give us the order to return. And he said unto us, "I will send with you one of the great amîrs whom I have here with me to give an answer to King Arghun"; and the king gave Rabban Sauma gifts and apparel of great price.

RABBAN SAUMA GOES TO THE KING OF ENGLAND [*i.e.* EDWARD I].

And they went forth from that place, that is to say, from Paris, to go to the king of England, to Gascony. And having arrived in twenty days at their city, Bordeaux, the inhabitants of the city went forth to meet them, and they asked them,

"Who are ye?" And Rabban Sauma and his companions replied, "We are ambassadors, and we have come from beyond the Eastern seas, and we are envoys of the king, and of the Patriarch, and the kings of the Mongols." And the people made haste and went to the king and informed him of their arrival, and the king welcomed them gladly, and the people introduced them into his presence. And those who were with Rabban Sauma straightway gave to the king the *Pukdânâ*, the letter of authorization of King Arghun, and the gifts which he had sent to him, and the letter of Mâr Catholicus. And King Edward rejoiced greatly, and he was especially glad when Rabban Sauma talked about the matter of Jerusalem. And he said, "We the kings of these cities bear upon our bodies the sign of the cross, and we have no subject of thought except this matter. And my mind is relieved on the subject about which I have been thinking, when I hear that King Arghun thinketh as I think." And the king commanded Rabban Sauma to celebrate the Eucharist, and he performed the glorious mysteries; and the king and his officers of state stood up, and the king partook of the Sacrament, and made a great feast that day.

Then Rabban Sauma said unto the king, "We beseech thee, O king, to give thy servants the order to show us whatever churches and shrines there are in this country, so that when we go back to the children of the East we may give them descriptions of them." And the king replied, "Thus shall ye say to King Arghun and unto all the Orientals: We have seen a thing than which there is nothing more wonderful, that is to say, that in the countries of the Franks there are not two Confessions of Faith, but only one Confession of Faith, namely, that which confesseth Jesus Christ; and all the Christians confess it." And King Edward gave us many gifts and money for the expenses of the road.

RABBAN SAUMA RETURNS TO ROME.

And from that place we came to the city of Genoa, in order to pass the winter there. And when we arrived there we saw a garden which resembled paradise; its winter is not too cold, and its summer is not too hot. Green foliage is found therein all the year round, and trees, the leaves of which do not fall, and which are not stripped of their fruit. There is in the city a kind of vine which yields grapes seven times a year, but the people do not press out wine from them.

At the end of the winter there came from the country of Allemagne a man of high degree, who was the "visitor" of Mâr Pâpâ, and who was on his way to Rome.[1] And when he heard that Rabban Sauma was there, he went to visit him and salute him. And when he entered his house they gave each other, "Peace!" and they kissed each other in the love of Christ. And the visitor said unto Rabban Sauma, "I have come to see thee. For I have heard concerning thee, that thou art a good and a wise man, and also that thou hast the desire to go to Rome." And Rabban Sauma said unto him, "What shall I say unto thee, O beloved and noble man? I have come on an embassy from King Arghun, and the Catholicus of the East to Mâr Pâpâ on the subject of Jerusalem. Behold I have been a year of days and a Pope hath not sat. When I go back what shall I say and what answer can I make to the Mongols? Those whose hearts are harder than flint [Muslims] wish to take the Holy City, and those to whom it belongeth never allow the matter to occupy their minds, and moreover, they do not consider this thing to be of any importance whatsoever! What we shall go and say we know not." Then the visitor said unto him, "Thy words are true. I myself will go and show in their integrity the cardinals all the words which thou hast spoken, and will urge them to appoint a pope."

[1] Probably John of Jerusalem, who, in 1286, went to Germany to arrange for the coronation of Rudolph of Habsburg.

And that visitor departed from him and went to Rome, and he explained the matter to the king, that is to say Mâr Pâpâ, and that same day the Pope sent a messenger to Rabban Sauma and his companions bidding them to go to him. And as soon as ever the messenger had arrived, they set out for Rome with the greatest readiness and they arrived there in fifteen days. And they asked, "Who is this Pope whom they have appointed?" And the people said, "It is the bishop who held converse with you when ye came here the first time, and his name is Nicholas IV [who was elected Pope in February, 1288]. And Rabban Sauma and his companions rejoiced greatly.

And when they arrived Mâr Pâpâ sent out a metropolitan bishop and a large company of men to meet them. And straightway Rabban Sauma went into the presence of Mâr Pâpâ, who was seated on his throne. And he drew nigh to the Pope, bowing down to the ground as he did so, and he kissed his feet and his hands, and he withdrew walking backwards, with his hands clasped on his breast. And he said to Mâr Pâpâ, "May thy throne stand forever, O our Father! And may it be blessed above all kings and nations! And may it make peace to reign in thy days throughout the Church to the uttermost ends of the earth! Now that I have seen thy face mine eyes are illumined, and I shall not go away brokenhearted to the countries of the East. I give thanks to the goodness of God who hath held me to be worthy to see thy face." Then Rabban Sauma presented unto him the gift of King Arghun and his letters, and the gift of the Catholicus, and his letter. And Mâr Pâpâ rejoiced and was glad, and he paid more honor to Rabban Sauma than was customary, and he said unto him, "It will be good if thou wilt keep the festival with us, for thou wilt see our use." Now that day marked the half of our Lord's Fast [*i.e.* Mid-Lent]. And Rabban Sauma made answer, "Your command is high and exalted." And Mâr Pâpâ assigned to him a mansion in which to dwell, and he appointed servants to give him everything that he might require.

Some days later Rabban Sauma said to Mâr Pâpâ, "I wish to celebrate the Eucharist so that ye may see our use"; and the Pope commanded him to do as he had asked. And on that day a very large number of people were gathered together in order to see how the ambassador of the Mongols celebrated the Eucharist. And when they had seen they rejoiced and said, "The language is different, but the use is the same." Now the day on which he celebrated was the Sunday on which the prayer beginning "Who is the physician" is recited. And having performed the mysteries, he went to Mâr Pâpâ and saluted him. And the Pope said unto Rabban Sauma, "May God receive thy offering, and bless thee, and pardon thy transgressions and sins." Then Rabban Sauma said, "Besides the pardon of my transgressions and sins which I have received from thee, O our Father, I beseech thy Fatherhood, O our holy Father, to let me receive the offering from thy hands, so that the remission of my sins may be complete." And the Pope said, "So let it be!"

And on the following first day of the week, which was the Festival of Hosannas, Palm Sunday, from the break of day onwards, countless thousands and tens of thousands of people gathered together before the papal throne, and brought branches of olives, which the Pope blessed and gave to the cardinals, and then to the metropolitans and then to the bishops, and then to the amîrs, and then to the nobles, and then he cast them among all the people. And he rose up from the throne and they brought him into the church with great ceremony. And he went into the apse of the altar and changed his apparel, and he put on a red vestment with threads of gold, and ornamented with precious stones, and jacinths [sapphires?] and pearls, down to the soles of his feet, that is to say, sandals.

And he went to the altar, and then went forth to the pulpit, and addressed the people and admonished them. And he consecrated the mysteries and gave the Eucharistic mystery to Rabban Sauma first of all—he having confessed his sins—and the Pope pardoned his transgressions and his sins and those of his fathers. And Rabban Sauma rejoiced greatly in receiving the Eucharistic mystery from the hand of Mâr Pâpâ. And he received it with tears and sobs, giving thanks to God and meditating upon the mercies which had been poured out upon him.

Afterwards, on the day of the holy Passover (Thursday) Mâr Pâpâ went to the church of Mâr John the Baptist, where a large number of people had gathered together. He went up into a great furnished and decorated chamber which was there—and before this upper chamber there was a large open space—and the cardinals, and the metropolitans, and the bishops went with him; and they began to recite a prayer. And when the prayer was ended, Mâr Pâpâ addressed and admonished the congregation, according to custom; and by reason of the great multitude of people that was there not one word could be heard except "amen." And when "amen" was uttered, the ground shook through the outcries of the people. Then Mâr Pâpâ came down from that place and stood before the altar, and he consecrated the oil of anointing. And afterwards he consecrated the mysteries which bestow pardon, and gave the Eucharistic mystery to the people. And he went forth from that place and entered the nave, and gave to each of the reverend fathers two gold "leaves" and thirty silver coins, and then went out. And Mâr Pâpâ gathered together the people of his palace household, and he washed their feet, and he wiped them with a napkin which he had wrapped round his loins, to the end. And when he had finished all the service of the Passover, at midday he made a great feast, and the servants placed before every man his portion of food. Now those who sat at meat were two thousand, more or less. And when they removed the bread from the table only three hours of the day were left.

And on the following day, which was the Passion of our Redeemer, Mâr Pâpâ put on a black cloak, and all the reverend fathers did likewise. And they went forth barefooted and walked to the church of my Lord, the Adorable Cross; and Mâr Pâpâ did homage to it, and kissed it, and gave it to each one of the reverend fathers. And when the crowds of people saw it they uncovered their heads, and they knelt down on their knees and adored it. Then Mâr Pâpâ addressed and admonished the people, and at the same time he made the sign of the cross over the four quarters of the world. And when the service of prayer was concluded, he brought some of the Paschal Offering, and set wine with it, and Mâr Pâpâ partook by himself of that offering (now it is not customary for Christians to offer up the offering on the day of the Passion of our Redeemer), and went back to his palace.

And on the day of the Sabbath of Light Mâr Pâpâ went to the church, and they read the books of the Prophets, and the prophecies concerning the Messiah. And he placed in position the baptismal font, and arranged branches of myrtle around about it, and Mâr Pâpâ consecrated the baptism water and baptized three children, and signed them with the sign of the cross. Then he went to the apse and changed his apparel of the Passion and he put on his ceremonial vestments, to state the price of which is beyond the power of words, and he celebrated the holy mysteries.

And on the day of the Sunday of the Resurrection Mâr Pâpâ went to the holy church of my Lady Mary. And he and the cardinals, and the metropolitans, and the bishops, and the members of the congregation saluted each other, and they kissed each other on the mouth, and he celebrated the mysteries, and they received the Eucharistic mystery, and then he returned to his palace. And he made a great feast, and there was infinite gladness. And on the following Sunday Mâr Pâpâ performed the laying on of hands, and he consecrated three bishops. And Rabban Sauma and his companions saw the use followed, and they celebrated the blessed festivals with them.

And when these things had taken place Rabban Sauma asked Mâr Pâpâ for his command to return. And Mâr Pâpâ said unto him, "We wish thee to remain with us, and to abide with us, and we will guard thee like the pupil of our eye." But Rabban Sauma replied, "O our Father, I came on an embassy for your service. If my coming had been the result of my personal wish, I would willingly bring to an end the days of this my useless life in your service at the outer door of your palace. But I must return, and I believe that when I go back and show the kings who are there the benefits which thou hast conferred upon my poor person, that the Christians will gain great content thereby. Now I beseech Your Holiness to bestow upon me some of the relics of the saints which ye have with you."

And Mâr Pâpâ said, "If we had been in the habit of giving away these relics to the people who come in myriads, even though the relics were as large as the mountains, they would have come to an end long ago. But since thou hast come from a far country, we will give thee a few." And he gave to Rabban Sauma a small piece of the apparel of our Lord Christ, and a piece of the kerchief of my Lady Mary, and some small fragments of the bodies of the saints that were there. And he sent to Mâr Yahbhallâhâ a crown for his head which was of fine gold, and was inlaid with precious stones; and sacred vestments made of red cloth through which ran threads of gold; and socks and sandals on which real pearls were sewn;

and the ring from his finger; and a bull which authorized him to exercise patriarchal dominion over all the children of the East. And he gave to Rabban Sauma a bull which authorized him to act as visitor-general over all Christians. And Mâr Pâpâ blessed him, and he caused to be assigned to him for expenses on the road one thousand, five hundred *mathkâlê* [$2,100] of red gold. And to King Arghun he sent certain gifts. And he embraced Rabban Sauma and kissed him and dismissed him. And Rabban Sauma thanked our Lord who had held him to be worthy of such blessings as these.

And Rabban Sauma returned. He crossed the seas which he crossed when he came, and he arrived in peace at the place where King Arghun was, sound in body, and with soul safely kept. And he gave to him the letter of blessings, and the gifts which he had brought from Mâr Pâpâ and from all the kings of the Franks. And he showed him how they had welcomed him with love, and how they had hearkened gladly to the royal dispatches which he had carried to them, and he related the wonderful things which he had seen, and the power of their kingdoms. And King Arghun rejoiced, and was glad, and thanked him, and said unto him, "We have made thee to suffer great fatigue, for thou art an old man. In future we shall not permit thee to leave us; nay, we will set up a church at the gate of our kingdom [*i.e.* palace], and thou shalt minister therein and recite prayers." And Rabban Sauma said, "If my lord the king would command Mâr Yahbhallâhâ, the Catholicus, to come and receive the gifts which have been sent to him by Mâr Pâpâ, and the sacred vestments which he destined for him, he could set up the church which the king is going to set up at the door of his kingdom, and consecrate it." And these things took place in this way.

CHAPTER SIX

RECOLLECTIONS OF THE CUSTOMS OF CAMBODIA

RECOLLECTIONS OF THE CUSTOMS OF CAMBODIA[1]

INTRODUCTION

Chen-la, as the country is called by the Chinese, is also called Chan-la (after it had conquered Champa in 1199). Locally its name is Cambodia. [An early ninth-century historian says the royal family took its name from the name of a fruit: red and white, round and streaked with three lines, it had the traits thought desirable in the women of Kamboja.]

Embarking at Wen-chou and sailing south-southwest, one passes the cities which lie on the coast of Tonkin and Kwang-tung; one crosses the Sea of Paracels and the Sea of Chiao-chih and arrives at Champa. Thence, with a good wind, in fifteen days it is possible to reach Chen-pu, the frontier of Cambodia. From Chen-pu, steering southwest by west, one crosses the Sea of K'un-lun and comes to the delta of a river. Of the score of mouths through which the river debouches, only the fourth has a channel; all the others have sand banks on which large boats can run aground. All that meets the eye are high rushes, dead trees, yellow sand, and white reeds; there are no land-marks and even mariners have trouble locating the real channel. From the beginning of the channel a gentle current permits a ship to reach Ch'a-nan, one of the Cambodian provinces in the north, in about fifteen days. At Ch'a-nan one changes to a smaller boat, and with a favoring current, one passes the midway village of Pan-lu-ts'un, then the village of

[1] By Chou Ta-kuan, A.D. 1296. Translation from Pelliot, *Bulletin de l'École Française d'Extreme Orient,* No. 1 (123), 1902, pp. 137–177.

Buddha, called Fo-ts'un, and so traversing the Tonle-sap, a name derived from the Cambodian word for fresh-water pond, one arrives at Gan-pang, about seventeen miles from the city. [Though Angkor is not mentioned by name, it is the city Chou Ta-kuan refers to.]

According to our Chinese text, *The Description of the Barbarians*, Cambodia measures some 2500 miles: to the north, after fifteen days' journey, one reaches Champa; to the southwest, at the same distance, is Siam; and ten days' journey farther south lies P'an-yu; to the east is the ocean. Formerly this country was engaged in active trade.

When our divine Chinese Dynasty received the august Mandate from Heaven and spread out over the four seas, the General So-tu was charged to bring law and order to Champa. He dispatched two officers with their sizable commands, but they were all captured and did not return. In the sixth month of 1295, our sacred emperor sent an ambassador with an official communication, and I was charged with the duty of accompanying him as commercial attaché. The second month of the following year I left Ming-chou and on the twentieth we embarked at Wen-chou; the fifteenth of the third month we arrived at Champa. From there we were so troubled by contrary winds that we only reached our destination in the autumn, the sixth month. We received homage before we returned to our ships. We stayed there almost a year. On the twelfth day of the eighth month, 1297, we dropped anchor at Ssu-ming. It goes without saying that the customs and the activities of the country cannot be completely known in so short a time, but it is possible to discern the principal traits.

THE WALLED CITY:

[Pelliot identifies this as Yasodharapura, the city, named for its builder, Yasovarman I, built around A.D. 900. Chou Ta-kuan's description is in remarkable agreement with what the archeologists have found.]

The wall around the town measures almost seven miles. It has five identical gates, each one flanked by two side gates; there is one gate on each side, except on the east side, where there are two. Above each gate are five stone Buddha heads; the faces are turned to the west and the central one is decorated with gold. Elephants carved in stone are on both sides of the gates. Outside the wall there is a wide moat crossed by impressive bridges which lead to causeways. On both sides of the bridges are fifty-four stone demons, that, like the statues of generals, look mighty and terrible. The bridge parapets are of stone, carved in the shape of nine-headed serpents. The fifty-four demons hold the serpents in their hands as though to prevent their escaping. The wall is about twenty-four feet high and is made of stone blocks fitted very carefully together so as to leave no cracks where wild grasses can take root. There are no battlements. Certain places on the ramparts are sown with a special plant [*Caryota ochlaudra*, one of the fish-tail palms]. At intervals there are tiny empty houses. On the interior of the wall are ramps more than one hundred feet long with large gates at the summit; these are closed at night and opened in the morning. Gatekeepers prevent slaves and criminals who have had their toes cut off from passing. The walls form a square and in each corner four stone towers rise. At the center of the royal city is a tower of gold surrounded by more than twenty stone towers and hundreds of stone cells. On the east side, two golden lions flank a bridge of gold and eight gold Buddhas are placed at the foot of stone cells.

A third of a mile to the north of the gold tower and even higher than it is a copper tower from where the view is truly impressive. At its foot are more than ten small stone houses. Another third of a mile to the north is the king's residence and attached to his sleeping quarters is still another tower of gold. It is such monuments, we think, which from the first have inspired Chinese merchants to praise Cambodia, as a land rich and noble. On leaving from the south gate one soon comes to a stone tower. This, it is said, was erected in one night by Lu Pan. [Chou Ta-kuan's reference to Angkor Vat as the tomb of Lu Pan, the Chinese legendary patron god of architects, was the Chinese version of a local legend that attributed the building of so great a structure to Visnukarman the divine artisan, and architect of the Indians. Pelliot suggests that Chou Ta-kuan's silence on Angkor Vat—he merely notes that it contains several hundred small, stone houses—creates the impression that Angkor Vat was forbidden to the Chinese.]

The eastern lake, about three miles beyond the east wall, is more than thirty miles in circumference. Rising above it is a stone tower and small, stone houses. Inside the tower is a bronze statue of the sleeping Buddha from whose navel water constantly flows.

About two miles to the north of the city is the north lake. It contains dozens of small, stone houses, a square tower of gold, a golden lion, a golden Buddha, and an elephant, bull and horse of bronze; nothing is missing.

HABITATIONS:

The palace, the official buildings, and the mansions of the nobles are oriented to the east. The palace, to the north of the tower of gold and the golden bridge, has many towers encircled by a wall some three miles long. The tiles of the private apartments are of lead, while those of the walls are of earth and yellow-colored. The bridge rests on gigantic piles; the Buddhas are carved and painted; the scale is magnificent. The long pavilion and covered corridors have an audacious irregularity; there is no enforced symmetry. The windows of the council hall are framed in gold and to the right and left of them are square columns on which are hung some forty or fifty mirrors. Beneath them is a frieze depicting elephants. I have heard it said that the interior of the palace has many marvels; but it is impossible to see them because the prohibitions against entering are very strict. Such is the golden tower in the palace on whose summit is the king's bedroom. The native inhabitants claim that in the tower lives the spirit of a nine-headed serpent, lord of the ground of the entire kingdom, who nightly assumes the form of a woman. It is with this supernatural being that the king first sleeps and then unites. Even the first wives of the king dare not enter the tower. Later, at the second watch, the king may leave and go to sleep with his wives and concubines. If one night the serpent spirit does not appear, it heralds the moment of the king's death; if for a single night the king fails to keep his appointment, some calamity will fall.

The residences of the princes and high officials are different in style and size from those of the ordinary people. The rank of each official determines the size of his home. All public buildings and special dwellings are covered with thatch; only the family shrine and private apartments can be roofed with tile. The homes of the ordinary people are covered with thatch and they would not dare use tiles. Again, their size depends on their owner's means, but in no case dare they imitate the style of the noble mansions.

CLOTHES:

All—from the nobles on down, men and women alike—wear their hair twisted in a chignon; their shoulders are bare. They simply wrap a piece of cloth around their loins. When they go out, they drape a large scarf over the smaller one. They have materials of many different qualities; that used by a noble is worth two or three ounces of gold—it is exquisite in color and sheerness of weave. Even though they weave cloth in this country, the fabrics used by the nobles are imported from Siam or Champa; those most highly prized are the gossamer pieces brought from the western sea (the muslins of Dacca).

Only the prince may wear patterned materials. His crown of gold is high and pointed like those on the heads of the mighty gods. When he does not wear his crown, he wreathes his chignon in garlands of sweet-scented jasmine. His neck is hung with ropes of huge pearls (they weigh almost three pounds); his wrists and ankles are loaded with bracelets and on his fingers are rings of gold set with cats' eyes. He goes barefoot—the soles of his feet, like the palms of his hands, are rouged with a red stuff. When he appears in public he carries the Gold Sword.

Among the people, women are allowed to tint the soles of their feet and the palms of their hands; men do not dare. High officials as well as the nobles are permitted to wear material on which there is a scattering of flowers; the palace attendants are permitted to use cloth with two sprigs of flowers, while among the common people, only women are permitted this. A Chinese, recently arrived, wore cloth decorated all over with flower sprigs—he was not punished because he did not know the rules.

FUNCTIONARIES:

In this country there are counselors, generals, astronomers, and so forth, and, under them, all kinds of minor officials. They differ from us only in their titles. Most of the time they choose nobles for the high positions. Otherwise, those who are appointed send their daughters to be royal concubines. Their insignia as well as their following is determined by rank: the highest dignitaries have palanquins with gold shafts and four gold-handled parasols; some of their followers have the same right to the gold-shafted palanquin but are limited to one gold-handled parasol; some have only the latter. Then come officials whose palanquins have silver shafts—it is the rank which dictates whether an official has the right to gold or to silver, to one or to many honorific parasols. These parasols are made of a red Chinese taffeta, and have thick fringes that hang to the ground. The umbrellas, which they also use, are made of oiled green taffeta and have short fringes.

THE THREE RELIGIONS:

[Chou Ta-kuan interpreted the local traditions to correspond with his own Chinese terms and customs.]

The three religions are those of the Scholars, the Monks, and the Taoists. [Pan-ch'i, which seems to indicate *pandit*, or Brahmans; Ch'ou-ku, Buddhist monks, and *pa-ssu-wei*, the Cambodian "Taoists," might be, Pelliot thinks, priests of a special cult of the Hindu god, Siva.] I do not know whom the scholars worship: they have nothing that resembles a school or any place of instruction whatsoever; it is difficult to know what books they read. Except for a white cord which is worn around the neck and which never leaves them as long as they live, they dress like everyone else. The *pan-ch'i* who assume duties become high officials.

The Buddhist monks, *ch'ou-ku*, shave their heads, wear yellow garments which leave their right shoulder bare; over the lower part of the body, they knot a skirt of yellow cloth. They go barefoot. Their temples are roofed with tile and contain a single statue which they call *Po-lai* and that in every respect resembles the Sakymuni Buddha. It is made out of clay, is painted vermilion and blue, and is dressed in red. These temple Buddhas are very different from those on the towers, which are cast bronze. There are no bells, no drums or cymbals, no offerings of silk hangings, no dais. The monks eat fish and meat, but drink no wine. In their offerings to Buddha, they include fish and meat. They have one daily meal with a family who invites them, because there is no kitchen in the monasteries. They recite from a great number of sacred texts written on palm leaves neatly piled up. On the leaves are black letters, but since they use neither paint brush nor ink, I do not know how they were written. Certain monks who have the right to use a palanquin with gold or silver shafts and to a parasol similarly ornamented are those whom the prince consults on grave matters. There are no Buddhist nuns.

The *pa-ssu-wei* are dressed like everyone else except for a red or white headcloth, which is like the *ku-ku* worn by Tartar women but is worn a little lower. Their temples, which may be tile, are smaller than those of the Buddhists and it does not seem that Taoism has achieved the prosperity of Buddhism. Their cult image is nothing but a block of stone, much like the altar stone of the God of the Soil in China. [Pelliot believes this is a *linga*.] I really do not know what God they worship. There are Taoist nuns. These Taoist priests do not share the food of other men and do not eat in public; they do not drink wine. I have never seen them recite prayers or perform acts of merit for others. The children of the laymen who attend school are taught by these priests; when they grow up they return to secular life. I was not able to learn the details of everything.

THE INHABITANTS:

The Cambodians remind me of the *Man*, our southern barbarians: they are coarse-featured and very dark. Whether they live in distant villages, or on the islands in the sea, or in the heart of the city—they all look alike. Only when one meets the people at the palace and the women of noble homes does one find many who are as white as jade, a condition probably due to their never going out in the sun. Women as well as men wear only a loin cloth and expose the upper part of their bodies; their breasts are as white as milk. They, too, wear their hair in a chignon and go barefoot, even the king's wives.

The king has five wives; one for the private apartment of which I spoke and the other four for the four cardinal directions. I have heard that the concubines and the palace girls number from three thousand to five thousand and are divided into several classes; they rarely appear outside the palace grounds. For my own part, I can say that each time I saw the king he was accompanied by his first wife and sat at the Golden Window of his private apartment. The courtiers ranged themselves on the veranda under the window on either side waiting their turn to look at them. I was able to catch a glimpse. Any family blessed with a beautiful daughter does not miss the opportunity to bring her to the palace. Of lower rank are the women who serve in the palace—not less than one or two thousand—who are married and live where they choose. They shave off the front part of their hair in the manner of the northern people and place a vermilion mark there as well as on both temples. This is their distinctive mark. These are the only women permitted to enter the palace; those of lower ranks dare not. There are always numbers of them on the road passing to and from the palace. Where the ordinary women do not wear hairpins, combs, or any other hair ornaments, or gold bangles, or gold rings, these palace women deck themselves out in all. Men and women anoint themselves with perfumes of sandalwood, musk, and other scents.

Everyone worships the Buddha.

In this country groups of homosexuals go to the market place every day where they try to attract the Chinese, hoping for expensive presents. It is hideous; it is undignified.

CHILDBIRTH:

When a woman has just given birth, she cooks rice, rolls it in salt, and applies it to her sexual parts. After a day and a night she removes it and thus her pregnancy has no unpleasant results; the woman preserves a girlish appearance. When I first heard this, I was astonished and could hardly believe it. But I was able to see this for myself when, in the family where I lived, a girl gave birth to a baby, and the very next day she carried her infant when she went to bathe in the river. It is really extraordinary!

It is said that the women of this country are very lascivious. A day or two after giving birth they sleep with their husbands. When a husband does not satisfy their desires, they abandon him. If the husband is called away for a lengthy period, the wife may remain faithful for several nights, but after a fortnight, she will usually say, "I'm not a ghost; how can I sleep alone?" To such lengths their depravity carries them! I have heard that there are some who do remain faithful. The women age rapidly; probably because they marry young and have children too early. At twenty or thirty, they look like Chinese women of forty and fifty.

THE YOUNG GIRLS:

The parents of a daughter generally offer up this prayer: "May you be desired by men! May a hundred thousand husbands ask your hand in marriage!"

When the daughter of a rich family is between seven and nine years—for the daughter of a poor man it is after she is eleven—they entrust her to a Buddhist or Taoist priest to be ceremonially deflowered. Each year an official sets a day in the early summer and it is announced throughout the land. Every family with an eligible daughter notifies the official, who gives the family a wax taper on which he has made a mark. On the designated day, when night falls, the taper is lit and, when it has burned down to the mark, the moment for the ceremony has come. A month, or fifteen days, to even ten days before, the family has selected a Buddhist or Taoist priest from those living near a Buddhist or Taoist temple. Certain monks have a regular clientele and those who are well known are preferred by the officials and the rich; for poor people there is no choice. Wealthy families and those in the official class present the monks with gifts of wine, rice, fabrics, silks, betel nut, and even money—as much as one hundred *piculs*, which is worth two to three hundred Chinese silver *taels*. The presents of the less well-to-do amount to ten, twenty, thirty, or forty *piculs*, according to their generosity. If a poor girl gets to be eleven years old without having had the ceremony, it is because her parents cannot afford it. For such unfortunates, there are priests who refuse presents and perform the ceremony without pay; theirs is considered a meritorious deed because a monk can deflower only one girl a year; once a monk has accepted, he cannot promise to perform the ceremony on any others.

The night itself is celebrated with music and a great feast is prepared for the relatives and neighbors. Outside the door a platform is erected on which many clay figurines of men and animals are placed; it is left up for a week. The poor do not observe this ancient custom. Then, with palanquins, parasols, and music they go out to call on the monk and bring him back with them. Two pavilions made out of many-colored silk have been set up—in one the young girl sits, in the other the monk. No one knows what they say to one another for the music is deafening. On that night it is not forbidden for music to disturb the peace.

I have been told that, when the moment comes, the monk enters the girl's pavilion; he deflowers her with his hand, which he then dips in wine. It is said that the father and mother, all the relatives and neighbors, use it to mark their foreheads. I have also been told that they taste it. Some say the monk actually unites with the young girl, others say he does not. Because the Chinese cannot witness the ceremony, they do not really know what happens. Just before daybreak the same procession of palanquins, parasols, and music escorts the monk. It is then, as if to redeem the young girl from the monk, that he is presented with gifts of fabrics and silks; otherwise she is considered to be his forever and will not be able to marry anyone else. When I was there, the ceremony took place in the early summer of 1297.

Sometimes more than ten families on the same street will be celebrating the ceremony and the parties who are conducting the monks pass each other. There is no place where the deafening music is not heard.

The girl, who before the ceremony had slept close to her parents, is now excluded from their room and goes where she wants without constraint or surveillance. When a marriage does take place, it is the custom to present the couple with gifts of fabrics, but it is a formality without much importance. Often men marry girls whom they have had as mistresses and this occasions neither shame nor astonishment.

THE SAVAGES:

There are two kinds of savages: those who know the language and are sold as slaves; the other are those who do not understand the language and could not adapt themselves to civilization. The latter have no permanent dwelling places, but, followed by their families, wander in the mountains carrying their few provisions in clay jars on their heads. If they find a wild animal, they will kill it with spears or bows and arrows, make a fire by striking stones together, cook the animal, eat it in common, and continue their wandering. Ferocious by nature, they use deadly poisons. Within their own band, they often kill one another. In recent times a few have started cultivating cardamom and cotton and weaving a cloth that is coarse and irregularly patterned.

SLAVES:

Savages are brought to do the work of servants. When they are young and strong, they fetch a hundred pieces of cloth; old and weak, from thirty to forty. Wealthy families may have more than a hundred; even those of modest means have ten or twenty; only the poor have none at all. The savages inhabit the wild mountains and belong to a different race; they are called *chuangs*, thieves. If, in a quarrel, a man calls another a *chuang*, it is a deadly insult, so despised are the savages, who are considered to be subhuman. Brought to the city, they never dare appear on the street. They are forced to live in the space under the houses which are built on stilts and when they come up into the house to do their work, they must first kneel and make the proper obeisance, prostrating themselves before they can advance. They call their owners "father" and "mother." If they make a mistake, they are beaten. They take their punishment with bent head and without making the slightest movement. The males and females [the words are those applied to animals] couple with each other. No master would ever want to sleep with a female slave. When—and it has happened—that a Chinese, alone and long resident in that country, has relations with a slave woman and this is discovered by her master, he will refuse henceforth to sit down with the Chinese because of what he has done. And if a slave is made pregnant by a stranger, the master does not care to learn the father's identity—he merely regards the infant as another slave to serve his household needs. When an escaped slave is recaptured, his face is marked with a blue sign. Sometimes an iron collar is fastened around his neck, sometimes his arms and legs are chained.

THE LANGUAGE:

This country has its own language. Even though the sounds are fairly similar, the people of Champa and of Siam do not understand each other. In a general way it can be said that they reverse the order of their words. [He gives examples, contrasting the Cambodian word order with that of the Chinese.] The officials have an official style for their deliberations; the scholars speak in a literary manner; the Buddhist monks and Taoist priests have their own language; and different villages speak differently. It is absolutely the same as in China.

WRITING:

Ordinary writing and official messages are written on the skins of deer or stags or sheep tinted black. The skins can be large or small as their fancy dictates. A powder resembling the Chinese "white earth" is pressed into blocks and with this white ink they write on the parchment in letters that do not rub off; to erase it, it must be wiped off with a damp cloth. When they have finished writing, they carry the writing block over their ears. A writer can be easily recognized by his script. Most of the letters resemble those of the Uighurs; writing is done from the left to right and not from top to bottom. Yeh-hsien Hia-ya has said that many of their letters are pronounced almost as those of the Mongols, only two or three are not the same. Formerly they had no seals. When people want to write petitions, they go to stalls where public scribes will write down their message.

NEW YEAR'S DAY AND THE SEASONS:
They chose as their first month the third month of the Chinese [March–April].

In front of the palace, they set up a grandstand capable of holding more than a thousand people and decorate it with lanterns and flowers. Opposite, and some paces away, they make a circle of wood posts about two hundred and fifty feet around and on them weave the scaffolding of a two-hundred-and-fifty-foot stupa. On the top they place fireworks and firecrackers. They may build as many as half a dozen in a single night. The expenditures are borne by the provinces and the nobles. They respectfully invite the king to join them in the festivities and when the night falls they set off the firecrackers and the rockets. The display can be seen for more than thirty miles. The firecrackers are the size of swivel guns and their explosion rocks the entire city.

The officials and nobles who pay for the festivities also distribute tapers and betel nut; their largesse is enormous. To see this spectacle, the king invites the foreign ambassadors. This goes on some fifteen days, and then stops.

Each month has its festival. In the fourth month they "Throw the Ball"; in the ninth they perform the Ya-lieh ceremony, when the entire population passes in review before the palace; on the fifth month they have the "Seek the Waters of the Buddha," when, in the king's presence, the Buddha statues are brought in from all parts of the country and bathed. At another ceremony, "Sailing Boats Over the Land," the king takes a part by appearing on a terrace. On the seventh month they have the festival of "Burning the Rice"; at this time newly ripened rice is burned outside the south gate as an offering to Buddha. Crowds of women, riding in carts or on elephants, celebrate this festival, but the king does not attend. The eighth month, when they dance the Ai-lan, the best musicians are called to the palace daily to furnish the music. During the festival's six days there are cock fights and pig fights and also elephant fights. To this the king again invites the foreign ambassadors. I do not remember exactly what ceremonies took place the other months.

In Cambodia there are men learned in astronomy who can calculate the eclipses of the sun and the moon. For the long months [thirty days] and short months [twenty-nine days] they calculate very differently from our astronomers. They too must have leap years, but they only intercalate the ninth, or the last, month and I do not know the reason. The night is divided into only four watches. Seven days form a cycle [the Indian week in which each day is named for one of the planets]. They have what in the Chinese calendar is called *k'ai-pi-pen-chou* [the twelve signs of good omen]. The twelve animals of the zodiac correspond to those of the Chinese, only their names differ.

These barbarians have neither a family name nor a personal name and do not remember their birth dates. Many take the name of the day on which they were born as their own name. They associate qualities with the days—thus the second day is very treacherous, the third neutral, the fourth inauspicious; on certain days one can travel to the east, and on others to the west. Even women know how to make such calculations.

JUSTICE:

Disputes that involve any of the subjects, no matter how insignificant, come before the king. Previously, they only leveled fines; they did not have any forms of corporal punishment. In very grave cases they do not decapitate or strangle; instead, outside the west gate they dig a ditch, put the criminal in, and fill it up with earth and stones well tamped down. Lesser crimes are punished by cutting off fingers or toes, or amputating an arm. Debauchery and gambling are not forbidden; but if a husband should catch his wife committing adultery, he can squeeze the feet of the lover in a wooden vise until the agony forces the lover to hand over all his wealth. They also have cheats and swindlers.

If a body is found in the street, they drag it off to a waste spot outside the city; no investigation is made. Whoever catches a thief can punish him as he wants.

But they do have one admirable procedure. If an object is lost and the person suspected of having stolen it denies his guilt, he can prove his innocence by submitting to a test. They boil some oil in a pot into which he plunges his hand: if he is guilty, his hand is completely burnt, if he is innocent, his skin appears quite untouched. Such is a method of these barbarians.

If two families quarrel, and it is impossible to say which is right or wrong, they make use of a dozen small, stone towers standing before the palace. Each of the adversaries sits on the top of one while the families cluster at the bottom to keep an eye on the other. After one, two, three, or four days the guilty party reveals himself in some way—either he has developed sores or boils, or he catches cold or a high fever. The innocent party is untouched and healthy. Thus they decide who is right and who is wrong. They call this "celestial justice"—in such ways the deities intervene in the human affairs of this country.

SICKNESS:

The Cambodians are ill frequently. I think this comes from their bathing too often and their incessant washing of their heads. Often they cure themselves. Many lepers are seen on the roads, and though people eat and sleep with them they do not contract their disease. From what they say it seems to be a disease familiar to them. Formerly a king contracted leprosy, but they did not think the less of him for this. It is my humble opinion that they are susceptible to this disease because of their excessive passion and their habit of taking too many baths. I have heard that the Cambodians bathe immediately after satisfying their desires.

Dysentery kills eight or nine out of every ten. Drugs are sold in the market, but they differ completely from those sold in China and I know nothing at all about them. They have sorcerers who practice black magic on the people and are quite laughable.

THE DEAD:

They have no coffins for their dead, only a kind of matting in which they are wrapped. In the funeral procession, they also have draped palls, banners, and musical instruments and scatter burnt rice along the route. Once outside the city, they leave the body in any remote, lonely spot and retire, waiting for vultures or wild beasts to come and devour it. If this is done quickly, they say that the dead relative has been rewarded for his good deeds; if it is not devoured quickly, or only partially, they say that this is due to some sin. Now there are some people who cremate their dead; they are the local descendants of Chinese. After a parent's death, the children do not wear mourning, but the sons shave their heads and the daughters cut the hair above their foreheads, somewhat in the style of our military; it is their mark of filial piety. The king is buried in a tower, but I do not know whether they bury his body or only his bones. [Pelliot notes that Chou Ta-kuan did not distinguish between their three kinds of burial; by fire, by being devoured by vultures, and by water.] After a body has been cremated, the ashes are collected and put into a container—silver or gold for the rich, pottery for the poor—which is then thrown into the river. As for the corpses left for the vultures, this is done as an act of piety in the same spirit that prompted the Buddha to give his flesh to save the life of a pigeon threatened by a famished tigress. Whatever the mode chosen, whether the bodies are cremated or exposed to the vultures, the bones gathered are put into an urn, and thrown into the water.

AGRICULTURE:

Generally, the Cambodians harvest three or four crops a year. Their whole year is like our summer months for they have neither frost nor snow. Half the year it rains every afternoon, the other half not a drop of rain falls. In the late summer and fall it rains every afternoon and the waters of the Great Lake flood until the mighty trees are drowned and only their very tops show. Those who live near the lake take to the mountains. When the rain stops—and not a drop falls in the spring—the Great Lake is only accessible by means of little boats, for the deepest parts are only some three to five feet deep. Then the lake dwellers return.

The cultivators calculate the exact time when the rice is ripe, the time of the flood crest, how much land it will cover, and, following the location of their fields, they sow. They do not use buffalo to plow. Their plows, sickles, and hoes are the same kind as ours but made differently. They also have fields where the harvest comes without sowing, where, as the waters rise, the rice plants also grow. I think it is a special variety. [It is the well-known aquatic rice whose heads float constantly on the surface no matter how rapidly and high the water rises.]

To fertilize their fields, they plant legumes; they do not use animal manure, disdaining it as impure. The Chinese who live there do not talk to them about this, and I think the

Cambodians consider the Chinese method of fertilizing disgusting. Two or three families dig a ditch into which they throw grasses; when the ditch is filled with mulch, they cover it up and scoop out another.

After they have relieved themselves, they go to the pond to wash themselves with their left hands—their right hand is kept clean for eating—and when they see the Chinese, who wipe themselves with paper, they ridicule them and shun them. There are also women who urinate while standing up; it is ridiculous. [This distinction between the impure left hand and the clean right hand was remarked on by the Chinese; it spread from India to Indo-China and the islands.]

PHYSICAL CONFIGURATION OF THE COUNTRY:
After the entry at Chen-pu, the frontier of Cambodia, there is nothing but thickets of low forests; the large estuaries of the mighty river, a hundred miles long, flow through the deep shade of a jungle of old trees and high cane. A concert of animal cries is heard. Midway up the river one sees for the first time the immense plain in which there is not even a stick of wood. As far as one can see there is nothing but grass. There the wild buffalo graze by the hundreds and thousands. Then come avenues of bamboo which stretch for another hundred miles. The trunks of this bamboo have sharp thorns and their young shoots have a very bitter taste. High mountains frame the horizon everywhere.

PRODUCTS:
Many strange trees are found in the mountains and in the clearings, herds of rhinoceros and elephants live, rare birds and many unusual animals are to be found. The most precious articles are the feathers of the kingfisher [valued in Canton to ornament gold jewelry], ivory, rhinoceros horn, and bees-

wax; cardamom and other forest products are more common.

The kingfisher is quite difficult to catch. In the thick woods are ponds and in the ponds are fish. The kingfisher leaves the forest to catch fish. Hidden under the leaves, by the side of the water, the Cambodian crouches. In a cage he has a female bird to attract the male and in his hand a small net. He waits until the bird comes and then catches him in his net. Some days he can catch as many as five; other days he waits vainly for a kingfisher.

Ivory is collected by the hill people. From a dead elephant one secures two tusks. Formerly it was thought that the elephant shed his tusks every year; this is not true. The ivory taken from an animal killed by a spear is the best. Then comes that which is found shortly after the animal has died a natural death; the least valued is that which is found in the mountains years after the death of the elephant.

Beeswax is found in rotted trees standing in the villages. It is produced by winged insects that have thin antlike waists. The Cambodians take it away from the insects; a boatload can carry from two to three thousand honeycombs.

Rhinoceros horn that is white and veined is the most valued; the black variety is of inferior quality.

Cardamom is cultivated in the mountains by the savages. Pepper is also found occasionally. It climbs up bushes and entwines itself like a common weed. The green-blue variety is the most bitter.

TRADE:

In Cambodia, women attend to trade. Even a Chinese who arrives there and takes a woman will profit greatly from her trading abilities. They do not have permanent stores, but simply spread a piece of mat on the ground. Everyone has her own spot. I have heard that they pay an official for the right to a location. In small transactions, one pays in rice, grain, Chinese goods, and, lastly, fabrics; in large transactions they use gold and silver.

In a general way, the country people are very naïve. When they see a Chinese, they address him timidly, respectfully, calling him Fo—Buddha. As soon as they catch sight of him, they throw themselves on the ground and prostrate themselves. Lately some of them have cheated the Chinese and harmed them. This has happened to numbers of those who have gone into the villages.

CHINESE MERCHANDISE DESIRED IN CAMBODIA:
I do not think that Cambodia produces either gold or silver; and what the Cambodians value most is Chinese silver and gold, then silks, lightly patterned in two-toned threads. After these items comes the pewter of Chen-chou, lacquerware from Wen-chou, the blue porcelain of Ch'üan-chou [it was famous in the Middle Ages under the Arab name Zayton], mercury, vermilion, paper, sulphur, saltpeter, sandalwood, irisroot, musk, hemp cloth, umbrellas, iron pots, copper platters, sieves, wood combs, and needles. That which they desire most of all is beans and wheat—but their exportation is forbidden.

PLANTS:
Only pomegranates, sugar cane, lotus flowers and roots, taro, peaches, and bananas are common to Cambodia and China. The lichee and the orange resemble one another, but they are acid. All the other plants are not seen in China. The kinds of trees are many, the flowers even more abundant, beautiful, and sweet-scented; there are a thousand kinds of aquatic flowers, but I do not know their names. They do not have various kinds of plums, apricots, pine, cypress, firs, junipers, pear trees, poplars, willows, cinnamon, orchids, chrysanthemums. At the

beginning of the Chinese year, the lotus flower is already blooming in Cambodia.

BIRDS:

Among the birds the peacock, the kingfisher, the parrot are unknown in China. The others, like the falcon, crow, egret, sparrow, cormorant, swan, crane, wild duck, canary, we also have. They do not have the magpie, the oriole, the swallow, and the pigeon.

ANIMALS:

Their animals are the rhinoceros, elephant, wild buffalo, and the "mountain horse," which are not found in China. There are a great many tigers, panthers, bears, wild boar, deer, stags, wild goats, gibbon, fox, a few lions [now entirely gone], and the *hsing-hsing* [a mythical large ape possessed of extraordinary qualities]. It is needless to mention chickens, ducks, cattle, horses, pigs, and sheep. Their horses are very small, the buffalo abundant, and they are ridden. When the buffalo dies it is neither eaten nor skinned, but left to rot because it is thought that the animals have spent all their strength in man's service. They will work only if yoked to a cart. Formerly they did not have geese, but, thanks to sailors who brought them from China, they have lately acquired some. Their rats are as large as cats; they also have a species of rat whose head is exactly like a dog's.

EDIBLE PLANTS:

Among their edible plants are onions, mustard, leeks, eggplant, melons, pumpkins; they do not have radishes, lettuce, chicory, or spinach. They have gourds by the first of the year; the plants continue to yield for several years. The cotton tree grows higher than their houses; it lasts more than ten years.

They also have many vegetables whose name I do not know; and also many edible aquatic plants.

FISH AND REPTILES:

Among the fish and turtles it is the black carp which is in greatest plenty. The false carp are also plentiful. There are "spitting fish" [dolphins], the big ones weighing a great deal. I do not know the names of all of the fish found in the Great Lake; they also have numbers of sea fish of all kinds and eels and congers. The Cambodians do not eat the frogs which croak along the roads the whole night. Tortoises and lizards they eat; the crayfish are huge. There are crocodiles as large as a canoe; they have four feet and look just like a dragon without horns. In the Great Lake one can gather bivalves —oysters, clams, mussels. Crabs are not seen; I think there are crabs but that the people do not eat them.

FERMENTED DRINKS:

They have four kinds of wine. The first, which the Chinese call "honey wine," is made by fermenting a mixture of half honey, half water. The second, which the Cambodians call *p'eng-ya-ssu,* takes its name and composition from its being made from the leaves of the tree of that name. The third is a rice wine, made from either raw or cooked rice. The last kind is a wine made out of sugar cane. In addition, the people who live far inland have a wine made by fermenting the juice of the *chiao,* a plant which grows along the river banks.

SALT, VINEGAR, SOY, LEAVENING:

No obstacles are put in the way of the production of salt. At several places along the seacoast, they evaporate the water by cooking. In the mountains a mineral which gives a salt flavor is found; it is hard enough to be carved in any shape.

The Cambodians do not know how to make vinegar. When they want a liquid with an acid flavor, they use a concoction of the leaves of the *hsien-p'ing* tree. If the tree has buds, or shoots, they use them; if the tree has run to seed, they use the seeds. They do not have any way to prepare soy, lacking both the necessary grain and bean. They do not ferment any of their grains.

RAISING SILKWORMS:

The Cambodians do not raise silkworms. Recently the Siamese have taught them how to raise silkworms; the mulberry trees and silkworms came from Siam. Their women do not know the art of sewing but only how to weave cotton cloth. Furthermore, they spin by hand, having no spinning wheels; nor do they have proper looms for weaving. Instead, they attach one end of the cloth to their belt and do their weaving at the other. A bamboo sliver serves as a shuttle. They do not have *ramie* [a plant of the nettle family whose fine fibers are woven] but only a kind of hemp. It is the Siamese who weave a kind of dark silk tussah for their clothes and who also know how to sew and mend. When a Cambodian tears his clothes, he hires a Siamese to repair them.

UTENSILS:

Middle-class people have houses but no table or bench, pan or pail. To cook their rice they use an earthen pot; to prepare the sauce, they cook on an earthen stove. Three stones set in the ground form their hearths and a coconut shell is their soup ladle. They serve rice either on Chinese plates of pottery or copper. They put the sauce into little cups made of a twisted leaf, which, even when filled with liquid, holds it without letting it spill. The leaves of the *chiao* are made into a little spoon and pusher, and when they are through using them, they throw them away. They do the same when they make their offering to Buddha and the spirits. At mealtime, they have a basin of pewter or earthenware by their side into which they dip their fingers before taking the rice. If they did not wet their hands the rice would stick to their fingers and make it impossible for them to handle the morsels of rice. [Chopsticks, first mentioned in the third century, was an important invention in the history of manners. Their use indicated that the Chinese had progressed beyond the level of eating with their fingers.]

Wine is drunk from pewter goblets; earthen porringers are used by the poor. In the homes of the nobles and wealthy, they use sometimes silver goblets, sometimes golden ones. Golden containers of many sizes and different shapes are used in the numerous Cambodian festivals.

They spread fine mats, or skins of tiger, panther, and deer, or even rush mats on the ground, though lately they have started using low tables, about a foot high. They sleep on matting spread over wooden planks, but they are beginning to use beds usually made by the Chinese. They cover their table utensils with a cloth; in the palace the king uses gold brocades presented to him by foreign merchants.

They do not use millstones to husk the rice, but mortars.

CARRIAGES AND PALANQUINS:

The Cambodian palanquins are fashioned out of a single piece of wood which is bent in the middle and raised at both ends. Carved with flower motifs, they are then covered with sheets of gold or silver foil to make what they call a gold or silver palanquin. About a foot from each end a hook is driven in and to these hooks they tie on a large piece of pleated material; in this hammocklike conveyance a passenger is carried by two men. In addition to this two-man palanquin, they have another kind, where the hammock is larger than the sail of a ship and decorated with figured silk. Four men carry this, following the smaller one on the run. When they take a long trip, they go on elephantback, horseback, and in carts, the same as in other countries, only the horses have no saddles and the elephants no howdah for the rider.

BOATS AND OARS:

The large boats are made out of hardwood planks. Because the shipwrights have no saws and rely solely on the ax, their work is long and difficult. For carving out of wood—even to decorate a house—they use the chisel. In boat building they use iron nails and cover the hulk with *chiao* leaves, held together by palm lathes. A boat of this kind is called a *sin-na* and is moved by oars. The boats are caulked with a mixture made out of fish fat and a heated mineral. Small boats are hollowed out of a large tree which has been softened by fire and scraped by wood; these boats are deep and commodious in the center and pointed at both ends. They can carry several persons; they have no sail and are steered by a paddle. They are called *p'i-lan*.

VASSAL GOVERNMENTS:

There are more than ninety vassal states: Chen-p'u, Ch'a-nan, Pa-chien, Mu-liang, Pa-hsieh, P'u-mai, Chih-ku, Mu-chin-po, Lai-kan-k'eng, and Pa-ssu-li. I cannot recall the others. Each one has its officials and each is protected by a wooden palisade.

VILLAGES:

Every village has a temple or stupa. However small the population, they have an official called *mai-shih*. There are rest houses along the main routes, as we have for our postal relays. These are called *sen-mou*. In the recent war with Siam the country was utterly devastated.

HARVEST OF GALL:

Formerly, in the eighth month gall was collected. This was done because every year the king of Champa demanded a jar filled with human gall; gall from thousands of persons was needed for the amount required. Men were stationed in many places in the cities and villages and when they found anyone abroad at night, they threw a bag over the victim's head, pulled the string tight, and with a little knife extracted the gall from the right side of his back. They kept this up until they had secured enough to offer the king. They never take the gall from a Chinese, because one year they did and when they mixed it with that of the others the whole jarful spoilt and could not be used.

Recently this custom has been abolished, but there still exists an official collector of gall who lives in the city near the north gate. [Pelliot notes that this custom actually took place in Indo-China. They held the Far Eastern belief that the gall bladder was the seat of courage—in Chinese they are the same word. The gall of animals, like that of humans, had an honored place in the Chinese pharmacopoeia.]

PHENOMENON:

In the city, by the east gate, there was a Cambodian barbarian who had incestuous relations with his sister. The two bodies remained united, and after three days passed without their taking any nourishment, they both died. A Chinese who has lived here more than thirty years affirms that he has seen this happen twice. Nevertheless, all this does not prove the supernatural intervention of the Buddha.

BATHS:

Cambodia is terribly hot: it is unthinkable to let a day pass without bathing several times and even once or twice during the night. Formerly, there were no bathhouses or tubs; either a family had a kind of pool, or two or three families shared one in which everyone went naked, men and women together. However, when the father, the mother, or the older people were in the pool, the sons and daughters or other young people did not enter. Or, if the young people were already bathing, the older ones would leave them alone. But those of the same age are not squeamish—a person simply covers his or her sex with the left hand, slips into the water, and that is that.

Every few days small groups of city women go to the river outside the walls. On the river bank, they untie the cloth they have worn and, quite naked, go into the water. Even noblewomen go there to swim and feel no shame; everyone can see them from head to feet. So in the large river outside the city there is never a day in which this does not take place. The Chinese, on their day of leisure, often go there to watch. I have heard that there are some people who while in the water take advantage of the opportunity.

The water is always as hot as though heated over a fire; only at the last night watch does it cool off a little. As soon as the sun rises, it again becomes very warm.

THE ARMY:

The troops go naked and barefoot. They hold a lance in their right hand and a shield in their left. The Cambodians have neither bows nor arrows, war machines nor bullets, helmets nor armor. It is said that in the war against the Siamese everyone was obliged to fight, but they had no knowledge of tactics or strategy.

THE PRINCE'S APPEARANCES IN PUBLIC:

I have heard it said that in earlier times the ruler never set foot outside his palace; if by some chance he did, even his footprints were respected.

The new king is the son-in-law of the old one. Having made

his career in the army, he had married one of the king's favorite daughters, who stole her father's Golden Sword (insignia of power) and presented it to her husband. The king's son, robbed of his succession, plotted to raise troops; when the new king learned of this he cut off the prince's toes and had him confined to a dark prison. The new king wears a suit of iron armor which even daggers or arrows cannot pierce. With this to protect him, he dares to go out. In the year I spent in Cambodia I saw him go out four or five times.

When the king leaves the palace, first comes the cavalry, leading his escort, followed by an array of standards, banners, and music. Next comes a troupe of palace girls, anywhere from three to five hundred, dressed in flowered material, their heads garlanded with flowers and holding large candles lighted even in broad daylight. After them come more palace girls bearing the royal utensils of gold and silver and an assortment of all kinds of ornaments whose usage I don't understand. Then come the palace girls who, armed with lance and shield, form the king's private bodyguard; they, too, form a troupe. They are followed by carriages ornamented in gold and drawn by goats and horses. Ministers and nobles mounted on elephants look straight ahead, while clustered around them are their many, many red parasols of rank. After them in palanquins, carriages, and on elephants come the king's wives and concubines; they have more than a hundred parasols decorated in gold. Behind them comes the king. Holding the precious sword, he stands on the royal elephant, whose tusks are encased in gold. More than twenty white parasols, gold-trimmed and with golden handles, surround him. A great many elephants form a cordon around the king and the cavalry guards him.

If the king leaves the palace for a nearby visit, he uses only a golden palanquin, which is carried by four palace girls.

Most of such visits are made to a small gold pagoda before which is a gold Buddha. Those who see the king must prostrate themselves and touch the ground with their foreheads. They call this obeisance *san-pa.* Anyone who fails to show proper respect is seized by the attendant guards, who punish the offender before releasing him.

Twice each day the king holds an audience to conduct the affairs of government. There is no set procedure. Whoever desires to see the king—either officials or any private person—sits on the ground and awaits him. After a little while, one hears, far off in the palace, distant music; outside they blow on conchs to announce his approach. I have heard that he uses only a gold palanquin and does not come from very far away. An instant later, two palace girls lift the curtain on the Golden Window and the king, sword in his hand, appears. All those present—ministers and people—clasp their hands together and beat their foreheads on the ground. As the sound of the conchs ceases, they can raise their heads. At the king's pleasure, they may approach and sit down on a lion skin, which is considered a royal object. When all matters are disposed of, the king retires, the two palace girls let the curtain fall; everyone rises. Thus one sees that, though this country is barbarous and strange, they do not fail to know what it is to be a king.

CHAPTER SEVEN

CHENG HO'S NAVAL EXPEDITIONS

CHENG HO'S NAVAL EXPEDITIONS[1]

Sea travel was mentioned as early as the Earlier Han Dynasty (202 B.C.–A.D. 9); a description of overseas contacts made during the time of the Emperor Wu (140–86 B.C.) reads: "From the barriers of Jih-nan [Upper Annam], and from Hsü-wen and Ho-p'u [south coast of Kuang-tung], going by boat about five months, there is the country of Tu-yuan. Going again by boat about four months, there is the country of Yi-lu-mo. Going again by boat twenty odd days, there is the country of Shen-li. Going by land about ten odd days, there is the country of Fu-kan-tu-lu. From the country of Fu-kan-tu-lu, going by boat about more than two months, there is the country of Huang-chih. The customs of the people resemble somewhat those of Chu-yai [prefecture in Kuang-tung].

"These water-encircled lands [continents or islands] are large, the population is numerous, and there are many curious products."

After enumerating the countries with whom they engaged in trade, the notice indicates how this trade was organized; certain institutions established in those days were still operative fifteen hundred years later in Ming times (1368–1644). "From the time of Emperor Wu they have all offered tribute. There are at the Chinese court, chiefs of interpreters who are dependent on the 'Yellow Gate' [the Department of Eunuchs]; together with those who volunteer, they go out into the sea

[1] Excerpted from J. J. L. Duyvendak, *China's Discovery of Africa* (London, 1949); and George Phillips, "The Seaports of India and Ceylon," *Journal of the North China Branch of the Royal Asiatic Society*, Vol. 20 N.S., 1885, pp. 209–226.

to buy pearls, glass, rare stones, and curious products, for which they give gold and various silks. The countries where they arrive provide food and companionship. The merchant ships of the barbarians transport [transship] them so as to make them reach their destination; the barbarians also draw profit from the trade and sometimes they loot and kill the people. Moreover there is the hardship that one may meet storms and die by drowning. If these misfortunes do not happen, the voyage out and back takes several years. The big pearls have a circumference of two inches at most. . . .

"In the period Yüan-shih of the Emperor P'ing (A.D. 1–6), Wang Mang [who succeeded as the only emperor of the Hsin Dynasty, A.D. 9–23] desired to exalt the luster of the imperial virtue. He sent rich gifts to the king of Huang-chih, causing him to send an envoy to present a live rhinoceros." The gift is confirmed by a statement in the *Annals:* in A.D. 2, in the spring, the throne's prestige was enhanced by a rhinoceros from Huang-chih and a white pheasant presented by Yüeh-shang (in Indo-China). Whether Huang-chih was also located in Indo-China or in India is not clear; in either case it meant that at that early date the Chinese had trade relations with countries of the Indian Ocean. Of course the entire route was not completed by one ship; the text explicitly says that there were many transshipments in the trade between China and the distant lands of the Indian Ocean.

During the T'ang Dynasty (618–907), sea travel between China and the Western countries increased: Buddhist pilgrims and missionaries came and went—as early as 411 the Chinese monk Fa-hsien returned from India aboard a foreign ship—adding to the knowledge of the Western lands. In a work written by a scholar, who died in 863, and published in a seventeenth-century compilation, appears the first definite information of a country to the west of India, in this case Berbera on the Somali coast.

"The country of Po-po-la is in the southwestern sea. The people do not eat any of the five grains but eat only meat. They often stick a needle into the veins of cattle and draw blood which they drink raw, mixed with milk. They wear no clothes except that they cover the parts below their loins with sheepskins. Their women are clean and chaste. The inhabitants themselves kidnap them, and if they sell them to foreign merchants, they fetch several times their price. The country produces only ivory and ambergris. . . . From olden times they were not subject to any foreign country. In fighting they use elephants' tusks and ribs and the horns of wild buffaloes as lances and they wear cuirasses and use bows and arrows. They have twenty thousand foot soldiers. The Arabs make frequent raids on them."

Po-po-la is mentioned in a much later work (completed about 1226, but utilizing material from an earlier account). It has "four department cities and for the rest the people are all settled in villages which try to gain the supremacy over the others by violence. They serve heaven and do not serve the Buddha [presumably indicating that they were Muslims]. The country produces many camels and sheep and they have camels' meat and milk as well as baked cakes for their regular food. The country produces dragons' saliva [ambergris], big elephants' tusks, and big rhinoceros horns. Some elephant tusks weigh more than a hundred catties [133 pounds] and some rhinoceros horns more than ten catties. There is also much *putchuk* [root of a plant used by Chinese for making joss sticks]; liquid storax gum [fragrant gum resin]; myrrh; and tortoise shell, which is extremely thick and which people from other countries all come to buy. Among the products there is further the so-called camel-crane [ostrich] whose body to the crown is six or seven feet high. It has wings and can fly but not to any great height. Among quadrupeds there is the so-called *tsu-la* [giraffe], striped like a camel and in size like an ox. It is yellow in color. Its front legs are five feet high and its hind legs only three feet. Its head is high up and is turned upwards. Its skin is an inch thick. There is also a mule with red, black, and white stripes wound as girdles around the body. Both these kinds of animals are of the mountains wild. The inhabitants are fond of hunting and from time to time they catch them with poisoned arrows."

The account has a short entry on another African territory, Ma-lin [Melinda, the African port where Vasco da Gama hired Hindu pilots on the first trip to India]. "Southwest from Fu-lin [as the Chinese called the Roman Orient of which Alexandria was the western border] after one traverses the desert for two thousand miles is a country called Ma-lin. Its people are black and their nature is fierce. The land is pestilential and has no herbs, no trees, and no cereals. They feed the horses on dried fish; the people eat *hu-mang* [the Persian date]. They are not ashamed of debauching the concubines of their fathers or chiefs; they are in this respect the worst of the barbarians. They call this: to seek out the proper master and subject. In the seventh moon they rest completely [i.e., Ramadan]. They then do not send out or receive any merchandise in trade and they sit drinking all night long."

During the Southern Sung Dynasty (1127–1279) not only did maritime trade increase considerably but the navy grew from a small service of some 3000 men to an impressive number of squadrons with more than 50,000 men. It was then that the Chinese took control of the coastal sea-lanes and, displacing the Arabs, who had dominated the Indian Ocean trade, carried on a lively commerce with the Malabar coast. Quilon, the port at which Marco Polo's homeward-bound ship called, and Cambay, the busy Gujarat entrepôt, were for a while their farthest trading places. To pay for the luxuries she imported —elephants' tusks and rhinoceros horns, strings of pearls, aromatics, and incense—China exported gold, silver, and copper cash, silks and porcelain. [This last, originally sent as ballast for the light, valuable silk stuffs, quickly created its own market; Chinese Sung porcelain has been dug up in Java, South India, Zanzibar, and the east coast of Africa.]

The three main types of ships, which seem to have already existed in the earlier T'ang times, are classified in the Sung *History:* the largest were called "one-mast ships" and had a tonnage of 1000 *po-lam,* [about 200 tons]; the second class, one third this size, were called "ox-head ships." The third class, one third the tonnage of the second class, were usually foreign craft built for coastal and riverine transport. The early practice of transshipment—costly in time, money, and energy—was not needed when traders had ships capable of sailing the entire distance. We know that Arab traders allowed two years for the voyage to China and back; from Persia to China was a 130- to 140-day voyage. Similarly, a Chinese source states that a ship starting from China in mid-winter would arrive at Lambri, the northwest corner of Sumatra, in about forty days, would spend the summer trading, and, the following season, catching the northeast monsoon, would sail to the country of the Arabs in sixty days. "All sea ships start in the eleventh and twelfth moon with the north wind and come in the fifth and the sixth moon with the south wind."

The enormous expansion of the navy encouraged naval architecture. At the end of the twelfth century, shipwrights had perfected two important inventions, the sternpost rudder and hulls divided into watertight compartments. A Chinese described these fine ocean-going craft. "The ships which sail the Southern Sea and south of it are like houses. When their sails are spread they are like great clouds in the sky. Their rudders are several tens of feet long. A single ship carries several hundred men. It has stored on board a year's supply of grain." Foreigners, too, spoke admiringly of them. Odoric of Pordenona, who visited China in Mongol times, 1260–1368, marveled at ships that carried seven hundred souls in comfort and safety; and Ibn Battuta voyaged on one carrying one thousand. They were broad and almost square—as capacious as the European cogs—and were armed against pirate attacks. These ships had two kinds of sails, cloth and mat, and went before the wind at a steady six knots; Marco Polo says there were usually four masts but some ships had five or six. When there was no wind, the crew had to row. There were four men to an oar and eight to ten oars. Ibn Battuta speaks of a ship with twenty oars. Each ship was furnished with two anchors, stones tied with rattan ropes and worked by a pulley.

Most important was their haven-finding art. In European literature, the first authentic record of the mariner's compass appears at the end of the twelfth century, and no earlier mention has been found in Arabic literature. In China, on the other hand, the polarity of the magnetic needle, as well as its declination, was known in the eighth century, for the Buddhist priest and astronomer Yi-hsing mentioned both properties. Shen Kuo in his "Dream Pool Essay" (about 1086) gave more detailed information: "Taoist geomancers rub the point of a needle with a lodestone, so that it acquires the property of pointing south. But it always declines slightly to the east and is not due south. . . . The best scheme is to suspend it [the needle] by a silk fiber, as follows: take a single thread from a new skein of silk, attach it with wax of the size of a mustard seed to the middle of the needle, and suspend it on a place where there is no wind. Then the needle will always point south. Some are so magnetized as to point north. In my family we have both the south- and the north-pointing needles. The property of the lodestone to point south, like that of the cypress tree to point west, can be explained by nobody."

Though it is clear that the compass was used on land by geomancers, the earliest description of its use by sailors says: "The shipmaster to ascertain his geographic position by night looks at the stars; by day he looks at the sun; in dark weather he looks at the south-pointing needle." [This oft-quoted passage is in a book whose preface is dated 1225; but the writer's information came from his father, who had been governor at Canton from 1099–1102; this, the first date recorded for the use of the mariner's compass by the Chinese, is earlier than any we have for its use by Arab or Mediterranean navigators.]

An offshoot of Chinese trade with the Arab countries was the African goods bought there. During the Sung period there is no evidence that the Chinese themselves ever visited the east coast of Africa. They were, however, aware of the existence of countries far to the west, whose products they loaded on their junks at Arab and Indian ports, and they wrote down whatever information they could glean of African lands and peoples. Thus, the inspector of trade, who had mentioned Berbera, passed on what he had learned of Chung-li:

"Its inhabitants go bareheaded and barefoot. They wrap a cloth around themselves but they dare not wear jackets. Only ministers and the king's courtiers wear jackets and turbans on their heads as a mark of distinction. The king's residence is masoned out of large bricks and slabs of stone; the people's houses are made of palm leaves and are covered with thatch. Their daily fare consists of baked flour cakes, sheep's and camel's milk. Cattle, sheep, and camels are plentiful, and even their 'big food' [food eaten on special occasions] is only this. The country produces frankincense. Many people are addicted to magical tricks: they can change their bodies into the shapes of birds and beasts or aquatic animals, and they frighten or bewilder the ignorant people. If while trading with a foreign ship there is a quarrel, the sorcerers bewitch the ship so it can neither move backward nor forward, and not until the parties to the quarrel have been wise enough to settle the dispute, is it released. The government of the country has strictly forbidden this.

"Every year towards the end of spring, countless numbers of birds of passage alight outside the suburbs. As soon as the sun rises they disappear without a trace. The inhabitants catch them with nets and eat them; their taste is delicious. When summer comes they disappear and are not seen until the following year.

"When one of the inhabitants dies and the body has been placed in a coffin, and they are about to bury him, the kinsmen from far and near come to condole. Swinging swords, they all ask the chief mourners the cause of the death and say, 'If he was killed by the hand of man, we shall revenge him and kill his murderer with this sword.' If the chief mourner replies that the deceased was not murdered, but that he died as the natural result of heaven's decree, then they throw down their swords and burst into violent wailing.

"Every year, regularly, big dead fish are driven on the neighboring coast; they are more than two hundred feet in length and twenty feet high in diameter. The inhabitants do not eat the [whale's] flesh; instead they cut away the brains and marrow as well as the eyes to make oil, getting more than three hundred *teng*. They mix this oil with lime to caulk their boats or use it for their lamps. Poor people use the ribs of these fish to make rafters for their huts, the backbones for door leaves, and they cut off the vertebrae to fashion them into mortars. The country has mountains which are contiguous with Po-po-la [Berbera]. In circumference it is about 4000 *li;* for the most part it is not populated. The mountains produce dragon's blood [the exudation of a leguminous tree, *kati* in Arabic] and aloes, and the waters of the sea produce tortoise shell and ambergris. It is not known where the ambergris comes from; suddenly lumps, sometimes three to five, sometimes ten catties, in weight are washed up on the shore, driven by the wind. The natives vie with one another in dividing it. Sometimes a ship at sea runs across it and picks it up."

[Ambergris, formerly used in cookery but now only in perfumery, is a waxy substance, ashy in color, found floating in tropical seas; it is a morbid secretion in the intestines of the sperm whale. Where on the east coast of Africa Chung-li was, is not certain. Duyvendak believes it did border on the mountains of Berbera (Po-po-la), but he also notes that the practice of using whale oil to caulk ships was known to the people of Yemen, Aden, and Fars, and that huts made of whale bones are mentioned on the Makran coast.]

The text also describes the large island of Madagascar "in the southwestern sea. There are regularly great *p'eng* birds [the now extinct dodo remembered in tales of the legendary roc]. When they fly they obscure the sun for a short time. There are wild camels and if the *p'eng* birds meet them, they swallow them up. If one finds a feather of the *p'eng* bird, by cutting the quill, one can make a water jar of it. [This quill water jar, thought to be the *langana* used by the coast tribes of Madagascar, is a bamboo about six inches in diameter. By perforating all the knots except the one at the end it is converted into a water vessel.] The products of the country are big elephants' tusks and rhinoceros horns. . . . There are many savages. Their bodies are black as lacquer and they have frizzled hair. They are enticed by offers of food and then captured and sold as slaves to the Arabic countries, where they fetch a very high price. They are employed as gate keepers and it is said that they have no longing for their kinfolk."

Egypt, called Misr, also mentioned in a Chinese book, has

a mighty and marvelous river "of very clear and sweet water —the source whence springs this river is not known. If there is a year of drought, the rivers of all other countries get low, this river alone remains as usual, providing an abundance of water for farming purposes, and the people avail themselves of it in their agriculture. Each year it is thus and men of seventy or eighty years of age cannot recollect that it has rained."

All these notices were written before the Chinese had direct contact with the western lands of the African shores; the information they preserved came from the Indian and Arab merchants whom they questioned. Soon after the Ming Dynasty came to power, in an unparalleled effort on the part of the government to reopen distant overseas trade, the Chinese discovered Africa for themselves.

During the previous century (1260–1368), when the Mongols dominated Asia, traffic between East and West had been very lively; with their downfall and the break-up of the vast Mongol empire, the caravan routes were cut and the imports to which the Chinese had become accustomed ceased to flow. Chinese attitudes toward foreign trade were always mixed. From a practical point of view, foreign trade brought prosperity to the great numbers of people profitably engaged in it, especially to the southern provinces, and the treasury was enriched by the import duties. Although the outflow of cash was an evil, the advantages of foreign trade were considerable. Now all overseas commerce had chiefly to do with articles of luxury—precious stones, fragrant woods, spices, rare objects—and the consumers of these goods were the wealthy classes, especially and most markedly, the court and its harem ladies. Ideologically, however, this state of affairs was never admitted because the Confucian theory regarded trade as something inferior, almost sordid, with which the emperor could have nothing to do. Therefore trade relations with overseas nations always took the form of tribute-bearing: barbarians, attracted from afar, recognized the overlordship of the Son of Heaven by bringing tribute; after this they were graciously allowed to trade. In the past Chinese envoys had repeatedly been sent to induce foreign nations to come to China offering tribute, thus increasing the prestige of the Chinese emperor as well as their own. The greater the number of foreign envoys present at the New Year's court audiences, the more illustrious was the glory of the emperor, who, like the Duke of Chou of old, succeeded by his sage government in attracting foreign barbarians.

These mixed motives, the longing for the exotic and precious felt particularly at court and the desire to increase the imperial prestige by the traditional tribute gifts, must have prompted the third emperor of the Ming Dynasty to undertake a series of missions overseas. In the official annals another, a political motive, is given: to search for the emperor's young nephew to whom the throne had been bequeathed and who, when he had been deposed, disappeared. Because it was rumored that he had fled overseas, a fleet was sent out to try and bring him back from the country of the barbarians where he was supposed to be hiding. The excuse is transparent; to search for the deposed, missing heir, it would not have been necessary to send expeditions on so large a scale as sailed, not merely once, but at least seven times, not counting minor ones. Some of the fleets consisted of sixty-two vessels and carried 37,000 soldiers; more than thirty countries in the Indian Archipelago and Indian Ocean were visited, as well as ports in the Persian Gulf; the great markets of Aden and Mecca were visited; and the Chinese ships sailed all the way to Africa.

These fleets were placed under the command of a Chinese Muslim, native of the province of Yunnan, a court eunuch,

Cheng Ho, popularly known as the "three-jewel eunuch." The ships under his command were designated "jewel ships." [From the days of the Emperor Wu-ti (second century B.C.), eunuchs were entrusted with overseas expeditions. And just as in the case of those early eunuchs, Cheng Ho was put in command of these later expeditions because he was expected to procure luxury goods for the court. He went, as Duyvendak remarks, a-shopping for the ladies of the imperial harem.]

Unfortunately, the official reports of Cheng Ho's voyages no longer exist—a direct consequence of his having been a eunuch. Whereas the overland expeditions into Central Asia led by various generals are part of the nation's historical tradition and are regarded as deeds reflecting China's greatness, knowledge of Cheng Ho's expeditions, equally notable, was deliberately erased. It is said that, about 1480, another eunuch who had risen to great power wished to emulate Cheng Ho and lead a maritime expedition against Annam. When he attempted to organize an expedition and asked for Cheng Ho's official records, to frustrate him the records were destroyed with the connivance of the high officials of the War Office. For during the Ming Dynasty a strong rivalry existed between the eunuchs, who were privately employed by the emperor in various important functions, and the official classes, who, as good Confucians, despised trade and luxury and foreign barbarians. Thus the whole matter of overseas relations became a moral issue to the official classes, inextricably bound up with their deep sense of disapproval of the extravagances and usurpation of power by the notorious eunuchs. In official eyes, China, economically self-sufficient, could very well do without the products of foreign countries which were nothing but curiosities. And it was indeed true that the expeditions were expensive and unprofitable.

These expeditions then, a major event in Chinese history,

are only known in a most fragmentary way; it was a fortunate accident that enabled us at least to fix the dates of the various expeditions with certainty and to ascertain the places visited by each of them. The accident ultimately rests on a miracle.

Some years ago in the yamen at Ch'ang-lo, in the province of Fukien, a stele was discovered; it had been brought there at an earlier date from the Temple of the Celestial Spouse in the same city. The official who discovered the stone wrote an account of his find in January 1937. The stone, he said, had been erected by Cheng Ho and his companions "on a lucky day in the second winter moon of the cyclical year *hsin-hai*, the sixth year of Hsüan-te [December 5, 1431–January 2, 1432]." Two years earlier, in 1935, the text of another inscription, now no longer extant, had become known; it was on a stele erected by Cheng Ho in the Temple of the Celestial Spouse at Liu-chia-kang, near Shanghai, where the fleet assembled for the expeditions. Ch'ang-lo, where the first inscription was found, was the port where the expedition waited for the favorable wind and collected the necessary provisions. Why were both inscriptions placed in the Temple of the Celestial Spouse (a goddess in the Taoist pantheon)? The texts give the answer. That at Ch'ang-lo reads:

"The Imperial Ming Dynasty, in unifying the seas and continents, surpassing the three dynasties, even goes beyond the Han and T'ang Dynasties. The countries beyond the horizon and at the ends of the earth have all become subjects; and to the most western of the western or the most northern of the northern countries, however far they may be, the distances and the routes may be calculated. Thus the barbarians from beyond the seas, though their countries are truly distant, with double translation have come to audience bearing precious objects and presents.

"The emperor, approving of their loyalty and sincerity, has

ordered us [Cheng Ho] and others at the head of several tens of thousands of officers and flag troops to ascend more than a hundred large ships to go and confer presents on them in order to make manifest the transforming power of the Imperial Virtue and to treat distant people with kindness. From the third year of Yung-lo [1405] till now we have several times received the commission of ambassadors to the countries of the Western Ocean. The barbarian countries we have visited are: by way of Chan-ch'eng [Champa], Chao-wa [Java], San-fo-ch'i [Palembang], and Hsien-lo [Siam], crossing straight over to Hsi-lan-shan [Ceylon]; in South India, Ku-li [Calicut, not Calcutta] and K'o-chih [Cochin]; we have gone to the western regions of Hu-lu-mo-ssu [Hormuz], A-tan [Aden], Mu-ku-tu-shu [Mogadishu, in Africa], all together more than thirty countries large and small. We have traversed more than one hundred thousand *li* of immense water spaces and have beheld in the ocean huge waves like mountains rising sky-high, and we have set eyes on barbarian regions far away hidden in a blue transparency of light vapors, while our sails, loftily unfurled like clouds, day and night continued their course, rapid like that of a star [the designation for an Imperial Embassy], traversing the savage waves as if we were treading a public thoroughfare. Truly, this was due to the majesty and good fortune of the court and moreover we owe it to the protecting virtue of the Celestial Spouse.

"The power of the goddess having been manifested in previous times has been abundantly revealed in the present generation. In the midst of the rushing waters it happened when there was a hurricane, that suddenly there appeared a divine lantern shining in the mast; as soon as this miraculous light appeared the danger was appeased, so that even in the peril of capsizing one felt reassured that there was no cause for fear."

The "divine lantern" in the mast was the well-known St.

Elmo's Fire; but to the men caught in a hurricane it was a sign of celestial protection. This miracle, which occurred on the first voyage, inspired the inscription which preserved knowledge of these maritime expeditions. By imperial decree the Celestial Spouse was given a title of twelve characters: "Protector of the Country and Defender of the People, whose miraculous power manifestly answers prayers and whose vast benevolence saves universally."

At the end of the inscription, the different expeditions are carefully listed. The first expedition (1405–07) visited Champa, Java, Sumatra, Lambri, Ceylon, and Calicut; the second (1407–09) and the third (1409–11) revisited many of these places and went to others in Indonesia and on the coast of India; on the third voyage, there was some trouble with the king of Ceylon, who was taken prisoner and brought to China. The fourth voyage (1413–15) also called at the previous ports, but went all the way to Hormuz while some of the ships were detached from the main fleet and called at Bengal. Muslim interpreters accompanied this voyage. The fifth (1417–19) went even farther, visiting, in addition to the now familiar places, Aden and even Melinda on the African coast. Avowedly, this was to escort home the many foreign envoys who had traveled to China as a result of the earlier expeditions. The sixth voyage (1421–22), undertaken for the same reason, went as far as Brawa and Mogadisho on the African coast. Finally, the seventh (1431–33) went to Hormuz.

This was an intensive exploration of Western lands and waters. Many of the countries were visited for the first time by Chinese missions, and first-hand observations were made about their exact location, their conditions, and customs. Upon the return of the first expedition, a school was founded to promote the study of the languages of the barbarians which continued for many centuries; we still have some of the bilingual works published, such as word lists in Malay and Chinese. The loss of Cheng Ho's own reports is partly compensated for by the accounts written by four of the admiral's staff drawn from the ranks of other highly placed eunuchs and important military officers; their books describe the peoples they visited and the products of the many lands they called at. The first was the *Record of the Barbarian Countries in the Western Ocean* by Kung Chen (1434), followed, two years later, by Fei Hsin's *Triumphant Visions of the Starry Raft,* [as ships carrying ambassadors were called]. Fei Hsin's other volume, a picture book which he presented to the emperor, unfortunately has not survived. The third account, *Triumphant Visions of the Boundless Ocean,* dated 1451, was written by the interpreter Ma Huan, who, like Cheng Ho, was a Chinese Muslim from Yunnan. In the fourth account, *Record of the Tribute-Paying Western Countries* (1520) were "compass directions," and a mariner's chart incorporating the maritime knowledge acquired by Cheng Ho's expeditions. (See frontispiece map.) Again, the preservation of this important map was due to a fortunate accident: it was included in a book called *Records of Military Preparedness,* offered to the throne in 1628 (its preface is dated seven years earlier) by the grandson of a governor of Fukien, who lived from 1511–1601. It happened that the governor, charged with the suppression of Japanese pirates, had avidly collected everything he could find pertaining to coastal geography. After relating this in his "Introductory Note," the governor's grandson refers briefly to Cheng Ho's magnificent pioneering: "His maps record carefully and correctly the distances of the road and the various countries and I have inserted them for the information of posterity and as a memento of military achievements."

Ma Huan's descriptions have a kind of journalistic flavor, reporting the practical and provocative. Thus he presents the

Nicobars, a group of small islands in the Bay of Bengal between Lambri, on Sumatra, and the islands of Ceylon. "These islands are three or four in number, and one of them, the largest, has the name Sambelong [?]. Its inhabitants live in the hollows of trees and caves. Both men and women there go about stark naked, like wild beasts, without a stitch of clothing on them. No rice grows there. The people subsist solely on wild yams, jack fruit, and plantains, or upon the fish which they catch. There is a legend current among them that, if they were to wear the smallest scrap of clothing, their bodies would break out into sores and ulcers, owing to their ancestors having been cursed by Sakyamuni [Buddha] for having stolen and hidden his clothes while he was bathing, at the time when he passed over from Ceylon and stopped at these islands. Continuing your voyage and sailing westward from here for ten days, the Hawk's Beak Hill is sighted, and in another two or three days the Buddhist Temple Hill is reached near [Dondere Head?] which is the anchorage of the port of Ceylon. On landing, there is to be seen on the shining rock, at the base of the cliff, an impress of a foot, two or more feet in length. The legend attached to it is, that it is the imprint of Sakyamuni's foot, made when he landed at this place. There is a little water in the hollow of the imprint of this foot which never evaporates. People dip their hands in it and wash their faces, and rub their eyes with it, saying, 'This is Buddha's water, which will make us pure and clean.'

"Buddhist temples abound there. In one of them there is to be seen a full length recumbent figure of Sakyamuni, still in a very good state of preservation.

"The dais on which the figure reposes is inlaid with all kinds of precious stones. It is made of sandalwood and is very handsome. The temple contains a Buddha's tooth and other relics. This must certainly be the place where Sakyamuni entered nirvana. Four or five *li* distant from here, in a northerly direction, is the capital of the kingdom. The king is a most earnest believer in the Buddhist religion, and one who treats elephants and cows with a feeling of veneration. The people of this country are in the habit of taking cow dung and burning it, which when reduced to ashes they rub over their whole bodies.

"They do not venture to eat cow's flesh, they merely drink the milk. When a cow dies they bury it. It is capital punishment for anyone to secretly kill a cow; he who does so can however escape punishment by paying a ransom of a cow's head made of solid gold. Every morning, all those, of whatever degree, residing in the king's palace, take cow dung and mix it with water, which they smear everywhere over the floor of their houses, and upon which they afterwards prostrate themselves, and perform their religious rites.

"Near to the king's residence there is a lofty mountain reaching to the skies. On the top of this mountain there is the impress of a man's foot, which is sunk two feet deep in the rock, and is some eight or more feet long. This is said to be the impress of the foot of the ancestor of mankind, a holy man called A-tan [Adam], or P'an Ku.

"This mountain abounds with rubies of all kinds and other precious stones. These gems are being continually washed out of the ground by heavy rains, and are sought for and found in the sand carried down the hill by the torrents. It is currently reported among the people that these precious stones are the congealed tears of Buddha.

"In the sea off the island there is a bank of snowy white sand, which, with the sun or moon shining on it, sparkles with dazzling brightness. Pearl oysters are continually collecting on this bank.

"The king has had an [artificial] pearl pond dug, into which every two or three years he orders pearl oysters to be thrown, and he appoints men to keep watch over it. Those who fish for these oysters, and take them to the authorities for the king's use, sometimes steal and fraudulently sell them.

"The kingdom of Ceylon is extensive, and thickly populated and somewhat resembles Java. The people are abundantly supplied with all the necessaries of life. They go about naked, except that they wear a green handkerchief around their loins, fastened with a waistband. Their bodies are clean-shaven and only the hair of their heads is left. They wear a white cloth twisted around their heads. When either of their parents die they allow their beards to grow. This is how they show their filial respect. The women twist their hair up into a knot at the back of the head, and wear a white cloth around their middles. Newly born male children have their heads shaven; the head of a female child is not shaven; the hair is done up into a tuft and is left so until she is grown up. They take no meal without butter and milk; if they have none and wish to eat, they do so unobserved and in private. The betel nut is never out of their mouths. They have no wheat, but have rice, sesame, and peas. The coconut, which they have in abundance, supplies them with oil, wine, sugar, and food. They burn their dead and bury the ashes. It is the custom in a family in which a death has occurred for the relatives' and neighbors' wives to assemble together and smite their breasts with their hands, and at the same time make loud lamentation and weeping.

"Among their fruits, they number the plantain and the jack fruit; they have also the sugar cane, melons, herbs, and garden plants. Cows, sheep, fowls, and ducks are not wanting. The king has a gold coin in circulation weighing one candareen six cash. Chinese musk, colored taffetas, blue porcelain basins and cups, copper cash and camphor are much esteemed by them, against which they barter pearls and precious stones. Chinese vessels on their homeward voyages are constantly bringing envoys from their king, who are bearers of presents of precious stones as tribute to the imperial court."

In sharp contrast to the ruby-rich island of Ceylon is Djube on the east coast of Africa, which Fei Hsin described. "The country is situated in a remote corner of the west. The inhabitants live in solitary and dispersed villages. The walls are made of piled-up bricks and the houses are masoned in high blocks. The customs are very simple. There grow neither herbs nor trees. Men and women wear their hair in rolls; when they go out they wear a linen hood. The mountains are uncultivated and the land is wide; it rains very rarely. There are deep wells worked by means of cog wheels. Fish are caught in the sea with nets. The products of the country are lions, gold-spotted leopards, and camel-birds [ostriches], which are six or seven feet tall. There are dragon saliva [ambergris], incense, and golden amber. As merchandise are used vermilion, colored silks [silk weavings of the Ming period have been found in Egypt], gold, silver, porcelains, pepper, colored satins, rice, and other cereals." The officer ended with a brief poem. "If one's eyes wander over this country one meets only sighs and sulky glances; desolation—the entire land nothing but hills!" Similar descriptions of Mogadishu and Brawa are equally chilling: of the former, Fei Hsin states that the houses are four or five stories high; the inhabitants quarrelsome and given to archery practice; the wealthy know navigation and engage in trade with distant countries. "Camels, horses, cattle, and sheep all eat fish," is his concluding sentence.

What could have attracted the Chinese to a region so dismal, poor, and barbaric? The answer to that question brings us full circle to the rhinoceros sent to the Han emperor. From olden times, strange animals were counted among the rare and precious tribute-objects; and now, after each of Cheng Ho's expeditions, foreign envoys arrived with wonderful presents. Egypt distinguished itself when its ambassador brought lions, tigers, oryxes, nilgais, zebras, and ostriches for the imperial zoological garden in the emperor's capital. It was a major event when in 1414 Bengal presented a giraffe. Obviously (since giraffes do not grow in Bengal) the giraffe had been among the gifts given to a new king on his ascending the throne of Bengal and by him sent on to the Chinese emperor. The following year, Melinda, a country that had never had contact with China, came to court presenting a giraffe. The Melinda ambassadors had to be conducted home and so Cheng Ho's fifth voyage (1417–19) included that African port. It was, as Duyvendak says, the giraffe that caused the Chinese to sail to Africa.

It was not merely that the giraffe is an outstanding animal to have in any zoo; there was a very special reason that made it so desirable. In the Somali language, the giraffe is called *girin*, which to Chinese ears sounded like *ch'i-lin*, the fabulous "unicorn." The appearance of the unicorn was a happy omen; it was a sign of heaven's favor and proof of the emperor's virtue. Furthermore, there was a superficial resemblance between the giraffe and the *ch'i-lin* which was supposed to have "the body of a deer and the tail of an ox," to eat only herbs and to harm no living being. For the eunuchs, the leaders of the expeditions, professional flatterers as they were, this resemblance of form and sound of the name was enough; the presentation of a *ch'i-lin* would be supreme flattery to the emperor. In the previous years several supernatural appearances had already been reported, such as vegetarian tigers, extraordinarily large ears of grain, sweet dew, etc. A *ch'i-lin* would cap this series in a masterly fashion. Not knowing whether the giraffe from Bengal would stand the hardships of the transportation, they made sure that the following year the Melinda people would present another sample.

When the giraffe from Bengal arrived at court on September 20, 1414, under the guise of a *ch'i-lin*, or unicorn, it caused quite a stir. The Board of Rites asked to be allowed to present a Memorial of Congratulation. The emperor declined, saying, "Let the ministers but early and late exert themselves in assisting the government for the welfare of the world. If the world is at peace, even without *ch'i-lins* there is nothing that hinders good government. Let congratulations be omitted."

When, however, in the following year the giraffe from Melinda arrived, a similar request was made, and, although the emperor again declined, he went out to the Feng-t'ien Gate to receive the animal in great state, together with a "celestial horse" [zebra] and a "celestial stag" [oryx?], and all the officials prostrated themselves and offered congratulations.

SECTION OF THE MAP INCLUDED IN *Records of Military Preparedness*[2]

This is a true mariner's chart. Its cartographic language differs from that of contemporary European portolano charts, for instead of the familiar rhumb lines drawn from an arbitrarily chosen point, this has written compass bearings. In addition to compass bearings, the legend inscribed along the sea routes includes distances measured by "watches," the distance traversed with a favorable wind in one day and one night, and such pertinent information as prevailing winds, ports and havens, half-tide reefs and shoals, etc. East, not north, is at the top of the page.

This chart also differs from the Chinese maps drawn on grids—parallel lines in two dimensions—which depict the

[2] See frontispiece map in this volume.

correct relationship of the various parts. Its extreme schematization has been likened to the diagrams used in metropolitan transportation systems, air routes, etc. Thus, the Indian Ocean and the Arabian Sea are tightly constricted in order to show both the Indian and African ports at which the fleet called; while the length of the littoral from the Bay of Bengal to the Persian Gulf is similarly compressed. Constriction and compression rather than scale were used to present the routes of the extended sea voyages in so small a space.

In this section, the uppermost track on the far right indicates the route along the east coast of India: 45 and 46 are the Ganges delta; 48 and 49 are Orissa (the great temple at Konarak). On the lower side, the opening between 60, the island of Socotra, and 62, Aden, is Bab el-Mandeb, the strait connecting the Arabian Sea and the Red Sea. Some of the other points that have been identified are: 16, Chittagong, and 17, Calcutta (?), in the Bay of Bengal; 19, 20, 22, 23, 26, and 27, places on Ceylon; 41, Cochin, 53, Calicut, 67, Bombay, and 71, Cambay are Indian ports on the west coast; 25, Melinda, 29, Mombassa, 38, Pu-la-wa (Brawa), and 39, Mogadishu, are settlements on the east coast of Africa; and 81 is Muscat on the Arabian coast.

CHAPTER EIGHT

THE HAI-LU: AN EIGHTEENTH-CENTURY SEAMAN

THE HAI-LU:
AN EIGHTEENTH-CENTURY SEAMAN[1]

During the seventeenth and eighteenth centuries, Europe's knowledge of China was being constantly enlarged by a growing body of accounts written by religious, mercantile, and sea-faring travelers who visited there. Whether it was from the writings of Jesuits who in their long residence in China learned the language and penetrated to the rich strata of Chinese civilization, or from the Voyages *of navigators who from limited contacts in commercial ports presented China as a benighted, squalid nation, Europeans had a literature that could give them some picture of China. All this time China's knowledge of Europe remained almost nonexistent. During the centuries when Europeans were poking and prying into all the corners of the earth, when societies were founded for the promotion of exploration and colonization, when trading companies were formed, the Chinese, on their side, were discouraged from leaving China for foreign lands. The few Chinese who did leave to study and work in European countries do not seem to have left any accounts of their reactions to Western civilization. We are thus left with a gap, the more serious since the Chinese who went abroad were unusual and serious men; we have little more than their names and the most fleeting knowledge of where they studied and traveled.*

There was Cheng Ma-no, who, accompanying Martin Mar-

[1] From Kenneth Ch'en: *Monumenta Serica,* Vol. 7, 1942, pp. 208–226.

tini when he returned to Europe in 1650, studied philosophy and theology at the Collegium Romanum (Rome) and became the first Chinese Jesuit father. Shen Fu-tsung left China with Father Philippe Couplet in 1681 and with him toured the principal European centers of Chinese studies; four years later he was in England assisting Thomas Hyde in building up the Chinese collection in the Bodleian Library. A Chinese Christian named Huang went to Paris in 1703 with the Vicar Apostolic of Szechuan and there worked with Ponchartrain on a Chinese dictionary. Other young Chinese were sent by the Jesuits to study in Europe: Louis Fan went to Rome, and, upon completing his studies, joined the Jesuit Society in 1709; but the greater number went to France (1740–65) and, in addition to their theological work, studied Latin and French, the humanities and Western science. A brief notation in Thomas Percy's diary (March 2, 1775) tells of a conversation he had with a young Cantonese who discussed Chinese painting. When Father Ripa (he engraved the great Atlas *the Jesuits made of the Manchu Empire) left China in 1723, he took four Chinese students with him; nine years later he started an evangelical training center in Naples, where, though the number of Chinese was always small, the college continued to function; in 1792 Macartney, leading England's first mission to China, secured two of its students to act as his interpreters.*

A brief account written in 1723 by a Manchu sent as the Chinese envoy to the Tangut Tartars (inhabiting the region north of the Caspian Sea) described the Russian cities he had visited during 1712–15. Mr. Ch'en summarizes the envoy's general impressions of Russia.

Russia ". . . is a large, cold and damp country with a sparse population. Whenever a person of inferior status meets his superior, he would have to remove his hat and bow. If a male meets a female, then the male would remove his hat while the female would bow. In marriage a go-between is still resorted to, and on the date of the marriage, the bride and the groom go to the church to conclude the ceremonies. Russians are fond of drinking, and wine is the favorite beverage brought out for guests and relatives. Tea is not known. Wheat is the main staple, while fish and meat are also eaten. No rice is to be had, however. In eating, the people use spoons and forks. Merchants outnumber the farmers in this country. The inhabitants are inclined to boastfulness and avariciousness. Ordinarily they like to joke and pass their lives peacefully. On festival days, the men gather together for drinking bouts, after which they would sing and dance. The womenfolk also have their own forms of festivities and merriment. On the whole, the people are industrious, thrifty, and law-abiding, with a strong aversion for warfare. Their dwelling places are, however, stuffy and filthy."

The Hai-lu, *therefore, has considerable importance as the first description of the Western world; here, an illiterate Chinese tells what he saw with his own eyes.* Hai-lu *means ocean record, or overseas records.*

The traveler was Hsieh Ch'ing-kao, born in 1765 in the district of Kwangtung. At the age of eighteen he boarded a foreign trading vessel and spent the next fourteen years visiting all the principal ports of Europe, America (North and South) and Asia. Blind at thirty-one, he returned to China and settled at Macao, where he died in 1822, at the age of fifty-seven.

Not only was Hsieh blind, he was also illiterate and could not write down his experiences. Two years before he died, a visitor from his home town came to see him; with Yang Ping-nan he talked of his foreign travels and the old, blind man urged his young friend to write down what he had related. Of the Western countries he visited, Portugal has the longest description, which suggests that Hsieh took service on a Portuguese ship.

Portugal (called Ta-hsi-yang, or Pu-lu-chi-shih) ". . . has a climate colder than that of Fukien and Kwangtung. Her chief seaport [*Lisbon*] faces the south and is protected by two forts manned by 2000 soldiers and equipped with about four or five hundred cannons. Whenever any ship calls at the port, it is first examined by officials to see whether there is any case of smallpox on board. If there is not, the ship is permitted to enter; otherwise, the ship must wait outside the harbor until all traces of the disease have disappeared. Places of importance are seven in all: Lisbon, Coimbra, Guarda, Vizeu, Villa Real, A-la-chia [*?*], and Chaves. All these towns are densely settled, garrisoned by heavy forces, and are connected by good land and water routes.

"The people are white in color, and are fond of cleanliness. As to the dress, the men usually wear trousers and short upper clothes, both very much tight-fitting. On special occasions, another piece is worn over the shirt, short in the front and long in the back, just like the wings of a cicada. Women also wear short and tight-fitting upper clothes, but instead of trousers they wear skirts which are sometimes eight or nine folds deep. Among the poor this is made of cotton; among the rich, silk. When rich women go out they often wear a veil made of fine black silk. Both men and women wear leather shoes.

"Monogamy is the prevailing practice. It is only when either the husband or wife has died that the other may remarry. The family of the prospective bridegroom takes particular pains to find out the size of the bride's dowry before marrying her. Marriages between persons of the same surname are permitted but they are prohibited between children of the same parents. All marriages must receive the sanction of the Church, and it is only after the priest has pronounced his benediction on the couple that a marriage is considered concluded. The marriage ceremonies usually take place in the church.

"Religion plays a dominant part in the lives of these people. Whenever anyone would commit a crime, he would go to the priest in the church and confess his sins and repent, after which he would be absolved by the priest. The priest is strictly forbidden to tell others what he has heard; he would be hanged if he did so. When a king ascends the throne, he does not take a new reign title, but follows the Christian calendar. There are also womenfolk who withdraw from the world and live apart in convents.

"The king of the country is called *li—rei.* His eldest son is called *li-fan-tieh* [*l'infante*]; his other sons, *pi-lin-hsi-pi* [*principes*]; his daughters, *pi-lin-so-shih* [*princezas*]. The Prime Minister is called *kan-tieh* [*conde*]; the commander-in-chief of the army, *ma-la-chi-tsa* [*marquesado*]. [*He then lists all the grades of officials in the court, army, and navy.*] . . . These officers are usually selected from among the leading citizens of the local community. In order to assist the local officials in their administration of affairs, the home government usually sends out a military official to each region. If the possession is a large one, then three or four officials are sent. If any problem arises, a conference is held of the four local officials and the two central officials from home to decide on the solution and this solution must be in conformity with local customs and habits." [*Obviously this refers to Portuguese overseas possessions; especially Macao, which Hsieh had observed.*]

Spain ". . . is said to be north-northwest of Portugal and could be reached by sailing in that direction for about eight or nine days from Portugal [*one of Hsieh's mistakes in indicating direction.*] The area of this country is larger than that of Portugal; the people are fierce and wicked. Catholicism is the main religion. Its products are gold, silver, copper, iron, wine, glass, and watches, etc. The silver dollars used in China are manufactured in this country."

France [like the short description of Spain, this, too, is equally unsatisfactory] ". . . is located north-northwest of Spain. The people are sincere and honest, also inquisitive and ingenious. The watches they make are superior to any other in the world. Their wine is also very excellent. In religion, customs, and habits, the country is similar to Spain. The coins used are either triangular or square, with a cross on the surface." [*All French coins then were round.*]

Holland [Hsieh speaks of the revolt of the Dutch against Spain and the establishment of a new religion to replace the Catholic one] has no monarch, ". . . for the royal line has ceased to exist. Instead, the reins of government are held by four ministers, who do not hold the office by reason of heredity.

"Governmental affairs are so well handled that even possessions thousands of miles away dare not disobey the orders of the central authorities. Social customs are the same as in the surrounding countries with the exception of the following. Before a rich person dies, he must first draw up a will and present it to the governmental officials, telling how he proposes to have his wealth distributed. After death, this will must be obeyed, otherwise the wealth would be confiscated."

Other countries, not clearly identifiable, are mentioned. Rome—Lang-ma, Roma—is "the headquarters of the church which numerous worshipers visit every day. Portugal, Spain, France, Austria, and Prussia embrace this faith, while Ying-lan-ni-shih and Ya-li-p'i-hua do not." *Then* Hai-lu *moves on to Tu-ku—Turkey. It is back of Portugal, Spain, and France, and is* ". . . very large geographically. The inhabitants are Mohammedans, are strong and flourishing, wear clothes with big sleeves, and wrap their heads with turbans. Other European countries have very little to do with them."

Austria and Prussia are ". . . brotherly nations which aid each other in times of trouble. Austria is called 'Double Eagle' by the Cantonese because the ships coming from that country to trade at Canton carry a flag with a double-eagle design, while Prussia is called 'Single Eagle' because of that design on her flag."

Russia, to the north of Prussia, has social customs ". . . similar to those of the Moslems. The climate is so cold that the inhabitants have to go about wearing furs and skins, which also serve as blankets during the night."

England ". . . is located southwest [sic] of France and could be reached by sailing north from St. Helena for about two months. It is a sparsely settled island, separated from the mainland, with a large number of rich families. The dwelling houses have more than one story. Maritime commerce is one of the chief occupations of the English, and wherever there is a region in which profits could be reaped by trading, these people strive for them, with the result that their commercial vessels are to be seen on the seven seas. Commercial traders are to be found all over the country. Male inhabitants from the ages of fifteen to sixty are conscripted into the service of the king as soldiers. Moreover, a large foreign mercenary army is also maintained. Consequently, although the country is small, it has such a large military force that foreign nations are afraid of it.

"Near the sea is Lun-lun [*London*], which is one of the largest cities in the country. In this city is a fine system of waterworks. From the river, which flows through the city, water is raised by means of revolving wheels, installed at three different places, and poured into pipes which carry it to all parts of the city. Anyone desirous of securing water would just have to lay a pipe between his house and the water mains, and water would be available. The water tax for each family is calculated on the number of persons in that family.

"Men and women all wear white ordinarily; for mourning, however, black is used. The army wears a red uniform. Women wear long dresses that sweep the floor, with the upper part tight and the lower part loose. At the waist is a tight belt with a buckle. Whenever there is a celebration of festive occasion, then some young and beautiful girls would be asked to sing and dance to the accompaniment of music. Girls of rich and noble families start to learn these arts when they are very young.

"Whenever English ships meet on the ocean a ship in dire straits, they must rescue all persons on the ill-fated ship, feed and clothe them, and then provide them with sufficient funds to take them back to their native lands. Any captains neglecting to perform such a task would be liable to punishment.

"Among the minerals produced here are gold, silver, copper, tin, and iron. Manufactured articles include tin plate, cotton and woolen goods, clocks, watches, wine, and glass."

Sweden ". . . can be reached by sailing about ten days or more from Holland and about six or seven days from England. The inhabitants of the country are more honest and simple than the English. Her trading vessels carry a blue flag with a white cross. Northwest of Sweden . . . and on the same island and connected with it by land routes is Yung-li-ma-lu-chia [*Denmark, which then included the present Norway*]. The people here have a slightly larger and stronger physique than the Swedes and their customs and habits are similar to those in Sweden. This is the country whose ships fly the yellow flag in Canton.

"*Mieh-li-kan* [*America*] is a small isolated island in the middle of the ocean. It could be reached by sailing west for about ten days from England. Formerly it was part of England but now is an independent country, although the customs and practices of the two countries still remain alike. This land is called Hua-ch'i by the Cantonese. [*Hua-ch'i, "Flowery Flag," refers to the United States flag flown from the ships.*]

"Minerals found in the country include gold, silver, copper, iron, lead, and tin. Manufactured products include tin plate, glass, snuff, wine, woolen and cotton goods. Water transportation in this country is done by means of boats which have wheels on the side and a fire engine in the center. When a strong fire is generated, the wheels are set in motion, thereby propelling the boat forward. The construction of such a boat is clever and ingenious, and other countries are following the example."

Ya-mieh-li-ko, [*South America*], is briefly alluded to. "The natives here have smooth hair and are simple and honest by nature. The entire region is divided into many small countries, with each having a ruler of its own. The climate is extremely hot. Within the country is a mountain called *Yen-ni-lu* [*Andes or Rio de Janeiro's Sugar Loaf?*]. A journey of ten days or more from the mountain brings one to *Ming-mai-i-yeh* [*Bahia?*], governed by Portugal, and further on is *Pi-ku-ta-li* [*?*] governed by England. The remaining countries are taken over by Holland, Spain, and France."

Of the countries of the West which he has visited and described, all are "resourceful, shrewd, and tricky. The inhabitants depend largely upon maritime commerce for their livelihood. Monogamy is the prevailing practice. Trading vessels which come from these countries to China have to sail south until they pass the Cape of Good Hope and then turn to the southeast."

This work, so glaring in the paucity of the information it presents, "constitutes a convenient landmark to gauge the extent of geographical knowledge in China concerning the West at the end of the Ch'ien-lung period (1736–95) of self-sufficiency and the beginning of the modern period, heralded by the thunder of British guns along the coast of China." *Thus Kenneth Ch'en gives* Hai-lu *its proper significance in the history of Chinese-European interchanges.*

CHAPTER NINE

SCHOLARS, STUDENTS, AND AMBASSADORS

SCHOLARS, STUDENTS, AND AMBASSADORS

INTRODUCTION

The Age of Exploration, the spatial expression of Europe's rise to pre-eminence and power, saw nothing comparable in China. By the nineteenth century the scientific, technological, and industrial revolutions had made the West dominant while isolation, stagnation, and the moribund Ch'ing Dynasty (1644–1912) made China, so rich, populous, and productive, a helpless victim. This tragic imbalance brought out the worst elements in both sides as they met. On the one hand, the Chinese court and its advisers, preoccupied with fidelity to the distant past, sought to quarantine the intrusive Westerners: Canton was the only port permitted to foreign ships and a small association of brokers (the hong *merchants) were given the monopoly of foreign trade. The West, on the other hand, commercially predatory and immeasurably superior in military strength, imposed treaties which lifted the strict quarantine. Of the many conditions to which the Chinese were unwillingly forced to acquiesce, certainly the least offensive were the rights granted to foreigners to travel inside the empire and to study the Chinese language. Like an organisim mobilizing its defenses to localize an infection that threatens to spread, the Chinese closed in around the concessions won from them. Any association with foreigners was dangerous and viewed with suspicion; and a special category of officials dealt with the foreigners in the new treaty ports. They became specialists in the "barbarian problem," as the Chinese called (and considered) all non-Chinese matters.*

From China's Response to the West, *by Ssu-yü Teng and John K. Fairbank (Cambridge, Harvard University Press, 1954), I have selected a few accounts written by Chinese about the West. The first shows how native scholars, imbued with the high traditions of their eighteenth-century excellence in historical and literary criticism, began to read Western books and respond to new ideas and information. It was a kind of preparation, a self-taught homework, a brave view of a world forbidden, dangerous, and alien.*

One of the most competent of these men was the scholar-official Hsü Chi-yü (1795–1873). His grandfather had been a provincial graduate and his father a metropolitan graduate, which Hsü Chi-yü also became in 1826, so that his unorthodox interest in the West was that of a reputable scion of the established order. After service in the Hanlin Academy at Peking and as a censor, he became the chief "barbarian controller" in Fukien, holding the posts successively of financial commissioner and governor between 1843 and 1851. His first foreign contact appears to have occurred at Amoy early in 1844, where an unfortunate British acting-consul was having a hard time doing business with the local Chinese authorities: lacking a competent interpreter, the Englishman in an interview would address his remarks in English to a Singapore Chinese, who would repeat them in Fukienese to a local Chinese, who would then state them in Mandarin (Pekinese) to the officials. The local American missionary, Rev. David Abeel, who could understand "a good deal" of Mandarin though not speak it, was called in to help stave off the resulting chaos. Thus is happened that Hsü Chi-yü met a Westerner of literary interests, who showed him an atlas of the world. After borrowing Abeel's atlas, Hsü took up world geography as a hobby. Abeel. . . . gave him instruction in geography and history and other foreigners also helped him.

Hsü's eventual product, *A Brief Description of the Ocean Circuit*, was completed in 1848 and printed in 1850. It was a straight summary of world geography based on Western sources; it was more handy and succinct—one might say "scientific." Hsü's maps, for example, were careful copies of Western maps, vastly more accurate than the old-style sketch-maps.

Hsü Chi-yü fitted into the post-treaty phase of conciliation, for he was concerned less with military strategy against the British invasion than with the study of Western society as a proper subject of scholarly interest. While his official memorials inveighed against the twin evils of foreign opium and missionaries in the fashion of the period, he is known to have gone rather far in friendly contact with foreigners.

The extracts translated below on Britain and the United States are in the form of digested statements, evidently based rather directly on Western sources. Governor Hsü's researchers laid before his countrymen enough data on the economy and political institutions of the West to make it plain that the Western barbarians represented an entirely different and very powerful society. The difficulty lay in absorbing the lesson of this difference and applying it to statecraft.

HSÜ CHI-YÜ'S ACCEPTANCE OF WESTERN GEOGRAPHY, 1848

[*On Britain and her empire*] The population of England is dense and the food insufficient. It is necessary for them to import from other countries. More than 490,000 people are engaged in weaving. The weaving machine is made of iron, and is operated by a steam engine, so it can move automatically. Thus labor is saved and the cost of production is low. Each year more than 400,000 piculs [1 picul equals 133 lbs.] of cotton are used, all of which are shipped in from the five parts of India and America. . . . Silk is purchased and shipped from China and Italy. The work of manufacturing guns, cannon, knives, swords, clocks, watches, and various kinds of utensils and tools for daily use is done by about 300,000 people. Each year the income from the various products is worth approximately ten million taels or more. Their commercial ships are in the four seas; there is no spot which they do not reach. The great profits go to the merchants and dealers, while the workers are poor. . . .

England consists merely of three islands, simply a handful of stones in the Western ocean. Her area is estimated to be about the same as Taiwan and Ch'iung-chou [Hainan] . . . Even if the soil is all fertile, how much can be produced locally? The reason for her becoming suddenly rich and strong, exerting political influence here and there beyond tens of thousands of *li*, is that in the west she obtained America and in the east she obtained the various parts of India. The land of America hangs isolated on the globe, and since ancient times it has been little known. In the Wan-li period (1573–1620) of the Ming, it was discovered, and then a rich soil of ten thousand *li* was added to Great Britain, soon making her immensely rich. Even though the land of America is separated from England by ten thousand *li*, the British are skilled in ocean navigation, and make the voyage as easily as crossing a marshy ground with weeds. When the southern part was ceded to the United States of America, the northern part [i.e., Canada] which, though vast, is as barren and cold as Chinese Mongolia [was retained by the British]. After England lost this part [U. S. A.], she almost lost her prosperity [lit., color].

The five Indias lie on the southwest of China. . . . In 1755 Bengal was annexed, and taking advantage of their victories the English stealthily encroached on the various states like silkworms eating mulberry leaves. The various parts, scattered and weak, could not resist, and consequently more than half became British colonies. The land produces cotton and also opium. After opium became popular in China, ten-fold profits were made. The revenue collected by the English in large measure comes from the five Indias. To have lost in the west [America] and yet to have made it up in the east [India]—how fortunate she is!

After the English obtained the five Indias, they gradually expanded toward the southeast. Along the eastern coast of the Indian Ocean, ports were opened everywhere. . . . Malacca and Hsi-li [Singapore] were exchanged with Holland. Eighty or ninety per cent of the wealth of the Small Western Ocean [the Indian Ocean] came under British control. In the farther East, of the states on the various islands in the southern ocean of China, except Luzon which belongs to Spain, the rest are all trading ports of Holland. The luxurious places like Ko-lo-pa [Javal], the strategic areas like Manila [Luzon] also were coveted by the English. Unfortunately other people already possessed them; she had no reason to take them by force. And yet, she goes to and fro on the Eastern sailing route, using the two places as her hostelries, and Spain and Holland dare not offend her in the least. . . . At the present time, what Britain relies upon to be her outside treasury and to extend the power of her nation lies in the five Indias. The territory is on the southwest of further Tibet, whence it only takes twenty or thirty days to go to Canton by sea. This colony of the British has been for a long time close to our southern frontier, and yet our critics merely know that England proper is over 70,000 *li* away.

England herself is geographically small in area, but very numerous in population. The arable land is not sufficient to supply food for one tenth of the population. Before the ceding of North America, the unemployed British subjects usually sailed westward to seek sustenance. After the ceding of America, the remaining land of England in the northern region [i.e., Canada] was too cold for farming. Even though the large territory of the five Indias was obtained, there were originally inhabitants in that area, and there was no unoccupied territory. Although many English people went to live there, after all they could not reverse their guest position to become the hosts, and therefore they were anxious to find new places. In recent years, the great island of New Holland [New Zealand] has been obtained. The grass and weeds have been cut down in order that criminals may be banished to that place. The poor people, who have no means of making a living, were also taken there for settlement. In moving these people over a distance of 80,000 *li*, it was a hard and painstaking job [for the government] to plan to feed and accommodate the people.

The size of the regular army of England proper is 90,000 men. In India, the British soldiers are 30,000, and the local troops 230,000, who are called "sepoy" soldiers. She has more than 600 warships, large and small, and more than 100 steamships. Their sailors wear blue uniforms and their army wear red. The navy is stressed but the army is slighted. They depend entirely upon rifles and guns, and are not skillful in boxing. Excepting knives and swords, they have no other weapons.

[*On the American Revolution and the U. S. A.*]

In the middle of the Ch'ien-lung period (1736–95), England and France were engaged in a war which lasted for years without being settled. Hundreds of methods had been used to raise provisions, and the rate of taxation was doubled. According to the old regulation, the seller of tea had to pay a tax; the British then ordered the purchasers also to pay a tax. The Americans could not bear this. In 1775, the local gentry gathered together in a public building, wanting to discuss the problem with their resident chieftain. The chieftain [i.e., British official] drove away the petitioners and urged the levy of the tax even more harshly. The multitude of the people were so irritated that they threw the tea from the ships into the sea, and they planned to raise an army to fight against the British.

There was a certain Washington [*Hua-sheng-tun;* note: also written *Wang-hsing-t'eng* and *Wa-sheng-tun*], a native of another part of America [i.e., not of Massachusetts], born in 1731 [1732]. When he was ten he lost his father, and his mother educated him and brought him up. He had cherished great ambitions in youth and was gifted in both literary and military matters. He was unusually gallant and robust. Once he served as a British military officer. . . . When the time came for the multitude of the people to revolt against the British, they urged Washington [lit., *Tun,* i.e., taking the last syllable as surname] to be their commander. . . . The army of Washington was defeated, and his followers were so discouraged that they wished to be disbanded and to go away. Washington maintained his spirit as usual. He gathered his forces and grouped them into an army to fight again, and he was victorious. Thus in eight years of bloody war, he was repeatedly defeated, but he also repeatedly refused to be discouraged. . . .

After Washington settled his country's affairs, he gave up arms and intended to return to his farm. The multitude could not bear to leave him, but insisted on electing him the head of the state. Then Washington held a discussion with the multitude, saying that to establish a state and to hand it down to his descendants would be selfish; the duty of looking after the people should be carried on by selecting those who have virtue. The traditional divisions [*pu,* parts] were set up as individual states, and each state has a commander [i.e., governor]. . . .

The leaders of the villages and towns write down the names of those whom they are going to elect and put them in a box. After this is finished, the box is opened, and the one who has obtained the most votes is established as governor. Whether he is an officer or of the common people, there is no restriction according to his previous status, and after retirement, the governor is still considered an equal of the common people. . . .

The whole continent of America reaches the great Western [i.e., Atlantic] ocean in the East, and the great ocean sea [i.e., Pacific Ocean] in the West. The United States are all in the eastern part. . . . The uncultivated region in the west is all occupied by the aborigines. Whenever new territory is to be opened, at first hunters are employed to kill the bears, deer, and wild oxen, and then the unemployed people are allowed to cultivate the land. When forty thousand inhabitants have been gathered together or born in the region, then a city is built which is given a name as a territory [*pu*] attached to the whole group of states. At present, apart from the states, three territories have been added.

The various states of America have an equable and normal climate. In the north it is like Chihli and Shansi and in the south it is like Kiangsu and Chekiang. The river currents are gentle and the soil is good. There is no desert and little plague. (Note: in the south there is a pestilential vapor, but it is not very poisonous.) The land is level and fertile and suitable for the five grains. Cotton is the best and the most produced, whence the various countries like England and France all get their supplies. There are all kinds of vegetables and fruits. Tobacco leaves are extremely good and are circulated far and wide. In the mountains coal, salt, iron, and white lead are produced. Within the country there are many small rivers, and the Americans have dredged them from place to place in order to facilitate water transportation. Steam locomotives [lit., fire-wheel carts] are also made. Stones are used to pave the road bed and they melt iron and pour it like a liquid in order to smooth the running of the train. Within one day it can run more than 300 *li* [about 100 miles]. Steamships are even more numerous, running back and forth on the rivers and seas like shuttles, because the land produces much coal. . . .

Once every two years, one person is elected for his outstanding ability and point of view out of every 47,700 people to stay at the capital city to participate in and discuss the national affairs. In the capital, where the president lives, there is a congress (*kung-hui*) representing all the states, each of which elects two wise men to participate in this congress and decide great political issues such as making an alliance, declaring war or adopting defensive measures, determining the rate of customs and taxes on trading transactions and the like. The full term is six years. In each state there are six judges to take charge of making verdicts or imprisonments. They are also elected to fill these positions. If there is anyone who is prejudiced or unfair, he may be removed by public opinion. . . .

The standing army of the United States of America is not more than 10,000, who are distributed among various forts and strategic points. Except for scholars, physicians, and astronomers, the rest of the people—farmers, workers, and merchants—from twenty to forty years old are subject to selection by the officials to serve as militia [*ming-ping*] and are issued registration cards. . . . The militia system of about 1,700,000 men is fundamentally identical with the method of our ancient people who quartered troops on the farmers.

In the United States of America, all the white men have immigrated to live there; there are people from all countries of Europe but those coming from England, Holland, and France are the most numerous. Among these three countries, England again provided more than one half. Therefore, the spoken and written language is the same as that of England. . . . The business and transportation work is all done by the white people. The people are docile, good-natured, mild, and honest. They do not have the fierce and cruel bearing of birds of prey. They work very hard in making a living and their merchant ships sail the four seas. All the states of America accept the religion of Jesus [i.e., Protestant Christianity], and are fond of academic discussions and activities. Everywhere there are schools. Their scholars in general are divided into three kinds: namely, academic, studying astronomy, geography, and the tenets of Christianity; medical, for curing diseases; and legal, for training lawyers and judges.

Feng Kuei-fen (1809–74), a scholar from Soochow, was another who from within China recognized the fact that the changing modern world had become much larger, more complex, and vastly different from anything ever imagined in ancient China. Some forty essays written before 1860, "Personal Protests from the Study of Chiao-pin," dealt with governmental, financial, educational, and other aspects of China's modernization. At his suggestion a school of Western languages and sciences was established in Shanghai in 1863 and its curriculum showed Feng's interest and high competence in mathematics, philology, astronomy, geography, agriculture, and other subjects. His insistence on the importance of Western science as a necessary auxiliary to Chinese knowledge was part of his realistic appreciation of the importance of genuine learning. His contempt for the Canton-style "linguists," through whom Western lore had been murkily filtered into China, springs from his deep understanding that the fundamental principles of mathematics and the sciences were the sources from which the barbarians got their power.

This is part of his essay "On the Adoption of Western Knowledge" (pp. 51-52).

The world today is not to be compared with that of the Three Dynasties (of ancient China). . . . Now the globe is ninety-thousand *li* around, and every spot may be reached by ships or wheeled vehicles. . . . According to what is listed on the maps by the Westerners, there are not less than one hundred countries. From these one hundred countries, only the books of Italy, at the end of the Ming Dynasty [1368–1644], and now those of England have been translated in Chinese, altogether several tens of books. Those which expound the doctrine of Jesus are generally vulgar, nor worth mentioning. Apart from these, Western books on mathematics, mechanics, optics, light, chemistry, and other subjects contain the best principles of the natural sciences. In the books on geography, the mountains, rivers, strategic points, customs, and native products of the hundred countries are fully listed. Most of this information is beyond the reach of our people.

Nowadays those familiar with barbarian affairs are called "linguists." These men are generally frivolous rascals and loafers in the cities and are despised in their villages and communities. They serve as interpreters only because they have no other means of making a livelihood. Their nature is boorish, their knowledge shallow, and furthermore, their moral principles are mean. They know nothing except sensual pleasures and material profit. Moreover, their ability consists of nothing more than a slight knowledge of the barbarian language and occasional recognition of barbarian characters, which is limited to names of commodities, numerical figures, some slang expressions, and a little simple grammar. How can we expect them to pay attention to scholarly studies? . . .

If today we wish to select and use Western knowledge, we should establish official translation offices at Canton and Shanghai. Brilliant students up to fifteen years of age should be selected from those areas to live and study in these schools on double rations. Westerners should be invited to teach them the spoken and written languages of the various nations, and famous Chinese teachers should also be engaged to teach them classics, history, and other subjects. At the same time they should learn mathematics. (Note: All Western knowledge is derived from mathematics. Every Westerner of ten years of age or more studies mathematics. If we now wish to adopt Western knowledge, naturally we cannot but learn mathematics. . . .)

I have heard that there are large collections of books in the Mei-hua shu-kuan [American Presbyterian Press] and in the Mo-hai shu-kuan [London Missionary Society's Printing Office]. Moreover, in 1847 the Russian barbarians presented us with more than one thousand books which are preserved in the Fang-lueh-kuen [Military Archives Office, in Peking]. These books should be sent to the new schools so that the valuable ones may be selected and translated. . . .

After three years all students who can recite with ease the books of the various nations should be permitted to become licentiates; and if there are some precocious ones who are able to make changes or improvements which can be put into practice, they should be recommended by the superintendent of trade to be imperially granted a *chü-jen* degree as a reward. As we have said before, there are many brilliant people in China; there must be some who can learn from the barbarians and surpass them. . . .

If we let Chinese ethics and famous [Confucian] teachings serve as an original foundation, and let them be supplemented by the methods used by the various nations for the attainment of prosperity and strength, would it not be the best of all procedures?

Moreover, during the last twenty years since the opening of trade, a great many of the foreign chiefs have learned our written and spoken language, and the best of them can even read our classics and histories. They are generally able to speak on our dynastic regulations and government administration, on our geography and the state of the populace. On the other hand, our officers from generals down, in regard to foreign countries are completely uninformed. In comparison, should we not feel ashamed? The Chinese officials have to rely upon the stupid and silly "linguists" as their eyes and ears. The mildness or severity, leisureliness or urgency of their way of stating things may obscure the officials' original intent after repeated interpretations. Thus frequently a small grudge may develop into a grave hostility. At the present time the most important administrative problem of the empire is to control the barbarians, yet the pivotal function is entrusted to these people. No wonder that we understand neither the foreigners nor ourselves, and cannot distinguish fact from unreality. Whether in peace negotiations or in deliberating for war, we can never achieve the essential guiding principles. . . .

MA CHIEN-CHUNG'S REPORT ON HIS STUDIES IN FRANCE, 1877

The last ten days of May were the examination period of the Political Institute. There were eight examination questions. . . . The third was on the commercial proceedings of all nations, dealing with the basis of credit for commercial organizations and bank drafts. From this we know that the wealth of Westerners in the last hundred years has not come purely from the creation and development of machines but essentially from the protection of commercial organizations. . . . Thus, even though the amount of capital required for railways, telegraph lines, steam engines, and mining is very great . . . and though there is a limit to gold and silver, there is no end to the use of money because, since the currency is represented by paper and guaranteed by credit, one coin may assume the usefulness of several hundred coins. . . .

The fifth question was on the differences and similarities of administrative methods, government, and education in the three countries, England, the United States, and France, the methods by which the upper and lower classes cooperate, what are the advantages and disadvantages of each method, and what are the reasons for England being able to maintain herself so long without changing, for America not changing though having many defects, for France repeatedly changing and frequently getting worse. . . .

The seventh one was on the similarities and differences of public administration in all nations, some of which are monarchies, some republics, and some partly monarchical and partly republican. The legislative, executive, and judicial powers are divided and are not given to one person. These three powers do not interfere with each other, and so the political situation is in good order, bright and presentable. The collection of taxes is not done by [police] officials, therefore bad officers have no way to fulfill their desires. The verdict for a crime is fixed by local juries; bad judges have no way to play on words. Everybody has the right to be independent, and seeks to be self-respecting.

The eighth question was on the levy of taxes and the amount of national debt. Western taxes are ten times heavier than those of China and yet the people are not resentful. The national debt is borrowed from the people and yet the people are not suspicious. Why?

For these eight questions the written examination took three days and I wrote more than twenty notebooks. . . . I answered them one by one in detail, and all received good grades from the professors, and were announced in the newspaper. They say I have understood these subjects very thoroughly and have grasped the broad outlines. Those who are merely bookworms cannot be compared with me. This praise is also caused by the fact that Westerners have had little contact with us Chinese and usually are scornful of us. Therefore, whenever there is a Chinese student who knows a little and understands half of what he has studied, he is praised as being extraordinary. This "being extraordinary" [as an individual] is just a sign of being despised [as a race]. I can only study hard, with strong determination. How dare I become proud of a little progress? . . .

I have been in Europe for more than a year. When I first came here, I thought that the wealth and power of all European nations lay exclusively in their fine manufacturing and strict discipline of troops. But when I worked on their laws and antecedents, and read their writings, I realized that their pursuit of wealth is based on the protection of commercial concerns, and that those who seek power consider it important to win the hearts of the people. When they protect commercial concerns, then taxes can be increased and their savings will naturally be more adequate. When popular support is won, then loyalty and patriotism will be doubled, and the people can be expected to unite against a national enemy. Other good things are the increase in the number of intelligent students after the spread of schools, and the communication of the opinions of the lower classes after the establishment of parliaments. As for manufacturing, the army and navy, and these various large items, they are all but unimportant details.

Thus, I thought the government of all Western nations was perfect. When I went to listen to the lectures in the Political Institute and discussed these things forwards and backwards with scholars and officials, I began to realize the truth of the statement that "It would be better to be without books than to give entire credit to them." England has a king and besides has an upper and lower house. It seems that all policies must originate there, but we know that the king only gives an endorsement and the upper and lower houses merely have empty discussions, the handle of policy is wielded by the premier and two or three chief ministers. Whenever they have to face a difficult matter, they use the parliament as a cover. The president of the United States is elected by the people themselves, and this seems to be just, without being selfish, but whenever it is time for an election, bribery is publicly practiced. When the president is changed, the whole list of government personnel is changed, and all officials are members of his party. How can they expect good administration? France is a republican nation where it appears that those who become officials need not come from aristocratic families, but we know they organize political factions among themselves, and except for those scholars such as Tien-yeh [Adolphe Thiers, 1797–1877, President of the Third French Republic, 1871–73] and others whose wisdom and ability are outstanding, it is very difficult for men who do not belong to the same faction to find a good job or get into a fine position. . . .

DIPLOMATIC MISSIONS ABROAD

Considering the efficiency and skill of many Chinese diplomatic representatives in the twentieth century, it seems amazing that the Ch'ing Dynasty should have delayed so long in dispatching envoys abroad. The first semiofficial venture in this direction was the mission chaperoned by Robert Hart in 1866. Headed by "an elderly Manchu official of low rank," this mission of investigation included three students from the T'ung-wen Kuan [Foreign Language Academy]. It visited nine European countries, but had little effect on its return. The famous "Burlingame mission," which visited the United States and Europe in 1868–70, appeared to the West to be primarily the achievement of the former American minister at Peking, Anson Burlingame, but the Chinese records make it clear that two Ch'ing officials, Chih-kang and Sun Chia-ku, were sent as his co-envoys with equal status. The Tientsin massacre of

1870 necessitated the sending of a special mission of apology to France, under the Manchu Ch'ung-hou; but this still did not constitute the establishment of a regular diplomatic legation. After much discussion and some false starts, a mission was finally established in England only in 1877; even then its immediate occasion was to present China's apology for the murder of a British representative, A. R. Margary, on the Burma border in 1875. The first Chinese legation in the United States was established in 1878 by Ch'en Lan-pin and Yung Wing, who had been in charge of the Educational Mission. Legations were also established in Germany (1877), France (1878), Russia and Spain (1879), and Peru (1880).

Kuo Sung-tao (1818–91), a highly competent, respected, and orthodox Chinese official, was the first envoy to Great Britain. It was while head of the Chinese legation in London that he wrote his personal observations, drawing a sharp contrast between Chinese conservatism and the rapid changes in Western society.

A LETTER OF KUO SUNG-TAO FROM LONDON, 1877

Here in England the circumstances of administration, education, and the social customs are changing every day. To trace the whole history of the nation—at first the king and the people struggled for political power and slaughtered one another. Great confusion lasted for several decades or a hundred years until the time of Jo-erh-jih [i.e., George I, 1714–27] when the situation became settled. Originally there was no time-honored accumulation of absolute virtue and excellent education (as there had been in China). . . . Their attainment of wealth and strength really began only after the Ch'ien-lung period (1736–95). Steamships were first built at the beginning of the Ch'ien-lung period, but at first they were not very profitable. Then in 1801 they began using them on the ocean.

The method was again followed in the building of locomotives, which had its beginning in 1813. Thereafter the study of electricity was pursued. Letters and messages were transmitted by a machine of magnetic-iron, until in 1838 a telegraph was first established in their national capital. . . . From the beginning of England's rise, it has been only several decades; while China was weak and declining they covered a distance of 70,000 *li* in the wink of an eye. . . . Chinese scholars and officials are presumptuous in their sanctuary and are trying to obstruct the changes of the universe; they can never succeed.

After several months here, I have actually seen the convenience of the railway train. A round trip of 300 or 400 *li* takes only half a day. In this country the local gentry strongly advise China to build railways; they say that the power and might of England are really based on them. At first they were also suspicious [like the Chinese populace] and tried to stop their construction. To speak first of the road between London and the seaport of Southampton—the coach transportation back and forth formerly used more than 30,000 horses, and the people concerned were afraid that this railroad would be detrimental to their livelihood. But when the railroad was opened as many as 60,000 or 70,000 horses were used. This was because the convenience of the railroad daily attracted more traffic and, since the train could run on only one route, those who were several tens of *li* away and came to take the train had to make use of more horses.

Last winter when I passed through Shanghai I saw a railroad map in the Academy of Natural Sciences on which there was shown a railroad from India directly to Yunnan; a branch . . . going eastward to Canton, etc., . . . Upon seeing it I was greatly surprised, saying that no sooner had trade relations with Yunnan been opened than the routes of railroads were immediately planned. . . .

When the Japanese minister saw me, he said that the natural resources of the universe can be developed by Westerners. They do the hard part—we do the easy part; can we waste more time in idleness? The vastness of China's territory and the number of her people are envied by all nations, but he has learned that until now not a single thing has been developed in China, which is a great pity. I was so embarrassed that I could make no reply. . . .

Personally I think there is something in the minds of the Chinese which is absolutely unintelligible. Among the injuries that Westerners do us there is nothing more serious than opium. Even the British gentlemen feel ashamed of having used this pernicious thing as a pretext for hostilities with China, and they are making a strong effort to eradicate it. Yet Chinese scholars and officials are willing to indulge complacently in it, without any sense of remorse. For several decades it has been the national humiliation, it has exhausted our financial power and poisoned and injured the lives of our people, but there is not a single person whose conscience is weighed down by it. Now clocks, watches, and toys are owned by all families, and woolen and cotton cloth and the like are prevalent in poor districts and the isolated countryside. The practice in Kiangsu and Chekiang even goes as far as to put aside the national currency for the exclusive use of foreign bank notes. . . . Nevertheless as soon as these people heard of the building of railroads and telegraph lines they became sorely disturbed and enraged, and arose in multitudes to create hindrances and difficulties. There are even people who regard foreign machines as an object of public hatred. Tseng Chi-tse, on account of a family funeral, took a small steamship [instead of walking home with a sorrowful face, according to custom] from Nanking to Changsha; this caused a great uproar among the local officials and gentry that lasted for several years. All this means they are willing to accept the harm from others and let the latter squeeze the marrow from their bones, but they use their whole strength to choke off the source of profits. I do not know what is in their minds. There have been foreign relations for thirty years, but the provincial authorities are entirely ignorant of them. They impose their ignorant ideas on the court under the guise of public opinion. The latter encourages them to do this and itself uses "public opinion" as a gloss for its own purposes.

There is a Mr. [George] Stephenson here who says that all countries are building more railroads. He particularly and indefatigably advises China to do this with dispatch.

. . . The critics merely say that wherever the machines of foreigners reach, the local geomantic harmony [*feng-shui*, lit., "wind and water"] is injured. This is a great error. Railways and telegraph lines are always built on level ground following the state roads. There is nothing to dig up or to destroy. As for the machinery used in opening coal mines and pumping water, it is for the purpose of making the mine deeper. The deeper one digs the better the quality of coal. When Chinese dig coal they like to penetrate from the sides; when foreigners dig coal they like to get it in depth. Both are opening the mine. The shallow method and deep method actually have the same result. What harm is there? Take for instance the natural resources in Hunan: the iron mines are mostly in Pao-ch'ing and the coal mines mostly in Heng-chou, and yet the people who are famous in passing high literary examinations are particularly numerous in these two districts. . . .

After several decades foreigners will arrive and then they will gradually build railways and develop [natural resources] for us. Their influence will be sufficient to control the people and the profit will be enough to bribe the wicked, the unruly, and the troublemakers, who will be employed in their service.

Then both the ownership and the profits will fall into the hands of foreigners and China will have nothing to depend upon. Mencius says, "When heaven produced these people, it made those who know beforehand teach those who know afterward, and those who perceive earlier inspire those who perceive later." The responsibility for foresight and perception must lie in the great ministers of the court.

Another able and outspoken Chinese envoy was Tseng Chi-tse (1839–90), known to the West as "Marquis Tseng," who had some grasp both of Western science and of the English language. After living in Europe, Marquis Tseng became not only a zealous advocate of Westernization, but a practitioner of Western ways, devoted to foreign clothes, utensils, and medicine, for all of which he was criticized by Chinese conservatives.

In 1878 he was appointed to succeed Kuo Sung-tao as minister to England and France. Before he sailed from Shanghai on November 22, 1878, he had an interview with the Empress Dowager Tz'u-hsi at Peking, after which he recorded in his diary the naïve and interesting conversation translated below. (Her declarative sentences were recorded as imperial decrees.)

TSENG CHI-TSE'S ACCOUNT OF HIS AUDIENCE WITH THE EMPRESS DOWAGER, 1878

On August 25, 1878, I received a decree granting me the privilege of wearing the peacock feather and appointing me Imperial Commissioner to England and France. . . . On the twenty-sixth, at the beginning of the *ch'ou* period [1–3 A.M.], I went to the court. . . . At the beginning of the *mao* period [5–7 A.M.], I entered the Ch'ien-ch'ing gate and sat for a long time in the room for intracourt interview. At the beginning of *ch'en* [7–9 A.M.] the grand councilors came out from their audience and the throne summoned me to the eastern apartment of the Yang-hsin Hall, which I entered by lifting up the curtain. I knelt on the ground to give thanks for celestial grace. I took off my hat and kotowed. Then I was ordered to put on my hat and stand up and to proceed to the front of the cushion where I knelt to listen to the sacred instruction. The Empress Dowager Tz'u-hsi asked, "When do you plan to start the trip?" The Empress Dowager Tz'u-an also asked the same question.

I replied, "Because there are public and private affairs that your minister must prepare well in Shanghai, it is necessary for him to leave the capital earlier. Now he plans to start the journey on the twenty-ninth of September."

Question: Are you going by way of Tientsin?

Answer: It is necessary to go via Tientsin and also to stay for some ten days to discuss various matters with Li Hung-chang.

Decree: Li Hung-chang is familiar with foreign affairs. You may take up the various matters with him in detail.

Answer: Yes.

Question: Are you going to spend some time in Shanghai?

Answer: It's a long way to go abroad. All the arrangements and all the things to be taken along must be well prepared in Shanghai. Moreover, the retinue which your minister is going to take along cannot be appointed until he has arrived at Shanghai, and therefore he will spend a considerable time there; probably he will have to stay for more than a month.

Question: Will you memorialize again about the staff members you are going to take along, after you have arrived in Shanghai?

Answer: Of your minister's retinue, some of them are going to travel with him from the capital, some are going to be transferred and appointed from the provinces outside the capital. As to the latter who are going to be appointed from outside provinces, whether they can go or not cannot be known in advance. He has to wait until the assignment is made and then he will assemble the information and submit a memorial for your approval.

Question: How many days will it take to go from Tientsin to Shanghai?

Answer: The speeds of the vessels of the China Merchants Company are not the same. The fastest from Tientsin to Shanghai takes only three and a half days.

Question: Are you going to England first or to France first?

Answer: Your minister plans to start the journey from Shanghai on November 22 aboard a French ship for Marseilles, where he will go ashore to take a train for Paris. Paris is the capital of France. When the French see the arrival of a Chinese minister they will certainly have someone perform ceremonies of welcome and entertainment. If your minister goes straight on without taking a look at Paris it will not be proper. He intends to send a telegram from Shanghai to Kuo Sung-tao asking him to come to Paris and hand him the seal. Your minister will receive the seal in Paris, and will immediately present his credentials to France first. Then he will go to London to present his credentials to England. London is the capital of England.

Question: Have the credentials been prepared and given to you?

Answer: He has already received them.

Question: How are you going to decide upon your living quarters?

Answer: Kuo Sung-tao has rented a house some time ago. When your minister goes there everything will be the same as before. Recently he has discussed with the princes and great ministers in the Tsungli Yamen whether in the future, if we have sufficient funds, it may be necessary to purchase a house in each country to be used as an embassy. The houses of foreign ministers in China are all purchased or built by themselves. It is indeed not a long-term plan for China's ministers to live in rented houses. Moreover, the rent is exorbitant and in the long run it is not economical. . . .

Question: Can you understand a foreign written and spoken language?

Answer: Your minister reads a little English and understands a little spoken English. He learned it from books and so it is comparatively easier for him to read the language but more difficult for him to understand it, because his mouth and ears are not accustomed to it.

Question: Is the common language English or French?

Answer: English is a commercial language. Foreigners stress business, therefore the people of the various countries can speak English. As for the language of France, it has been handed down for generations; therefore, in documents and official dispatches among various nations French is frequently used. For instance, the international treaties, ratifications of treaties, and so on, are often written in French.

Question: Since you understand both the spoken and written language, it is much more convenient. You do not need to rely on the translations of interpreters [do you?].

Answer: Although our minister can understand and read a little, he is not very familiar with it and he still has to depend upon interpreters . . . Understanding of a foreign written or spoken language and management of foreign affairs are two entirely different things. It is essential for those who manage foreign affairs to be familiar with treaties and with official procedures. It is not essential for them to concern themselves with the duties of interpreters. In the future when your minister discusses official business with foreigners even though he understands the language he still would wait for the restatement by the interpreter, partly because the procedure of the court ought to be so, partly because during the interval of re-statement by the interpreter he can take advantage of the pause to give thought to the language with which he should answer. The British Minister, Thomas Wade, can understand the Chinese written and spoken language. When he discusses official business he has to use interpreters to convey the meaning to him. That is the same idea.

Question: I have learned that Wade is going to come here soon. Have you heard about it?

Answer: During the summer your minister read a newspaper which said Wade would start his strip in the autumn; since then no exact news about him has been heard.

Decree: Wade is a very cunning person.

Answer: Wade can understand the Chinese written and spoken language. As a person he is very cunning and his temperament is very harsh. Foreigners also say that he is bad tempered.

Decree: It is very difficult to manage foreign affairs. I have heard that in Fukien there are again cases of the burning and destruction of churches and houses; in the future, there will be trouble again.

Answer: The difficulty in handling diplomatic affairs lies in the fact that foreigners are unreasonable, while Chinese are ignorant of current events and circumstances. Chinese ministers and people usually hate foreigners, as goes without saying, but we must plan gradually to make ourselves strong before anything can be done. The destruction of one church or the killing of one foreigner by no means avenges our grievances or wipes out our humiliation. At present many Chinese do not understand this principle and so there has been the Margary incident in Yunnan [February 1875], which caused the Empresses Dowager and the Emperor work and worry day and night.

Decree: It is true indeed. How can we forget our grievances for a single day? But we must gradually make ourselves strong, as you just stated very clearly. The killing of one person or the burning of one house definitely cannot be considered as having avenged our grievances.

Answer: Yes.

Decree: Very few persons understand this idea. If you manage such matters for the nation, there are bound to be times when people will scold you. You, however, should bear the toil and blame.

Answer: When your minister formerly studied the classics and came to the sentence, "To serve the ruler one must be able to offer one's life," he thought that a loyal minister would have reached the extreme point of loyalty if he devoted his whole life to it. After observing the recent situation and the course of negotiations between China and foreign countries, he has found that sometimes it is necessary to consider his life a secondary matter; and in the last analysis he even has to risk considering his reputation unimportant, before he can make the general situation secure on behalf of his country. For instance, at the time of the former Tientsin incident [June 1870] your minister's father, your deceased minister, Tseng Kuo-fan, before he started his trip from Pao-ting, was then on his sickbed and immediately he wrote his last will and testament to bid his family make arrangements as though he had already discarded his life. After he arrived at Tientsin and saw that the matter was so serious that it could not be satisfactorily concluded even by [the sacrifice of] his life, he made concessions and secured the best arrangement to obtain a peaceful settlement. At that time many scholars and officials in the capital condemned him. Your minister's father accepted the responsibility and blamed himself. In sending letters to his friends he frequently wrote the eight characters, "Outwardly I am ashamed of public criticism and inwardly I cannot live with my conscience." This shows how he struggled to protect the general situation by disregarding his own reputation. As a matter of fact, at that time there was no other way to deal with the case, apart from what had been done by Tseng Kuo-fan.

Decree: Tseng Kuo-fan was really a just and loyal man who took the nation into consideration. (Note: I took off my hat and kotowed, but did not make any reply.)

Decree: It is also bad luck for the nation that before long Tseng Kuo-fan departed from the world. Now there are many great officials in various places who are cowardly.

Answer: Li Hung-chang, Shen Pao-chen, Ting Pao-chen, and Tso Tsung-t'ang are all loyal and sincere ministers.

Decree: All of them are good but all are old troopers. The new ones all fail to equal them in ability; they have not kept abreast of new ideas.

Answer: Kuo Sung-tao is certainly an upright and straightforward person. This time he also risked damage to his reputation in order to manage affairs for the nation. In the future it is hoped that the special grace of the empresses and the emperor will protect him in every respect.

Decree: Up above [*shang-t'ou,* i.e., by the rulers] it is thoroughly understood. Kuo Sung-tao is a good man. Since his mission abroad he has managed many affairs but he has also received plenty of scolding from people.

Answer: Kuo Sung-tao is vexed by the fact that China cannot become strong immediately and he has frequently argued with people and therefore he has been scolded. After all he is a loyal minister. Fortunately the empresses dowager and the emperor understand him. Even though he has lost his reputation in the fight, still it is worthwhile.

Decree: We all know him. The princes and great ministers also understand him.

Answer: Yes.

Question: Are you now living in the Tsungli Yamen?

Answer: The affairs of the Tsungli Yamen must be kept confidential. Formerly your minister and others dared not participate. Now, since he has received the order to go abroad on a mission, he must thoroughly investigate the old and new documents in cases concerning England and France, and he must jot down some essential points. Even though the complete cases are now in the hands of Kuo Sung-tao, yet when your minister is on his journey, there are certain to be some foreigners who will meet and entertain him. If during the course of conversation he is ignorant of the facts of the case, it will be somewhat embarrassing.

Decree: You are really quite careful in handling public affairs. (Note: Reverent silence, no reply.)

Question: Are you going to take some students along from the T'ung-wen Kuan?

Answer: Your minister is going to take an English interpreter, a French interpreter, and a clerk. This will be reported when he reaches Shanghai.

Question: Are all of them good?

Answer: Your minister understands English only slightly. The English interpreter, Tso Ping-lung, your minister knows can be employed. The French interpreter, Lien-hsing, has not yet been carefully investigated by your minister, because your minister does not understand French. . . .

Question: Will the date for presentation of credentials be decided by you or by the foreigners?

Answer: We must wait until (your minister's) arrival in their country; then both sides can discuss the matter and deal with it.

Question: Is there also a Tsungli Yamen in foreign countries?

Answer: In foreign countries it is called a *Wai-pu* [or ministry of foreign affairs]. The matters it deals with are the same as the public business of the Chinese Tsungli Yamen. I have heard it said that recently England also changed the name to Tsungli Yamen, but in reality the name in a foreign language is entirely different; it is called neither "Wai-pu" nor "Tsungli Yamen." Only, if the work they do is the same, it is the same office.

Question: When can you arrive there?

Answer: If the Empresses Dowager and the Emperor wish him bon voyage [*I-lu-p'ing-an*] and if there are no delays en route, he should be able to reach the capital of France near the end of the year.

Question: You have never been in foreign countries. I presume you must have heard about these routes and their circumstances.

Answer: Some information has been obtained by consulting books and maps and some by inquiry.

Question: Is your ship going to cast anchor at Hongkong or not?

Answer: Your minister is going to board a French Company's steamship. The steamship must have cargo to be loaded or unloaded, passengers to embark or disembark, and so on. There will be delay in every harbor throughout the journey, but everything will be decided by the captain.

Decree: Now you kneel for greetings. (Note: I withdrew to my original position, knelt, and said) Your minister Tseng Chi-tse kneels and prays for the good health of the Sage.

Raising the curtain I withdrew. It was already the *ch'en* hour [9:00 A.M.].

THE 1890S: THREE DIARY ENTRIES

1.

Among my associates some talk about the honesty and magnanimity of the people of the United States. I think the Western countries today are at the pinnacle of their prosperity, which is caused by their good fortune in natural resources. At the beginning of the nation, the population of the United States was not very large, and these natural resources had not yet been unearthed. By nature the people are open and generous. This is because the development of America was later than that of Europe, and the development of Europe was later than that of China. Among the various European countries, again, some were developed later and some earlier; and accordingly the customs are good and bad. America is like the time of the Golden Age of Ancient China [lit., the time of Yü and Hsia]. Russia is like the time of Shang and Chou. England and Germany are like the two Han dynasties of China. France, Italy, Spain, and Holland are probably like Chinese T'ang and Sung. As for the inconstant and excitable spirit of the French, with their perpetual struggles among political factions, they resemble the age of the former Ming Dynasty. . . .

2.

The secret of the sudden rise of the various nations in Europe and America lies in the fact that day by day their knowledge progresses and their industry and commerce increase in prosperity. But the pivotal implements have all developed in the last hundred years. As for the means by which they cross the globe with no hindrance, the Westerners rely on steamships, trains, telegraphs, and the like, all of which were invented during the last sixty or seventy years. It is the same with other matters.

Nowadays some Chinese critics are either surprised at the strength and prosperity of other countries and praise them too much; or else hold that great China should not imitate Westerners, should reject their inventions, and condemn them severely. I think both are narrow-minded.

In general the Westerners' commercial administration, military methods, shipbuilding, machine manufacturing, agriculture, fishing, husbandry, mining and all such matters are indeed developed to a high point of excellence, and yet all are derived from studies of steam, light, electricity, and chemistry, by means of which they have obtained the methods of controlling water, fire, and electricity. These result from the ingenuity of the inventors, and there is no reason to expect that they can be kept secret for a long time. Famous experts of the West have been particularly entrusted with demonstrating them. The way revealed is one that belongs to all the universe; it is not a monopoly of the Westerners. The intelligence and energy of Chinese scholars are not necessarily inferior to those of Westerners. Unfortunately the energy of their youth has been mostly wasted on eight-legged essays, examination papers, and the calligraphy of small model characters. They are not like thousands and millions of Westerners who exert their intelligence and wisdom in pursuing their study of special subjects and so can at once achieve the best and finest. Certainly we should not deny this fact, and why, likewise, should we confine ourselves to what we are?

In ancient times inventions were concentrated in China. As spiritual sages arose in succession, they invented plows, hoes, boats and carriages, bows and arrows, fishing nets, clothes, and writing. At the time of primeval chaos and uncultivation, there suddenly arose this civilization. If we compare it with the European inventions today, was it not even more marvelous? But people are accustomed to our old civilization and do not realize this. As for the fixing of the four seasons . . . and the teaching of mathematics, . . . Western astronomy and mathematics may have been derived from both of these. How can we know that they have not patterned other matters useful to their nation and people after those of China? In antiquity, when there was not yet any invention in the universe, Chinese sages had observed what was above them and examined what was below and gradually Westerners imitated them. In modern times, Westerners have followed the inventions of Chinese sages, stepped after them, and elaborated upon them. Why should China not follow Westerners now? If we are afraid that they are ahead of us, and so do not want to reveal our shortcomings, that would be to conceal one's illness because of hating to see the doctor. If you say that it is not easy to follow in their steps and you fear that eventually you cannot overtake them, that is like stopping to eat on account of choking. In general, blue is distilled from indigo, but it is bluer than indigo; and ice is frozen from water, but it is colder than water. King Wu-ling adopted barbarian clothes and later wiped out the barbarians. Learning from others does not necessarily mean that there is no chance to surpass them. How can we know that after several thousand years the Chinese cannot carry further the knowledge of Westerners and develop once more the genius of creators, so that the Westerners will be astonished and dazzled by us?

3.

China has all four seasons and the climate is proportionally distributed. In parts of the West the heat and cold are unseasonable, the winter and summer change their normal order, and there are spots that from ancient down to modern times have never had frost or snow. . . .

As to human affairs, China emphasizes human relationships and honors benevolence and righteousness. In the West, on the contrary, a son does not take care of his father, a minister cheats his emperor, a wife is more honored than a husband; thus the bond of the three relationships is broken. Because the proper relationship between husband and wife is not cultivated, the marriage ceremony is neglected. As soon as a girl is twenty-one years old she is permitted to find a husband whom she likes, and there are those who make many selections or trials before they make a match. They do not consider sexual relations preceding marriage as a shame. Beautiful young girls are seeking for males everywhere; the hoary-headed and the widows can invite male companions as they like. The customs are bad to such a degree! . . .

As to other customs, the residence of the emperor is the same as that of ordinary people except that it is a little larger, and it lacks an awe-inspiring appearance and dignity. The pictures of the emperor and empress are hung up at random in the markets for sale and people can purchase them as toys. Thus there is no distinction between the noble and the mean. . . .

Speaking about official costumes, except in one country, Turkey, where the costume is strange, all other nations are the same. The noble and the mean use the same style, which makes it difficult to tell who is honorable and who is lowly. In summertime there is no linen or silk to make their bodies comfortable, and in winter there are rarely furs or padded coats to dress their bodies. They have to go to the trouble of taking a carriage or a horse, but do not have the comfort of sedan chairs. The skirts of their women are seven feet long, only good for sweeping dust. The bed curtain is hung ten feet high but it is hard to keep mosquitoes away.

As for food, there is no difference between winter and summer; they always sip cold water and juice. They cannot appreciate the culinary art, but like butter and mutton ribs. The amount of food served at meals is small, and they use many different kinds of utensils to cause servants a good deal of work. The kinds of soup are very limited. Delicious things are completely lacking.

In government, their taxes since antiquity have been unprecedentedly heavy and numerous. There is actually a levy of taxes of certain amounts according to the value of commodities. If smuggling is detected, the tax on the smuggled article is increased ten or a hundred times as a fine. In some places there is a land tax. Some have a poll tax, or property tax, or tax on trademarks. The government takes money from the people insatiably. How can the people bear it? Moreover, they worship their unorthodox religion and allow the Christian clergy to overrun the country, exhausting all the people's money in building churches, thus spending useful funds for a useless purpose.

As for the law, it has no articles for punishing adultery; a wife can have a concubine [i.e., a lover] and can accuse her husband. This is even more ridiculous. Apart from these there are other things which they improperly turn upside down. Their prisons, for instance, are as comfortable as the kingdom of heaven. It is not very easy for people to maintain their living, because the cost of food and utensils is as high as that of precious jewels. The five relationships are not cultivated, the five kinds of grains are incomplete, hundreds of herbs are unknown to them and hundreds of grasses or flowers are not fragrant. . . .

As the nineteenth century was ending, the Chinese responses to the West, whether experienced vicariously through books or directly through travel, were beginning to move away from the earlier preoccupation with superior armaments, railroads, and so forth, to individual evaluations. The Chinese were not to be stampeded into a wholesale acceptance of Western ways. Formed by a historically minded civilization, the Chinese surveyed the strangeness of the customs, attitudes, ideas, and goals of the newly opened Western world and even as they recognized their inadequacies and backwardness created by outworn institutions, they became conscious of their traditional strength and capabilities.

In the past Chinese travelers had brought back such diverse things as new crops and a new religion; in the coming decades travelers would return to add new disciplines and new ideologies to the fabric of their society. These later travelers belong to a very different story.